Buy and Hedge

The 5 Iron Rules for Investing Over the Long Term

Jay Pestrichelli
Wayne Ferbert

Vice President, Publisher: Tim Moore
Associate Publisher and Director of Marketing: Amy Neidlinger
Executive Editor: Jeanne Glasser
Editorial Assistant: Pamela Boland
Operations Manager: Gina Kanouse
Senior Marketing Manager: Julie Phifer
Publicity Manager: Laura Czaja
Assistant Marketing Manager: Megan Graue
Cover Designer: Alan Clements
Managing Editor: Kristy Hart
Project Editors: Samantha Sinkhorn and Jovana Shirley
Copy Editor: Gayle Johnson
Proofreader: Apostrophe Editing Services
Indexer: Lisa Stumpf
Compositor: Nonie Ratcliff
Manufacturing Buyer: Dan Uhrig

© 2012 by Jay Pestrichelli and Wayne Ferbert
Publishing as FT Press
Upper Saddle River, New Jersey 07458

FT Press offers excellent discounts on this book when ordered in quantity for bulk purchases or special sales. For more information, please contact U.S. Corporate and Government Sales, 1-800-382-3419, corpsales@pearsontechgroup.com. For sales outside the U.S., please contact International Sales at international@pearson.com.

Company and product names mentioned herein are the trademarks or registered trademarks of their respective owners.

Printed in the United States of America

Second Printing November 2011

ISBN-10: 0-13-282524-4
ISBN-13: 978-0-13-282524-5

Pearson Education LTD.
Pearson Education Australia PTY, Limited.
Pearson Education Singapore, Pte. Ltd.
Pearson Education Asia, Ltd.
Pearson Education Canada, Ltd.
Pearson Educatión de Mexico, S.A. de C.V.
Pearson Education—Japan
Pearson Education Malaysia, Pte. Ltd.

Library of Congress Cataloging-in-Publication Data

Pestrichelli, Jay, 1970-
  Buy and hedge : the 5 iron rules for investing over the long term /
Jay Pestrichelli, Wayne Ferbert.
    p. cm.
  ISBN 978-0-13-282524-5 (hbk. : alk. paper)
  1. Investments. 2. Portfolio management. 3. Hedging (Finance) I.
Ferbert, Wayne, 1971- II. Title.
  HG4521.P424 2012
  332.6--dc23
                          2011029879

To my girls: Abby, Ella, Grace, and Linda
—Wayne

To my wife and son, Lynn and Zander
—Jay

Contents

Foreword

Investing on your own can be intimidating. But remember when you were seven? So was learning to ride a bike. How did you feel about learning to drive? I remember when I moved to Chicago from Nebraska to start college; the thought of driving in Chicago traffic was mind-blowing. A few years later, I had a sales job in Chicago and was driving all over the city, focused on my next sales call and not the traffic. You could add flying for the first time, buying your first home, and a whole list of other things you have never done before. Or even if you *have* done them, you know you need to continue to learn to advance. You must play against a better racquetball player to improve, not against inferior opponents. The key to all these activities is that someone who knew what he or she was doing taught you the skill, and then you practiced it.

My family has been involved in the securities industry for more than 40 years. I grew up with it around the dining room table. I worked at our family company, Ameritrade, as a summer job and then for more than a decade. I am still on the board of directors. When I was the Chief Operating Officer for Ameritrade, Jay Pestrichelli and Wayne Ferbert worked for me. Jay oversaw our largest client segment and came to Ameritrade through one of our many acquisitions. Wayne ran our product development efforts. For years they were responsible for developing, building, and rolling out many of the products we delivered to our clients. They were a great team and always focused on putting the clients first. Wayne was so focused on his projects that, more than once, he forgot to change his bonus goals with me before the end of the bonus period when our priorities changed, to the detriment of his income. When Jay and Wayne approached me with the idea for this book, I was not surprised. Both had always been extremely interested in helping our clients learn how to invest more effectively.

The product of their collaboration is this book, *Buy and Hedge*, and it is a great one. I wish I had this book when I was learning to invest. It would have saved me a lot of money. It also would have been especially useful these last three or four years. At its simplest, this is a guide to how you can insure your portfolio against downturns in the market. That makes a tremendous amount of sense. We insure many of our large, important assets. We insure our car, our house, and even our lives. Why wouldn't we want to insure our nest eggs, retirement, savings—our securities investments?

I was educated at the University of Chicago, where Modern Portfolio Theory was born. The basic idea of Modern Portfolio Theory is diversification to reduce risk. This book takes that idea one step further. Yes, you want to diversify your investments, but you also want to hedge them against a downturn or insure them. Having been in the industry for so long, I have seen numerous ups and downs. The strategies that this book teaches are straightforward and essential to the self-directed, individual investor.

Two key themes are important in this book. The first, and most important, is discipline. Jay and Wayne state that the only successful investors they have seen are the ones with discipline, and I wholeheartedly agree. Discipline is the prerequisite for success. The individual investor who has a plan and follows it will have the best opportunity to acquire great returns. If you don't have a plan, or if you let your emotions influence your portfolio management decisions, your investment decisions will end up following the crowd. Following the crowd is a recipe for selling low and buying high and will lead to poor performance. The second key theme of this book is risk. Too many investors, including myself, fail to appreciate the times when we take on too much risk for the expected returns. This is, of course, understandable. As Jay and Wayne point out, it is relatively easy to measure the return, but getting a handle on the risk is something else entirely. The authors will teach you new ways to measure and monitor risk in your portfolio. This is truly a lost art in the world of retail investing. Too many other sources, and investment advisors, fail to even address it. The last few years have demonstrated this. You need to take risks to get a return, but too much risk leads to volatility in your portfolio and the potential for sleepless nights. Jay and Wayne help you think about how much risk you are taking and how to limit the volatility in your portfolio. This book is worth reading just for the methodology of thinking about risk.

Finally, this book is about not just theory but practical application. Although you might enjoy the intellectual stimulation that the market can provide, you invest to preserve and grow your capital. To help you reach your goals and implement their advice, the authors offer the Immutable Laws of Investing. These may seem like common sense, such as "After-tax returns are the ones that matter," but it is certainly worthwhile to articulate them and be reminded of them. Jay and Wayne also describe the Five Iron Rules (see, I told you—discipline!). These rules include how to hedge your investments, a detailed discussion of risk metrics, and how to calculate the risk in your portfolio. I guarantee you very few individual investors do this precisely. If you are one of the few who do, you will have a huge advantage over everyone else who doesn't. This part of the book alone is pure gold (which, if you haven't noticed, is going up like crazy!). In addition, the authors provide tactics and advanced tactics to make it all work. Have you used a married put before? What about a collar or a diagonal spread? One of the best features of their strategy is that you can implement it gradually, one position at a time if you like, and get a feel for how to use options to hedge a stock or ETF.

I wrote this foreword in August 2011 after one of the most volatile weeks the market had seen in years. This is a great reminder of why when we buy, we must hedge. With the markets becoming more unpredictable and more difficult to navigate, a book like this gives you the tools to succeed. Jay and Wayne are instructors who know what they are doing, and they can guide you through the process. Then it will be up to you to practice and gain experience. This is not a "get rich quick" book. You won't find any stock recommendations here. You will not find yourself asking, "If these guys are so smart, why don't they just do it instead of writing a book?" In fact, they *are* doing just what they explain in this book. And so are institutional investors. Now, the instruments are available to everyone, and the authors provide this how-to manual to teach you how to use them. In all, this is a must-read for the self-directed, individual investor. If you are a beginner, this book will introduce you to concepts you may never have considered in a straightforward, easy-to-understand manner. Even if you have been investing for yourself for years, you will still find the discussion of risk and the advanced tactics enlightening. *Buy and Hedge* is a great resource that you will consult time and again as you master each tactic. Enjoy reading it. I wish you the best with managing your portfolio. Remember, nobody is more interested in how you do than you are—and now you have the tools to be successful.

—Pete Ricketts, TD Ameritrade Board member
Chicago Cubs Board member
Former COO, Ameritrade

Acknowledgments

First and foremost, we want to thank our families for supporting us through our efforts to write this book and launch our new business. Our families worked around our schedule, and we appreciate it. Thank you, Lynn and Linda. And thank you, Zander, Abby, Ella, and Grace!

In creating the Buy and Hedge methodology, we routinely sought the opinions of our former colleagues at TD Ameritrade. The list is long, but we'd like to call out Mick Brokaw, Felix Davidson, Don Elliott, Bryce Engel, Joe Faber, Asiff Hirji, James Kostulias, Dave Lambert, Mike McGrath, Pete Ricketts, Matt Sadowsky, and Bill Wymer.

Thanks to the guys at Minyanville for giving us a platform for our content and making the introductions to our publisher. Thanks to Kevin Wassong and Todd Harrison. And thanks to our publisher, Pearson. In particular, we want to thank our executive editor, Jeanne Glasser, for her regular and positive feedback throughout the process.

We would like to thank the mentors who shaped our critical thinking skills and helped make us better investors: Jim Ditmore, Bryce Engel, Bill Gerber, Gig Graham, Asiff Hirji, Ellen Koplow, Joe Moglia, Pete Ricketts, and Larry Szczech.

Wayne would like to thank his parents for instilling in him a passion for learning that includes a shared appetite for reading.

Jay would like to thank his parents for teaching him the value of a strong work ethic and the power of an entrepreneurial spirit.

A wise man once said, "All a man has is his name and his word."

We want to thank our parents for teaching us how to properly honor our family name. And we thank our wives and children, who keep us true to our word. This wouldn't be possible without all of their encouragement.

About the Authors

For years, Wayne and Jay partnered at TD Ameritrade to launch innovative new products for its online clients. Today, Wayne and Jay have left TD Ameritrade to work with clients on a more personal level. Meeting your personal life goals requires you to meet your financial goals. This book is your key to meeting your financial goals.

Wayne Ferbert is a cofounder and principal of ZEGA Financial, LLC, a Registered Investment Advisor. He has spent his entire 17-year career in financial services, with 10 of them in the online brokerage segment with TD Ameritrade. In addition to managing business development as a member of the Senior Operating Committee at Ameritrade, which included M&A and market research, he ran product development. Prior to Ameritrade, he worked in planning and analysis roles at a Fortune 500 insurance firm and then a Fortune 500 bank. Wayne has an MBA in finance from Loyola University (Maryland) and a BSBA in finance from Bucknell University. He has his series 65 license. He resides in Ellicott City, Maryland, with his family. He has three daughters, ages 6, 8, and 9, and coaches their soccer team.

Jay Pestrichelli is a cofounder and principal of ZEGA Financial, LLC, a Registered Investment Advisor. He has 20 years of experience in business management, with 12 years in the online brokerage field with TD Ameritrade and Datek On-Line. As manager of the Active Trading business, he helped drive it to become number one in trade volume of U.S. brokers. During that time he was a regular contributor as a subject matter expert on CNBC's *Fast Money*, provided video interviews for CNN, and has been regularly quoted in publications such as *The Wall Street Journal* and *SmartMoney*. Licenses include series 7, 63, 65, 24, 4, and 3. Jay resides in Omaha, Nebraska, with his wife, Lynn, and 6-year-old son, Zander.

To contact Wayne and Jay visit www.zegafinancial.com or www.buyandhedge.com and click Contact Us. You can contact the authors by email at service@zegafinancial.com.

Introduction

Join the authors on a brief but instructional journey back in time—but not too far back. Think about the year 2008. More specifically, think about your investment portfolio in 2008. Warning: This journey might be upsetting and/or emotionally painful. If you are like most investors, your portfolio suffered losses that were historic in size and scope. Believe me, we are reluctant to take you on this journey. After all, this is the first paragraph of the first chapter of the first book we have ever written. Putting you in a bad mood in the first paragraph is a little risky. But we hope this exercise will prove enlightening.

Next, think about the investment destruction that continued through early 2009. Unbelievably, the markets sank to even lower lows. Along with these new market lows came historically high market volatility. Respected financial institutions were on the brink of failure. Every day was a new adventure in the market. Finally, mercifully, the markets recovered sharply in mid-2009, and they have been on a steady rise in the two years since.

Consider for a moment the investment climate back in the fall of 2008. The market crash was precipitous and calamitous. Think about the investment decisions you faced with your portfolio. If you are like most American investors, you thought about doing one or two of the following:

- Curling into the fetal position and hoping it would all go away
- Calling your investment adviser and screaming at him to do something
- Selling everything
- Looking for ways to find any tax advantages from your investment losses

For 90% of investor households in this country, one or several of these decisions were an implicit or explicit outcome of the 2008–2009 market collapse. But of these four actions, the only one that was even modestly productive was the last one. At least the investor who looked for tax efficiency from the losses might have saved himself a bit of money. But it's hard to save on taxes when you don't have any gains to offset the losses. You can at least admire the person who tried to find tax efficiency for his "glass half-full" attitude.

The other investment options would have been counterproductive. An investor who runs and hides from his portfolio might as well dismiss any chance he has for achieving his investment goals. Screaming at your adviser won't help, especially because he owns some of the responsibility for your portfolio's poor performance. Maybe yelling at him made you feel better. But did it make your portfolio perform better?

Last, selling everything in your portfolio is not a long-term solution. Pulling your money out of the market might have made you feel better in the short term. In fact, you might even have missed the continued market declines through early 2009 if you liquidated your portfolio right after the crash in September/October 2008. But did you get your portfolio reinvested in 2009 in time to enjoy the sharp reversal in the market? You probably didn't. Timing the market is a difficult proposition. The best traders in the world time the market—and the data says that fewer than half of them succeed. Is that the portfolio strategy you want to rely on? Always being right about timing the market?

The authors promise this painful journey is almost over. We have one last question for you to consider in light of the recent stock market performance. Do you think the recent activity, volatility, and turmoil in the market are the new normal? Or do you think we just survived the equivalent of the market's 100-year flood? Or do you think the answer lies somewhere in between?

If you think we just survived the 100-year flood, this book isn't for you. You can invest your money in the broad markets and sit back and wait for it to appreciate. You can put this book down. And, by the way, good luck!

If you think the market has the potential for significant turmoil and volatility, this book fits you like a glove. Even if you just think that the markets are uncertain, and you worry that it is possible that this is the new normal, this book will work for you. If you are just uncertain about the markets in general, the lessons you will learn in this book will work for you in any market.

The Buy and Hedge strategy is a new way to invest. It is an all-weather portfolio approach to help you beat the markets. Our Five Iron Rules of Buy and Hedge, when implemented effectively, will provide you with a portfolio that you can feel secure owning. And by "secure," we mean you will sleep well at night knowing that you have limited the potential destruction that market volatility can create in your portfolio.

Buy and Hedge the book is for the investor with a long-term outlook who wants to take control of his or her portfolio. It will teach you to build and manage a balanced, diversified, and *hedged* portfolio. By hedged, we mean a portfolio that limits its downside losses in a violent and volatile market. Hedge fund managers and professional money managers use these techniques. And we teach them in this book using straightforward and easy-to-understand language. Most important, the book shares techniques that can be implemented quickly and efficiently. In other words, you don't need to be a full-time money manager to make this portfolio work for you. It does help to have a basic understanding of financial markets and to already be a do-it-yourself investor.

The authors worked together at TD Ameritrade (TDA), where we were employed for over a decade. TDA is the largest online brokerage in terms of total investor transactions executed. We spent our time at TDA building the trading and investment platform that is used by millions of clients today. In fact, collectively we launched over 100 tools and enhancements while at TDA. And we led the initiatives that spent nearly 750 million acquiring several companies. Each of these companies was acquired so that we could unleash their new investment tools for our clients. We estimate that together we met more than 10,000 individual clients at client functions and events. Simply put, we were intimately involved in the expansion and growth of the fantastic online brokerage industry.

The main competitors in this space have really democratized the investing industry. The little guy can now manage his money in a way that only institutional investors could have achieved 10 to 15 years ago. The main players—TD Ameritrade, E*TRADE, Charles Schwab, and Fidelity—all deserve kudos for tearing down the barriers and reducing the friction for the individual investor to take control of his or her financial future.

In our combined 22-plus years in this new industry, we have learned an important series of lessons, which you will benefit from. The first lesson is that it is very difficult to beat the market. Even professional money managers have a hard time picking stocks that beat the market. We have tried—and we can attest to our scars and bruises. The second lesson is that it is supremely difficult to stay disciplined within an investment strategy. Discipline is the key to being a successful investor. And the third lesson is that we have never met an investor who consistently beat the market without following a disciplined investment strategy. We have met disciplined investors who did *not* beat the market. But we have never met an *undisciplined* investor who consistently beat the market over the long term.

We have experimented with many investment strategies over the years. In fact, our jobs at TDA encouraged us to use the tools and products. And being product developers at heart, experimenting with different trading systems and investment strategies came naturally at a company like TDA. Both of us will even tell you that we had a lot of fun being two of the more active users of the tools and products within the industry. After our testing and experimenting with different investment strategies, we developed the Buy and Hedge strategy and now endorse it for the do-it-yourself investor. We have successfully driven market-beating performance using this strategy for over three years now—and these were a very hard three years.

Buy and Hedge is your path to investment success!

Before you begin the first chapter, we want to explain a few terms we use:

- When we use the word "Option," we almost always capitalize it because we are referring to the financial instrument called an Option. An Option is a financial security that is a derivative that represents a contract sold by one party (the Option writer) to another party (the Option holder). The Option gives the holder the right to either buy or sell an underlying security for a set price by a set date. When "option" is not capitalized, the word is being used in the traditional sense: a choice between two or more things.

- This book often uses the words "investment" and "position," but we do not use them interchangeably, even though the industry often does. Instead, for clarity, we have created a hierarchy between the two. Investment is the parent of positions. An investment is made up of one or more positions. Here's an example: I am bullish on Microsoft, but with a small hedge. The positions could be 100 shares of MSFT *and* one Option contract on MSFT that provides the hedge. The investment is the exposure you want to create to some investment vehicle. The positions are the specific investment vehicles you want to own in your portfolio to make that investment a reality.

- This book uses the word "we." "We" always refers to the authors. It is not the collective "we." It is the authors only. When we use "you," "investor," or "one," we are referring to the reader—the individual investor who will implement the Buy and Hedge strategy after reading this book.

Part I
Introduction to Hedging and the Markets

This book is organized into five parts. As the book progresses, each part gets a little more prescriptive than the previous one. As a result, the book gets more technical as you move to the later chapters. The first three parts are a must-read for any investor, whether new to investing or not. Part I, "Introduction to Hedging and the Markets," and Part II, "The Immutable Laws of Investing," outline the basis of the Buy and Hedge investment approach. Part III, "The Five Iron Rules of Buy and Hedge," describes the rules that define the investment strategy we recommend. Follow these Five Iron Rules, and you will be a Buy and Hedge investor.

The last two parts of this book relate to your experience using Options or ETFs in your portfolio. If you don't know what these products are, Part IV, "The How-to and Basic Tactics of Hedging," will help you build a foundation for using these investment vehicles. If you are already very experienced with Options and ETFs, Part V, "Advanced Tactics," will help you learn more-advanced tactics. If your experience is somewhere in between, both parts can be instructional for you.

The model for learning in this book is well thought-out. The parts are organized this way for a reason:

- You will learn why hedging is an attractive strategy.
- Then you will learn the Immutable Laws that define the most important investor lessons.
- Knowing that these Laws inform the Iron Rules,
- And that the Iron Rules define the Buy and Hedge investment strategy,
- You'll learn the basic tactics for managing your portfolio,
- And you can move on to the advanced strategies with confidence.

1

Life Is a Series of Risk-and-Return Decisions—and So Is Investing

In the critically acclaimed movie *The World According to Garp*, T.S. Garp (played by Robin Williams) and his wife finish touring a home for sale with their realtor. As they stand in the front yard and debate whether to bid on the home, a prop plane with engine trouble crashes into the roof. With the smoldering plane's tail sticking out of the roof, Garp turns to his wife and realtor and says:

> "We'll take the house. Honey, the chances of another plane hitting this house are astronomical. It's been pre-disastered. We're going to be safe here."

Most of us never face a risk/reward decision as dramatic as the one made by Garp. It is equally unlikely that you are as consumed with risk avoidance as he was. If you've seen the movie, you remember that Garp's upbringing was—well, let's call it "eclectic." Even if your early years weren't "eclectic," your life involves risk/reward decisions every day.

You make decisions innately; doing so is wired into how you behave. People like positive rewards and have visceral responses to positive outcomes. And you take actions that help produce those positive outcomes, just as you take actions to avoid negative outcomes. And you do this all day long, in nearly every part of your life that you value.

How does that innately wired behavior affect your investment decisions? In investing, the entire return on your portfolio is linked to the amount of risk you design into your portfolio. Investing is all about risk and return. Many pundits make it sound a lot more complicated than that. In fact, Wall Street benefits from the fact that you think it's more complicated than that. But it isn't. Risk is the input to your portfolio. Return is the output. It's that straightforward.

Yet when it comes to investing, the average do-it-yourself investor often forgets to monitor the risk component and obsesses too much over its prettier sister, the returns. But if risk is the *input*, it is the aspect you can directly control. If return is the *output*, it is not the aspect you can directly control. But ask a friend at your next cocktail party to describe his investment portfolio. Chances are, he'll focus almost exclusively on the portfolio's returns, not the risk. Most individual investors cannot even describe the risk in their portfolio. Isn't it a bit surprising that investors don't focus on what they *can* control when asked to describe their investment approach?

Let's give the individual investor the benefit of the doubt. Let's assume he focuses on return because the output is the *reason* he invests. The investor wants his money to grow, so he takes risks to generate returns. Returns create wealth, and wealth enables the investor to achieve his life goals such as an education for his children or a comfortable retirement. So, let's change the experiment. Ask your friend about the risk in his investment portfolio. More than likely, the discussion will be identical to the first dialog. Your friend will begin talking vaguely about risk but will invariably discuss return instead, thinking the two are interchangeable.

Why do investors view risk and return so interchangeably? Money is a powerful motivator. In this case, it drives the investor to massage, in his own mind, his view of risk in exchange for a much more comfortable view of return. Let's face it—return is the prettier sister. It is easier to understand and even easier to measure. You either made money or you didn't. Your return can be measured in dollars and percentage. Both are easy to process for the average fifth-grade math student.

But risk is not nearly as easy to measure or understand when it comes to investments. Take the most common measure of risk—standard deviation. You didn't learn about standard deviation until tenth-grade math, but you learned about percentages and comparisons in the fifth grade. The language of risk when it comes to investing is more intimidating but not necessarily more difficult. When you finish this book, you'll be able to express the risk in your investments just as comfortably as you can express the return in your portfolio. Believe it!

Let's look at an example of risk-versus-return decision making in everyday life. Let's use one everyone can relate to, that is dynamic, and that requires a thoughtful analysis. Then, after you analyze this thought-making process, we'll put a twist on the risk/return paradigm.

The example: Should I change jobs?

Almost everyone has wrestled with this question. It is one of the biggest decisions you'll ever make. In fact, it is common to see people create lists of pros and cons when considering such a change. A pros/cons list is really just the risk/return continuum for this decision, written down.

You've seen these lists before. They include things like the following:

- Higher/lower pay or benefits
- Changing career fields
- Challenges of a new environment
- Shorter/longer commute
- Hate/love my current job
- Industry is attractive/unattractive

The list can be almost endless. But all of these decisions, when considered together, make for a dynamic decision process—and one that requires a lot of thought. Your life changes when you change employers. It is not a decision to be taken lightly.

When making investment decisions, should each portfolio decision be equally complex and involved? Of course not. If every portfolio decision were this time-consuming, you'd rarely get anything else done—and you'd agonize over so many of these decisions that you'd really struggle to be an effective investor.

But what if we told you that to be an effective do-it-yourself investor, your decision process for your portfolio must be just as *thoughtful* as the decision to change jobs? Faced with the stress and perceived risk of a job change, you elevate your thinking and come up with thoughtful risk-and-return analysis. That same level of elevated thinking is necessary to be a great investor—to make decisions on stocks and markets that will outperform.

This is a daunting task, but don't fret. Buy and Hedge doesn't believe that this level of thoughtfulness is easy to replicate on a continuous basis. In fact, we believe it is impossible. So, instead of teaching you how to be excessively thoughtful in your analysis, this book teaches you to change the investment game through hedging. Investing is about risk and return, so we need to change the risk/return paradigm to change the game.

Let's return to the example of changing jobs. Let's turn that game on its head and see how the risk/return process changes. Let's say you have been offered a new job. You really want to take it, but you have a few reservations. Most relate to the fact that your current job, although not ideal, is not half-bad either.

Also suppose that your prospective new employer and your current employer get together and make you a proposition. They offer you a chance to purchase a new employment contract with "optionality." This means that at any time in the first 90 days of your new job, if you don't like your new job or new employer, you can execute the "option" clause in your contract. You can return to your old employer, in the same job and at the same pay as before, no questions asked. You'll be welcomed back with open arms.

Of course, such contracts don't exist. But wouldn't this option clause completely change the dynamic of the decision to change jobs? Would you agonize over this decision if you knew you could reverse it and go back to your old job? Would the process involve nearly as much thought if the risk of being wrong could be contained, as it would be with the option contract? Wouldn't your analysis of the pros and cons switch instead to an analysis of the price of the employment contract you were offered compared to these perceived pros and cons?

The whole process would change! The entire risk/return dynamic would change. The game would be turned on its head. In fact, how you measure risk would change. The risk of loss now is contained to the cost of the option contract that protects your old job. Can you imagine such a product?

You don't need to imagine such a product in the world of investing because it already exists. It is called a derivative, and it serves a utilitarian purpose in the marketplace for individual investors. Derivatives permit an investor to *hedge* his positions. These derivatives can be used to create downside protection and to contain risk to a specific and measureable amount of money.

Hedging your investments changes how you measure risk in your portfolio. It simplifies the process. When you are hedged, you have controlled for your risk! Remember, risk is your *input!* You have created a portfolio that has a maximum downside exposure. So when measuring risk, you can always fall back on the simplest measure of all—the total amount of money you could lose in a worst-case scenario. This isn't the only measure of risk. It isn't even the only measure you will learn in this book. But it is always comforting to know that you can fall back on a well-defined measure of risk—and know that you have controlled for the only input you can control in your portfolio.

A well-constructed portfolio can create comfort. This is quite a dynamic given that comfort is a feeling and feelings are, by definition, emotional. Emotions play a key role in investing. Money is emotional—mostly because the ability to build wealth drives the ability to realize long-term goals. These goals often consume us, so we get emotional about our money. And, by extension, we get emotional about investing our money.

Emotion, however, more often has a destructive rather than constructive impact on a portfolio. The ability to control emotion and lessen its negative impact on your portfolio is a key part of becoming an effective investor. Luckily for you, hedging breaks down the negative impact that emotion has on investing. We'll examine that dynamic in the next chapter.

Chapter Lessons

- We control risk in our portfolio because it is our input.
- The return in our portfolio is the output.
- You must learn to measure both risk and return to be an effective investor.
- Hedging controls for risk in your portfolio and simplifies the measurement of risk.

2

Emotion Is Your Enemy,
So Bid It Good-Bye

"Are you crying? There's no crying! There's no crying in baseball!"

—Jimmy Dugan (played by Tom Hanks), coach of the Rockford Peaches in the movie *A League of Their Own* (1992)

Have you ever had a very important decision to make and thought, "If I could just let my emotions control my thinking, I bet I would be a better decision-maker"? Of course not. No one ever associates runaway emotions with thoughtful decision making. However, emotions often reside in your subconscious. In other words, emotions often affect your decision making without your realizing it.

Emotions play a role in every important decision you will ever make. Some people might be better at limiting the impact of emotion, but no one can truly eliminate it. Why? Because if something is important to you, it is most likely important for some strong reason. That reason might be visceral, instinctive, or even primitive. It means something to you because there is some perceived benefit to you. The benefit could be something you gain or some loss you avoid. But the benefit is real—and your brain processes the expectation of that benefit.

If it matters to you, why would you expect that emotions wouldn't play a role? In the world of investing, gains and avoided losses are measured in dollars. Of course, dollars are important to everyone. They are our everyday currency. They supply basic needs: food, water, shelter. So, of course, money drives emotions. Wealth and currency are prerequisites for many of the key activities that people plan for themselves and their families. The conclusion: Gaining or losing money drives emotional feelings because of what money allows you to do and accomplish. Wow. There is nothing earth-shattering in that conclusion. You knew that before you started reading this book.

But did you know that the feelings you get from gaining or losing money are not just a result of the logical conclusion that you have more or less money? They are visceral and primitive feelings as well. When you win money, such as in a raffle or poker game, you experience excitement. That excitement is further enhanced by the release of endorphins. That chemical release makes the "high" you get from the excitement last longer—and you feel even "higher." That is why you hear the expression "Money found is better than money earned." It is because of the endorphin release.

So, gaining a windfall releases chemicals and creates an even higher high. But what about losing money? Here is where the feelings get even *more* powerful. Studies have shown that losses are twice as powerful, psychologically, as gains. People would rather avoid a loss than acquire a gain. This concept is called *loss aversion*, and it is one of the most powerful forces in the markets. It is destructive, often leading to overly reactive portfolio decisions that destroy value.

If you don't believe that loss aversion exists, or that it is this powerful, let's look at an interesting study on loss aversion suffered by professional golfers on the PGA tour. In Moskowitz and Wertheim's recent best seller *Scorecasting*, two Wharton professors, Devin Pope and Maurice Schweitzer, examined the putting results for 421 golfers in over 230 tournaments held between 2004 and 2009. Over 2.5 million putts were laser-measured for accurate reporting. The study analyzed the success rate of nearly identical putts for birdie, par, and bogey across the PGA golf community.

Every hole has a stroke count that is called *par*. Par is the number of strokes the golfer is expected to require to hit the ball into the hole. A birdie means you completed the hole in one stroke less than par. A bogey results when the golfer needs one more stroke than par.

Of course, the golfer wants to record the lowest possible score on every hole, resulting in the lowest possible total score combined for all 18 holes. In the end, the only score that matters is the total for 18 holes. Getting par or birdie or bogey on an individual hole is not part of the formula for determining the winner. Only the total score matters.

Putting typically is a golfer's last act on every hole. When the ball comes to rest on the green, the golfer uses his putter to roll the ball into the hole. The resulting number of strokes for the hole is his score for that hole. Each putt on the green counts as an additional stroke on that hole—and therefore, one more stoke on the total.

So, putting is the last act on each hole. Check. Each putt counts as a stroke. Check. You want the fewest putts to keep your score as low as possible. Check. The lowest total score for 18 holes wins. Check. Scoring a birdie, par, or bogey on any individual hole is not part of determining the winner. Check.

You might expect nearly identical putts, one for birdie and one for par, to have identical success rates. But you would be wrong. Professional golfers are materially better putters when putting for par than when they are putting for birdie—even when you normalize the scenario to compare identical putts and identical conditions for the putt.

Why? Because PGA golfers suffer from loss aversion. When they approach a birdie putt, they believe they have taken the risk of a bad score off the table, so they putt with less care. As a result, they tend to leave the putt short of the hole more often than long. But when they putt for par from the identical location, they tend to sink the putt more often than when the putt is for birdie. They must focus better and are more aggressive with their putt. They are materially less likely to leave the putt short. A putt that doesn't reach the hole can't go in. And the loss aversion in this case is that they want to avert a bogey. A bogey is a bad score on the hole. So the golfer takes more care in his putting stroke.

But a professional golfer knows that each putt, whether a birdie or par, is worth the same on the scorecard. Surely a professional golfer knows the importance of making each and every putt. But the statistics clearly show that they don't. They let loss aversion get in the way. Clearly, if they viewed the putt objectively, they would view every putt the same. Even more surprising, in the PGA, a one-stroke improvement in their score for the average tournament would result in an increased average payout of over $10,000. Can you imagine?

Each putt is worth $10,000, and the golfers still don't treat each putt equally.

Loss aversion has been studied in the world of investing more than any other field. Losses in one's portfolio tend to hurt worse than the gains feel good, even when the dollar amounts are identical. And because of that feeling, the investor tends to make the worst mistakes when he lets loss aversion take over and influence his portfolio decisions. The single biggest mistake the investor makes is thinking that he has averted a loss just because he hasn't sold the stock yet. The investor mistakenly thinks he hasn't yet made the loss a reality.

This is where loss aversion really creates delusional thinking. If you buy a stock for $50,000, and three months later it is worth $25,000, you have already experienced the loss. Even though you don't sell the stock, the loss is still real—it is just not yet "realized" for tax purposes. In the industry, this is called holding on to losers.

Many investors hold on to this $25,000 loser of a stock hoping for a rebound. Most of the time, the stock keeps riding down and loses even more. Loss aversion causes some illogical behavior. Loss aversion is a psychological reaction, but scientists are unsure why almost everyone is afflicted by it. Something about society and our value systems causes us to prioritize loss avoidance over acquiring gains. Who knows why? Maybe it's chemical. Maybe we are hardwired for loss aversion. Whatever the reason, to become a successful investor, you need to find a way to overcome its destructive force.

Hedging is a cure for loss aversion. This cure doesn't treat the cause of loss aversion. Instead, it treats the symptoms. Treating the cause would be next to impossible because loss aversion is hard-wired into your psyche. But effective hedges restrict your portfolio's loss potential. This creates downside protection—and means that you don't have to dwell on losses—because your losses have been limited.

This benefit of hedging cannot be overstated. Loss aversion is one of the most powerful deterrents to an individual investor's success in managing a portfolio. And hedging can treat the symptoms of loss aversion. So, by hedging, you have a leg up on other individual investors because you can reduce or even eliminate the impact of loss aversion on your portfolio. How does it work?

Hedging, when executed the Buy and Hedge way, establishes downside protection in your portfolio. Your maximum possible loss for every investment is defined and controlled. So you should never "ride a loser" from $50,000 to $25,000. If you make a bad portfolio decision and it loses money, your losses will stop at a predetermined level. You establish that predetermined level based on your tolerance for risk and your expectations for that investment.

This benefit of hedging is not hard to imagine. While other investors are being whipsawed by the markets and the resulting loss aversion, your portfolio is more stable and less volatile. Your losses are capped. You do not experience losses like those of an identical portfolio that doesn't have hedges in place. Without steep losses, loss-aversion decisions occur less frequently. If you aren't forced to think about losses as often, you will not be influenced by the emotional toll that loss aversion has on your thinking process.

Hedging is all about building portfolios that have controlled for risk—and that have reduced volatility as a result. Hedge funds have recently given the concept of hedging a bad reputation. Why? Because many hedge funds today are extreme risk vehicles, not risk-control vehicles. The current 2%/20% fee arrangements for hedge funds encourage risky behavior from hedge fund managers because they share 20% of all profits. These managers swing for the fences or take shortcuts (such as insider trading) because the incentives are so strong.

The hedge fund industry was not created in the first half of the 20th century with these extreme risk vehicles in mind. Hedge funds did what their name says—they *hedged!* What a novel concept! Based on how the industry runs today, the term "hedge fund" is a misnomer. The word "hedge" implies risk abatement, but the industry doesn't seem to notice.

Don't let the word "hedging" throw you. Hedging is just a technique—a tool, if you will. But it is a powerful tool. Emotion is a very destructive force on portfolios, especially when it manifests itself through loss aversion. But hedging reduces your potential for losses and reduces the emotional impact on your portfolio. You can't eliminate emotion from the business of investing. This is impossible. But you *can* treat the symptoms—through hedging.

Chapter Lessons

- Emotions typically have destructive consequences for your portfolio.
- In particular, loss aversion is the most destructive force. This is when you take steps to avoid losses more than achieve gains because the power of a loss feels worse emotionally.
- Hedging has a psychological benefit: It reduces the likelihood that you will suffer from decisions influenced by loss aversion.
- Hedge funds have attracted bad press because they don't really hedge. Don't let that influence your approach to hedging.

3

Don't Forget Why You Invest

"How many yachts can you water-ski behind? How much is enough?"

—Bud Fox (played by Charlie Sheen) to Gordon Gekko (played by Michael Douglas) in the critically acclaimed movie *Wall Street* (1987)

Thought we'd keep using movie quotes and not include one from *Wall Street*?

Everyone invests for a reason. These reasons are most often life goals such as retirement, a second home, or a dream vacation. Maybe your retirement includes water-skiing behind interchangeable yachts. More likely, it involves a much simpler existence. But either way, this goal is probably a long-term goal. For you to achieve it, your assets must grow to provide you the buying power you need to fund that goal.

So let's agree that investing is a means to an end. It is not the end itself. Never forget that. Investing might be fun for some investors. Others might dread it. But never confuse it with the endgame. The endgame is realizing your life goal.

Life goals are most often long-term endeavors. For nine out of ten investors, the goal they are trying to fund is at least 10 years away. For some, the goal is more than 20 years away. For you to be able to spend your capital in this far-away future, it has to still be there. Capital preservation becomes critical to realizing your goals. Capital lost is capital that cannot grow. It is capital that cannot be spent when it is needed.

But investors often forget two key facts:

- Your goals are long-term goals.
- You must preserve your capital.

Let's examine why investors lose sight of these mostly obvious facts.

Having a Long-Term Horizon

Clients with long-term goals often invest with short-term horizons. They tend to buy and sell investments on very short turnaround times—even though they often bought the investment with a long-term hold time in mind. The leading cause of this incongruity is that they tend to "over-monitor" their portfolio. Individual investors tend to overanalyze and track their portfolio's performance too frequently and too closely. This behavior causes the investor to agonize over every little gain and loss—especially the losses. The investor creates high portfolio turnover when giving his portfolio this much attention. Human nature is to take action when presented with lots of data—even when the data changes only marginally.

When you're an investor with a long-term goal, your investment horizon should correspond to your goal's time horizon. So think about making investments with longer-term horizons. Think about making investments you would be comfortable holding for one to three years or longer. At a minimum, your expected hold time should be six months.

Equally important, do not over-monitor your positions after you purchase them. You should be well-versed in what you own, and you should monitor your portfolio values. But remember that you are now a Buy and Hedge practitioner. And you will learn two key lessons later in this book as a Buy and Hedge investor:

- Hedges outperform over the long term, not the short term.
- A well-constructed hedged portfolio has reduced volatility, so monitoring your portfolio on a daily basis is overkill.

Preserving Your Capital

The second issue that investors tend to undervalue is the preservation of capital. Hedging is a defensive strategy. Investors who practice hedging are wisely acknowledging the impact of risk and volatility on their portfolio. But fewer than 1% of retail investors purposely build hedged portfolios. Almost all retail investors want downside portfolio protection. Hedging creates downside protection in a portfolio, so anyone who hedges has established a basis for capital preservation.

But most retail investors fail to deploy any defensive tactics. It is as if the average retail investor is a head football coach who focuses only on the offensive players and playbook while ignoring the defensive coaches and players. This approach of constantly playing aggressive offense with no defensive consideration is a common malady among retail investors. In my experience, these clients can experience short-lived success, but long-term asset growth is elusive.

In all fairness to retail investors, building a defensive portfolio has not always been easy. The number of products for building a hedged portfolio has increased significantly in just the last ten years. And many of these products and tools continue to evolve every year. Some of these products, such as options, can be difficult to invest in at certain brokerage firms. The industry has even created requirements that retail investors must certify their knowledge of these tools before they are permitted to use them. There are some natural roadblocks here. But when you are done reading this book, you will know how to build a customized defensive portfolio.

If you wonder whether a portfolio with a built-in defense can really be successful for a retail investor, consider a 2010 study on client investing performance conducted by TD Ameritrade (TDA).[1] TDA identified two subsets of clients: those with the best portfolio performance, and those with the worst portfolio performance. Then TDA examined the demographic and investing behavioral characteristics of these two groups. Ideally, management hoped to find predictors of client success as a way to help clients become better investors.

---

[1]Used with permission of TD Ameritrade, Inc.

The results were remarkable. The clients were identical in every key demographic category:

- Nearly the same average age
- The same average wealth
- The same average education level
- The identical average investment experience

And they were identical in nearly every behavioral characteristic of importance:

- Both groups had the same average number of trades per year
- Both used the same types of investments (such as equities and mutual funds)
- Both logged in with the same frequency
- Both had similar average hold times for investments

But these client groups differed in one material area: The Successful investors used protection in their portfolios, and the worst investors did not. The best group tended to use stop orders, stop-limit orders, and/or Options to create loss protection in their portfolio. This is a significant finding. The best investors took the time to consider the worst-case scenario for their individual positions and designed protection for those positions. The clients with the worst performance tended to be identical in every other way to the best group, except that they did not build in downside protection.

The findings in this study are very telling. You can't conclude that building position protection into your portfolio will by itself make you a good investor. But the fact that the best investors differed from the worst investors in *only* this category makes you wonder whether the best investors are clued in to something that the worst investors have not figured out.

This study alone cannot lead to the conclusion that building in portfolio protection will make you a better long-term investor. But the authors of this book *have* come to that conclusion through independent study and experience. Chapters 5 through 9 explain in both qualitative and quantitative terms why this conclusion is true.

To understand the basis of this conclusion, you need to understand Mr. Market a bit better. So let's start to examine Mr. Market.

Chapter Lessons

- Life goals that require future wealth typically are long-term goals. Therefore, it is important to align your investment time horizon with your life goal time horizon.
- Capital lost is capital that cannot grow.
- In a study of retail investors, the best investors tended to use portfolio protection tactics, and the worst investors did not.

4

The Investment Game
Isn't Rigged, But...

John Nash: *"In competitive behavior, someone always loses."*

Charles: *"Well, my niece knows that, John, and she's about this high."*

—From the Academy Award-winning best picture
A Beautiful Mind (2001)

Without a doubt, investing in the market is a competitive undertaking. When you lose sight of this fact, you put your portfolio at great risk. For every buyer, there is a seller. And many in the markets believe for that very reason that the markets always have a winner and a loser. Some market pundits think this view is a bit cynical—but not the authors of this book. Buy and Hedge believes that the markets can be very unforgiving to the unprepared.

Wall Street firms spend billions of dollars on the technology needed to handle market data. These firms spend even more money on technology to analyze the data and execute the transactions. These firms spend the *most* money on the systems they believe give them an advantage in the market. The smart retail investor must acknowledge the built-in disadvantage he holds compared to the institutional firms on and off Wall Street. These firms have more information, and it is typically more detailed. They even have access to information that the retail investor does not.

These facts about the market might seem daunting:

- It is competitive.
- Retail investors are being outspent by Wall Street.
- Wall Street has access to more information.

In reality, these facts actually also work in the retail investor's favor. The proliferation of institutional investors has created significant volume in the markets. The increased volume makes the market more efficient. A more efficient market helps the retail investor with price discovery and better trade execution.

As shown in Figure 4.1, institutional traders dominate the total trade volume of U.S. securities. Nearly 97% of all trade volume is placed by institutions. The remaining 3% is placed by retail investors. This is good news for investors. It means that most trades being made are actually between two institutions. These institutions employ money managers and traders who make their living by making a profit. No institution gives away its money. These employees have a single report card: return on investment. Make money, or lose your job. As a result, they keep each other honest. They create an orderly and liquid market.

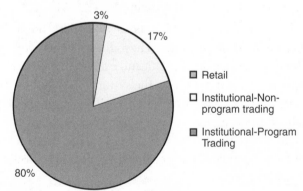

Estimate: Order flow by investor type dollar volume weighted

3%

17%

80%

☐ Retail

☐ Institutional-Non-program trading

☒ Institutional-Program Trading

Figure 4.1 Order flow: retail versus institutional

Retail investors benefit from the market efficiency created by institutions. In fact, many of these institutions are market makers that are required to buy and sell certain securities at market price for small trades. These small trade requirements are called automatic fill requirements. Small trades are the domain of the retail investor. Many online brokerages, such as TD Ameritrade, have negotiated these automatic fill requirements with market makers on behalf of their retail investor clients. So, although the institutions have an information and capital advantage, at least someone is looking out for you.

So, the market isn't rigged against retail investors, but it isn't designed primarily for retail investors either. But investors can take solace in the fact that the market is kept efficient by very powerful institutions. These institutions make markets and help with price discovery. If a market were ever to show inefficient pricing, you can be confident that an institution would step in and deploy its capital to take advantage of the inefficient pricing. Institutions are happy to exploit price discrepancies to make a profit. Along the way, they return the market to its equilibrium state, where it is efficient again.

The outcome of an efficient market backed by institutions is that retail investors can step into this market and feel confident building portfolios and making trades.

You might have the impression that all institutions are "smart money." This expression refers to people who make the smartest and best decisions when investing. But plenty of institutions go out of business all the time. Being big enough to be a financial institution doesn't make an institution smart money. It just means the firm has a lot of money. It means the firm spends on technology and has more information than the average investor. It doesn't mean these firms make the best decisions. For every successful institutional firm, at least two firms are struggling to make their investment strategies work.

Over the years, the authors have seen many investment strategies originate from a myriad of institutions. And we have used many of them in our portfolios. We have found three strategies that, when combined, create a compelling long-term portfolio advantage:

- Indexing
- Asset class allocation
- Defensive hedging

Individually each of these strategies has seen mixed results over the past ten years. Large institutions deploy these strategies—some to the tune of trillions of dollars in assets. None of these strategies is new; they are tried and true. The real power comes in combining them into one retail portfolio.

Indexing

This strategy has gained real momentum with investors over the past ten to 20 years. An investor who indexes is trying to emulate the identical performance of a broad market or sector index. The investor is not trying to beat the market; he's just trying to mimic the market's performance at the lowest cost possible. Many fund companies have created exchange traded securities that track the performance of the largest indexes. These securities are called exchange traded funds (ETFs). ETFs are very liquid and very low-cost.

Indexing is one of the authors' favorite investment strategies. It is low-cost and tax-efficient (because it enjoys low turnover). But over the last decade, indexing has not kept up with inflation. The major indexes for the last decade are all flat; the only return coming from dividend yield. So, to achieve our desired returns, we need to couple this with another strategy.

Asset Class Allocation

Financial advisors most often recommend asset allocation strategies to their clients. The advice usually includes a collection of mutual funds or ETFs to achieve the desired allocation. Asset classes are investment categories that are distinctly different. The most popular are equities (also known as stocks), fixed income (also known as bonds), and cash equivalents. Many asset allocation plans also consider real estate and commodities as additional asset classes.

An asset class allocation strategy invests the portfolio across the selected asset classes to create a portfolio with the client's desired risk profile. The advisor selects the allocations to optimize the return for the given risk the client can sustain. These asset classes typically have very different risk/return profiles and behave mostly independently in the market. When they are combined into one portfolio, the asset classes tend to counterbalance each other. This strategy has been around for over 50 years and is often called modern portfolio theory.

This strategy is fairly low-cost when implemented by a retail investor. The tax consequences are modest because turnover is moderate. But the performance of this strategy over the last ten years has been only slightly better than the market. The average annual return is between 3% and 4% for the most aggressive asset allocation strategies, which carry the most risk. Like indexing, as a strategy by itself, asset class allocation leaves the investor wanting more.

Defensive Hedging

Defensive hedging is deploying protection for your investments or portfolio. The investor can achieve this by purchasing positions that increase in value when another position decreases in value. Designing these kinds of portfolios and investments takes knowledge and practice. This book explains the process in great detail.

Notice that this strategy is called defensive hedging and not just hedging. The hedge fund industry has bastardized the definition of the word hedge. As a result, finding a market proxy for this strategy is difficult. The authors have deployed this strategy with great success. Imagine an investor who built a defensive hedge for every position held in 2008. Obviously, that investor would have avoided the worst market collapse in the last 75 years. That influence alone on your portfolio would have generated terrific market-beating returns.

But defensive hedging during a prolonged and sustained uptrending market reduces the investor's overall returns during the uptrend. In other words, hedging has a cost, just like homeowner's insurance, for example. If you expect someone to pay you to make up for a loss, you need to pay a premium along the way. The strategy of hedging cannot win in the market by itself. It must be combined with smart portfolio management technique.

Note that the costs of hedging are real. And hedging has higher-than-average turnover. So the tax consequences need to be managed closely. And since hedging has a cost, an investor needs to consider ways to overcome this cost. This book teaches you how to manage both the cost of a hedge and the tax consequences.

This book unites these three strategies to teach you how to build and manage your own portfolio. The strategy comes together as Buy and Hedge. How do you know these strategies work when combined? Well, the authors know they work for us. This book is being published because these strategies, when combined, have produced excellent returns for the last three-plus years. The authors have been running a personal portfolio that follows the Buy and Hedge philosophy since early 2008. That portfolio's performance is available for review at http://www.BuyAndHedge.com/Performance.

But most important, the authors have learned some key lessons from their years building investment tools for retail investors at the world's largest online brokerage. These lessons influenced our conclusions and the design of our Buy and Hedge strategy. These lessons are the Immutable Laws of Investing. These laws describe conditions that every investor must deal with to be successful. They are unavoidable. Part II, "The immutable Laws of Investing," focuses on these laws. When an investor understands these laws, the power of Buy and Hedge becomes clear.

Chapter Lessons

- Markets are kept efficient by institutions—efficient enough for retail investors to confidently invest in advanced strategies.
- When combined, indexing, asset class allocation, and defensive hedging create the strategy called Buy and Hedge.
- An investor who understands the Immutable Laws of Investing will understand the forces that make Buy and Hedge successful.

Part II
The Immutable Laws of Investing

Every investment book ever published was authored from experience. But the best do-it-yourself investment books effectively convey the key lessons the author has learned from his or her experience. An author feels strongly about a handful of key lessons and produces a story from those lessons. The authors of this book are no different—except that our lessons are more commonsense than most.

Both authors spent over ten years building and buying the online tools used by individual investors at the world's largest online brokerage. Many individual investors have used or seen a tool in the industry that was built or launched by the authors. During our time deploying these tools, we tried many investing and trading strategies. Some worked, but many didn't. More important, we developed the key lessons of this book. In fact, not only is the Buy and Hedge investment strategy influenced by these lessons—it originates from them!

These lessons are the Immutable Laws of Investing. These Laws are unavoidable when you're a retail investor. They impact every investor. You ignore them at your own peril. The authors learned these lessons and always keep them at the front of their thought process. Some of these lessons we learned the hard way. Many others we learned from our clients. Some were expensive lessons to learn.

The key is for you to realize that these Laws are the foundation of the Buy and Hedge investment strategy. After explaining these laws, this book will introduce the Five Iron Rules of Buy and Hedge. An investor who deploys these Rules will maintain an official Buy and Hedge portfolio.

To summarize:

- The Laws define the most important investor lessons.
- The Laws inform the Rules.
- The Rules define the Buy and Hedge strategy.

- Following the Rules is your path to investment success!

The Immutable Laws of Investing that you'll learn in Part II are

- Capital Lost Is Capital That Cannot Grow
- Risk Is the Input, and Return Is the Output
- Emotion Is the Enemy
- Volatility Is Kryptonite
- The Return That Matters Is After-Tax Return

5

Capital Lost Is Capital That Cannot Grow

"Say it! Say it! Say, 'I lost the nest-egg.' Go on, say it!

—David Howard (played by Albert Brooks) in *Coming to America* (1985)

This first Immutable Law of Investing probably seems somewhat trifling at first glance. After all, it is a blinding glimpse of the obvious (BGOTO, pronounced "buh-GO-tuh"). But when you think about it, aren't all the most powerful laws simple and straight to the point? Thou shalt not steal. Thou shalt not kill. These are short, straightforward, and downright pithy!

In the end, this is the most important law that drives the Buy and Hedge strategy. Hedging is the act of building downside loss protection into a portfolio or position. Hedging protects the investor from potential losses. Hedging becomes important because of this law. Capital losses are difficult to overcome. A portfolio that has suffered a significant loss must overcome the loss just to get back to even. None of us invest to break even. We invest so that we can fund future goals.

Capital is invested with one purpose in mind: *growth.* Investments come with some level of inherent risk—and in exchange, you expect some reciprocal level of return. Over time, the growth builds on itself and can evolve to a very impressive size. When growth builds on growth, this is called compounding. Compounding growth is one of the most powerful forces in the investment world. But don't take our word for it. Take Warren Buffet's word: "My wealth has come from a combination of living in America, some lucky genes, and compound interest."

A portfolio can grow through compounding only when the returns are positive. Negative returns result from losses. Hence, the Law is that capital lost is capital that cannot grow. If an investor can protect his capital, he gives himself a chance to see the power of compounding. Without positive returns, the portfolio will never reach sufficient size to fund its goal.

So, the key to investing is not to lose any money? This lesson probably still seems too basic. It is more complex than it probably appears. This book is a how-to on investing in the markets. You cannot invest in the markets without the risk of losing money. We are not proposing that you avoid all losses. That would be both impossible and rather irresponsible on our part. But you need to understand the impact of regular and repeated losses in the context of a market-invested portfolio.

Proper understanding of this law includes this context. Let's engage in a mathematical analysis to attempt to make this point using some market investments.

We'll examine the worst-performing periods in the S&P 500 over the ten years ending Dec 31, 2010. Then we'll examine the impact on a portfolio that is fully invested in the S&P 500 and that avoids these worst-performing periods.

Study #1: Avoiding the Ten Worst Days

The Facts

The ten worst days in the S&P 500 ranged from –5.22% to –9.84%. Eight of these days occurred in the second half of 2008. The other two occurred in 2009 and 2001, respectively. The arithmetic mean of the ten worst days was –6.88%.

The Data Analysis

$100,000 invested in the S&P 500 on January 1, 2001 would have been worth $113,692 on Dec 31, 2010.

$100,000 invested in the S&P 500 on January 1, 2001 that suffered no loss or gain on the ten worst-performing days in the market would have been worth $232,360 on Dec 31, 2010.

The Results

If an investor could have avoided the investment results from these ten days, the portfolio performance would have been dramatically increased. The results would have been a 132% gain versus the S&P's 13% gain. The arithmetic sum of the ten worst days that were avoided was –68.8%. But the winning portfolio outperformed by more than 119%!

The results are telling. This outperformance has two components: the losses avoided and the compounding effect. The losses avoided, as you just saw, were equal to –68.8%. But the rest of the portfolio outperformed because of the positive impact of compounding. The capital that was preserved was given a chance to grow because it was fully invested in the markets. And those market results were, by and large, positive—especially with the ten worst days avoided.

Let's perform a reality check: Avoiding the ten worst market days is impossible. After all, it is impossible to predict these days. This book does not advocate or teach day-trading techniques. We are not trying to time the markets in any way. This analysis is only meant to show you the destructive power of a loss when invested in the markets.

Let's examine the impact of losses on a portfolio that occur over a longer time period—three months. We can't predict what will happen in the market on one day, nor can we realistically build and manage hedges for one-day time periods. But we can build hedges for longer time periods, such as a quarter. Let's see what happens to our performance when we avoid the worst-performing quarters in the last ten years.

Study # 2: Avoiding the Four Worst Quarters

The Facts

The four worst quarters were the quarters ending December '08, September '08, June '02, and September '01. The average loss for these four quarters was –16.5%.

The Data Analysis

$100,000 invested in the S&P 500 on January 1, 2001 would have been worth $113,692 on Dec 31, 2010.

$100,000 invested in the S&P 500 on January 1, 2001 that suffered no loss or gain in the four worst-performing calendar quarters in the market would have been worth $226,627 on Dec 31, 2010.

The Results

The portfolio that avoided the four worst quarters again outperformed the portfolio that invested in the S&P 500: +126% return versus +13%. The cumulative arithmetic sum of the four quarterly losses was –66%. Again, the power of compounding enhanced the overall results materially beyond the 66 percentage points avoided from the losses.

The authors *still* are not advocating trying to time the market, even on a quarterly basis. Our years of experience tell us that is a loser's game. Instead, focus on the benefits of capital preservation and compounding growth. The lesson here is clear: If you can build a portfolio that lessens, mutes, or avoids market losses, your portfolio will benefit significantly. We'll teach you those techniques using hedges in later chapters.

The key to successful hedging is finding hedged techniques that can reduce your losses at a cost that is effective. For the cost to be effective, the total cost of the hedge when compared to the losses avoided still must yield overall returns that are higher when measured over the long term. This topic will be covered more later in the book.

Hopefully, you can now understand that avoiding a loss on capital provides greater benefit than solely the avoidance of the loss. The capital preserved is positioned to grow through compounding and create exponentially higher levels of growth in your portfolio.

Chapter Lessons

- Capital lost is capital that cannot grow.
- Compounding growth is one of the most powerful forces an investor can put to work for his portfolio.
- The gain from avoiding a loss is more than just the loss avoidance itself; it is also the benefits from compounded growth on the capital that is preserved.

6

Risk Is What You Buy;
Return Is What You Hope For

"If it weren't for people who took risks, where would we be in this world?"

—From the sequel *Wall Street: Money Never Sleeps* (2010)

In this Immutable Law of Investing, risk is the input, and return is the output.

Why do capital markets exist? Think about this for a moment. The answer is quite simple. Capital markets exist so that companies can raise funds from new and existing investors. When companies raise funds directly from investors this is called the primary market.

What will these companies do with those funds? The use of funds raised in capital markets is endless! The funds are often used for expansion: new plants, new products, new geographic markets, or a new marketing campaign. Another common use of the funds is the acquisition of other companies. And sometimes the capital is raised just to pay off early or original investors. In other words, sometimes the money raised is just handed to another investor, along with a pat on the back and a thank-you handshake.

What do these transactions in a primary market have in common? The investor who gives his money to the company has purchased an ownership stake in the company—through either equity or debt. And this is true in the secondary market as well. When you, the retail investor, purchase a company's stock or bonds in the public marketplace, you are buying an ownership stake in that company. In this case, you have bought your investment from another owner, not from the company directly. You now have an ownership stake in the company—albeit a small one.

So, what exactly have you bought when you buy a stake in this company? To put it simply, all you bought was *risk*. You might expect a return, but all you really bought was *risk*. Remember that there can be no expectation of a return without the risk. So, what you really bought was risk. You had control of what you bought—and what you sold. And what you bought was risk.

What do we mean by "all you bought was risk"? Think about your situation. You own a piece of this publicly traded company. As a retail investor, your ownership stake is small. As a result, you have no control over this company's resources or strategy. Your return on investment will be based on the performance of the company's stock or debt. That performance will be based on management's ability to execute. And you have no say in the decisions that influence that execution. In other words, you bought nothing but risk. The risk that things might go terribly wrong at this company. Or in this industry. Or in the broader markets.

The company's performance might be exceptional and drive excellent returns for its investors. Or the company might perform poorly and drive equally poor results. Or it might limp along without much return at all. Or it could go out of business, leaving its investors to fight in bankruptcy court over its assets. These are four very different return scenarios. When you purchase the security, you don't know which of these outcomes to expect. The investor has a hypothesis about which of these outcomes to expect—but no certainty. Securities do not come with money-back guarantees. If they did, it wouldn't be called investing.

When investors purchase securities, risk is the only certainty that has been purchased. Securities represent the ownership interest in some entity—and that entity has no guarantee that it will succeed or even survive. When investing, the investor buys risk, not return. Return is the outcome. Returns can be positive, negative, or zero. Return is a measurement. It is the output. The investor cannot control for return. The investor can only control for risk.

When building a portfolio, the risk is the input. The investor can control for risk—at least in the portfolio design. The investor is buying risk, and risk can be measured in many different ways. Risk has qualitative and quantitative measures. We'll teach these key measures in Chapter 11, "Know Your Risk Metrics."

When designing a Buy and Hedge portfolio, risk is front and center. Each security has a series of risk measures unique to that security. In the aggregate, the portfolio has an overall risk profile as well. The combination of all the risk metrics of the individual securities creates a different risk profile at a portfolio level. And the thoughtful investor will consider the change to the overall portfolio risk every time he adds a new investment with its own risk metrics.

The individual investor tends to obsess about return, with little focus on or discussion of risk. We opened this book with this discussion in Chapter 1, "Life Is a Series of Risk-and-Return Decisions—and So Is Investing." It's easy to get caught up in return, because our investment growth determines our investor success. Who doesn't like to review a real-time report card every time they get a chance? Your online brokerage account gives you a real-time report card every time you log in!

The temptation to focus on return is strong. But in the end, success rarely comes from a focus on the things you cannot control. Risk is the controllable factor in your portfolio, not return. The investor who lacks a healthy appreciation of risk lacks perspective. Even worse, that investor lacks control over his portfolio.

In the world of investing, risk and return have a contingent relationship. The investor takes on risk to achieve a desired return. Even more important to the individual investor, the contingent relationship includes a dependency on degree. Excess return cannot be achieved without excess risk. The inverse is true also—excess losses can only result from excess risk. Correspondingly, low risk levels should produce lower returns.

When presented with any sales pitch that describes excess returns that are married to low risk, an investor should run for the hills. This scenario doesn't exist in the real world of investing. If it did, it would be exploited very quickly until the opportunity dried up. More important, it wouldn't be offered to the retail investor. Why would someone offer the small investor that opportunity and not keep it for himself? In fact, nearly every case of fraud in the history of commerce has started with "I promise you X returns in exchange for risk that is significantly less than X." Risk and return are inextricably linked. Forget this lesson at your own peril.

This relationship between risk and return might seem like it fails at times. The markets have shown plenty of examples where a portfolio outperforms its perceived risk. These kinds of market displacements happen, and investors are always surprised. In reality, the return that occurred was always perfectly correlated to the risk of the investment—the *actual* risk, not the perceived risk. The winner in these scenarios is the investor who accurately assessed the actual risk and found a price discrepancy in the *perceived* risk. These kinds of scenarios happen routinely. But they are very difficult to spot.

The Buy and Hedge method does not spend time trying to find these kinds of scenarios. The investor who wants to focus on these scenarios might as well be hunting for a one-eyed polar bear. Instead of exploiting the difference between the market's perception of risk and your investment hypothesis, Buy and Hedge teaches the investor to modify and control for risk. This is where hedging comes in. The investor who learns to hedge can control for risk. As a result, that investor can design a custom risk-controlled portfolio built to outperform over the long term!

Chapter Lessons

- Retail investors tend to focus on return, but risk is the control factor in a portfolio.
- The investor ignores the measurement of risk at his own peril.
- Risk and return have a contingent relationship.

7

Emotion Is the Enemy

"Fear is the path to the dark side. Fear leads to anger. Anger leads to hate. Hate leads to suffering. I sense much fear in you."

—Yoda from *Star Wars–Episode I: The Phantom Menace* (1999)

This is the second chapter in this book that describes emotion as being the enemy. This is neither a misprint nor a coincidence. Too often, investors get caught up in the emotions surrounding investment gains and losses. The two most powerful forces that drive the markets are greed and fear. These "forces" are actually feelings—meaning that they are powered, in part, by emotion. Upward-moving markets tend to create updrafts that fan the flames of greed. Correspondingly, downdrafts tend to fan the flames of fear. In either case, these forces are shaped by feelings—the feelings of investors in the market.

Pundits like to debate which force is more powerful, fear or greed. The authors believe that debate is over. Fear wins. It isn't even close in our book! Recall the introduction of loss aversion in Chapter 2, "Emotion Is Your Enemy, So Bid It Good-Bye." Loss aversion is more closely linked with fear. The fear of incurring a loss drives the behavior to avoid the loss; hence, loss aversion occurs. Loss aversion is a powerful motivator for investor behavior in the market. Recent market performance is a constant reminder of the power of fear in the markets.

Maybe you aren't sold yet on the concept of loss aversion. In fact, you might even believe that loss aversion doesn't affect you. If you aren't convinced yet, maybe an empirical data analysis will change your mind. When you study the market over the last two decades, you clearly see the impact of fear and greed on the market.

The data analysis shows that market declines tend to be sharper and faster than market increases over the past two decades. When markets increase, the increases tend to occur over wider windows and be more steady. Meanwhile, market losses tend to be more sudden— even violent in the case of 2008. Let's take a closer look at the data.

We'll start by looking at the best and worst one-day market movements of the last two decades (see Table 8.1). The analysis uses the S&P 500 because it is a great proxy for the wider market movements.

Table 7.1 Best and Worst One-Day Market Movements over the Last 20 Years

Best One-Day Market Moves	Percentage Change	Worst One-Day Market Moves	Percentage Change
10/13/08	+11.6%	10/15/08	–9.0%
10/28/08	+10.8%	12/1/08	–8.9%
3/23/09	+7.1%	9/29/08	–8.8%
11/13/08	+6.9%	10/9/08	–7.6%
11/24/08	+6.5%	10/27/97	–6.9%
3/10/09	+6.4%	8/31/98	–6.8%
11/21/08	+6.3%	11/20/08	–6.7%
7/24/02	+5.7%	11/19/08	–6.1%
9/30/08	+5.4%	10/22/08	–6.1%
7/29/02	+5.4%	4/14/00	–5.8%
	Mean: +7.72%		Mean: –7.28%

At first glance, you would look at this data and say the two groups are very close. The worst days are similar in average to the best days. In fact, the list of the best days includes a wider range, with its top two days being 2 percentage points higher than the worst single day. But a closer examination of the data shows an ominous trend. Look at the dates.

Six of the best ten days occur in the fall of 2008, along with two more in the spring of 2009. I don't need to remind you about this time period in the markets. This was the single worst bear market since the Great Market Crash of 1929. Despite these positive days, no one in the market was feeling buoyed. Investors were mired in volatility and downward-trending violent market days.

In fact, the other two days on the list occurred in July 2002—another violent downward market move. The S&P 500 dropped over 300 points, from a high of 1168 in March 2002 to a low of 797 in July 2002 and a subsequent new low of 776 in October of that same year.

In other words, all the best days in the market were rebound days from terrible downward swings in the market. No investor felt good about these rebounds. The overall market feeling was one of malaise. In fact, loss aversion had an iron grip on the markets during these time periods.

To wrap up the data, look at the ten worst days in the market. The four worst days and seven of the ten worst days occurred during that same fall 2008 time period. This further supports the case about the violent nature of downswings in the market compared to upswings. The single-day upswings were not nearly as powerful as the downswings when you consider the market timing of the upswings and downswings. This data also tells us something about the volatility of the market, which is covered in the next chapter.

For some perspective, let's summarize the 20-year window ending December 31, 2010. The total market return was impressive. The S&P 500 opened on January 2, 1991 at $330.20 and closed on December 31, 2010 at $1,257.64. This is a +280% return over 20 years, or an average annual return of +6.9%. On January 2, 2001, the midpoint of this period, the S&P 500 opened at $1,320.28, or slightly higher than it closed at the end of the time period. This means that all the gains in the S&P 500 Index came in the first ten years—and none in the second decade. But both decades had tremendous swings in market values.

The first analysis looked at daily swings. But we don't invest day to day in the markets. We are long-term investors. So let's examine strong market moves over wider time periods.

As shown in Table 8.2, we examined every market rally and market decline of the last 20 years that represented a move of at least +/–10%. We measured from peak to trough and back again. And we further examined the time it took to reach 10% and to reach an eventual peak or trough. In addition, we examined the total magnitude of the move, from trough to peak and peak to trough. This analysis does not define a new uptrend or downtrend until the reverse equals a new

10% move in the opposite direction. In other words, we considered a new peak or trough only if the move was at least a 10% change in the value of the S&P 500. In this 20-year window, there were 51 periods where the market moved at least 10% from peak to trough or trough to peak—equaling 26 peaks and 25 troughs.

Table 7.2 S&P 500 Index Peaks and Troughs for 20 Years Ending January 1, 2011

Peak or Trough	S&P Price	Date	Days to Peak	Days to Trough
Peak 1	817.68	2/19/97	2,195	
Trough 1	733.54	4/14/97		55
Peak 2	983.12	10/7/97	173	
Trough 2	855.27	10/28/97		21
Peak 3	1,190.58	7/20/98	262	
Trough 3	939.98	9/1/98		41
Peak 4	1,066.11	9/24/98	23	
Trough 4	923.32	10/8/98		14
Peak 5	1,420.33	7/19/99	281	
Trough 5	1,233.70	10/18/99		89
Peak 6	1,478.00	1/3/00	75	
Trough 6	1,325.07	2/28/00		55
Peak 7	1,552.87	3/24/00	26	
Trough 7	1,339.40	4/14/00		20
Peak 8	1,530.09	9/1/00	137	
Trough 8	1,305.79	10/18/00		47
Peak 9	1,438.46	11/6/00	18	
Trough 9	1,254.07	12/21/00		45
Peak 10	1,383.37	1/31/01	40	
Trough 10	1,081.19	3/22/01		52
Peak 11	1,315.93	5/22/01	60	
Trough 11	944.75	9/21/01		119
Peak 12	1,176.97	1/7/02	106	
Trough 12	775.68	7/24/02		197
Peak 13	965.00	8/22/02	28	
Trough 13	768.63	10/10/02		48

Peak or Trough	S&P Price	Date	Days to Peak	Days to Trough
Peak 14	954.28	12/2/02	52	
Trough 14	788.90	3/12/03		100
Peak 15	1,555.90	7/16/07	1,564	
Trough 15	1,370.60	8/16/07		30
Peak 16	1,576.09	10/11/07	55	
Trough 16	1,256.98	3/17/08		156
Peak 17	1,440.24	5/19/08	62	
Trough 17	1,133.50	9/18/08		119
Peak 18	1,265.12	9/19/08	1	
Trough 18	839.80	10/10/08		21
Peak 19	1,044.31	10/14/08	4	
Trough 19	865.83	10/16/08		2
Peak 20	985.44	10/21/08	5	
Trough 20	845.27	10/28/08		7
Peak 21	1,007.51	11/4/08	6	
Trough 21	818.69	11/13/08		9
Peak 22	916.88	11/14/08	1	
Trough 22	741.02	11/21/08		7
Peak 23	943.85	1/6/09	45	
Trough 23	666.79	3/6/09		60
Peak 24	1,219.80	4/26/10	410	
Trough 24	1,065.79	5/6/10		10
Peak 25	1,173.57	5/13/10	7	
Trough 25	1,010.91	7/1/10		48
Peak 26	1,276.17	1/3/11	182	

Here are some key observations from this data:

The average length of time to go from a trough to a peak was 224 days, and the average time to go from a peak to a trough was 55 days. These averages are heavily influenced by two long and steady bull market periods that were 2,200 and 1,500 days. Even when these two bull markets are removed from the trough-to-peak calculation, the change is from 224 days average to 86 days. Eighty-six days is still materially more than the 55 days to move from peak to trough.

When examining the speed with which the peak or trough occurs, we examined how long it took to achieve at least 80% of the eventual gain or loss within the respective peak or trough. For the peaks, 80% of the overall gain was achieved on average within 179 days versus a 44-day average for the troughs to reach 80% of the overall loss.

The two decades examined here represent two distinct ten-year periods. The first decade was one of the greatest secular bull markets ever. Every market correction was small in magnitude and short in duration. The second decade is now known as the lost decade. It began with the significant dot-com bubble burst of 2000–2002. This was followed by another secular bull market that lasted five years, from October 2002 to October 2007, in which the market doubled. During that window, only two modest corrections occurred, and both were again short in duration.

Of course, you know that the decade ended with the worst market correction since the Great Market Crash of 1929. This correction was violent and included many of the worst one-day losses in market history. The market has enjoyed a nice rebound since, but it is still well under the $1,500 level of the S&P 500 high of October 2007.

In summary, market increases have tended to be steady and secular, meaning that they spread out over several years. Meanwhile, market decreases have tended to be shorter in duration and violent in their destruction, especially in the last ten years.

Why do we study these trends? Only to prove that fear is more powerful than greed in the markets. Fear makes investors sell and drive down prices with record acceleration. And fear is what drives loss aversion. An investor who thinks he or she is unaffected by loss aversion is not being honest. This market forces the investor to confront regular and dramatic market decreases. Faced with these market forces, loss aversion must be part of your planning. All investors are all subject to its disastrous impact.

All investors suffer from loss aversion, and this book promises a treatment for the symptoms of loss aversion. That treatment begins in Chapter 10, "Hedge Every Investment," which describes the first Iron Rule of Buy and Hedge. The more you understand the impact of fear on your portfolio, the better prepared you are to correct it.

This is why you should hedge your investments. Buy and Hedge investors remove the emotion of loss aversion by constructing portfolios that do not suffer wild market swings or dramatic losses. The volatility of these market moves is destructive. We'll address the impact of that destruction in the next chapter.

Chapter Lessons

- Emotions such as fear and greed destroy portfolio value.
- Empirical data shows that market downswings tend to occur very quickly and with significant market force, causing fear and loss aversion to drive markets further downward.
- Hedging is a structural approach to investing that reduces the impact of fear and loss aversion on your personal portfolio.

8

Volatility Is Kryptonite

"Fasten your seatbelts. It's going to be a bumpy night."

—Margo Channing (played by Bette Davis) in *All About Eve* (1950)

This is one of the most famous movie quotes of all time. This quote made the American Film Institute top 10 movie quotes from the last 100 years. The investment world for the past four years has been about as "bumpy" as it ever has been. The "bumps" in the market are called market volatility.

In the Immutable Law of Investing, volatility erodes investment returns.

Every few years, a survey is published that amounts to an investor "taste test"—just like the famous Coke versus Pepsi taste tests. Some college professor presents "blind" information about two investment portfolios to strangers and asks them to pick the portfolio they prefer. The study is typically designed to measure both investor knowledge and risk appetite.

We have an informal version of a portfolio "taste test" that we have used with friends, family, and colleagues through the years, as shown in Table 8.1. You must decide which of the two portfolios would have performed better assuming that each started with $100,000.

Table 8.1 Test #1

Portfolio A		Portfolio B	
Period	Performance	Period	Performance
Year 1	–30%	Year 1	–10%
Year 2	+30%	Year 2	+10%
Year 3	–30%	Year 3	–10%
Year 4	+30%	Year 4	+10%

More than two-thirds of the friends and colleagues decided that these two portfolios performed equally. Respondents typically pointed out that the performance amounts added up to 0% in each portfolio. So these investors assumed that each portfolio did not gain or lose money. Of course, these investors were wrong. Here are the actual portfolio values at the end of Year 4:

Portfolio A: $82,810

Portfolio B: $98,010

This is straightforward math, not investment voodoo. This version of a "taste test" would more accurately be called a "math" test. If one dollar declines by 30% in one year, it is worth 70 cents. Your investment is now worth 70 cents at the beginning of Year 2. If that investment increases by 30% in Year 2, it does not return to $1.00 in value. 70 cents increased by 30% would add 21 cents, resulting in 91 cents ($0.70 × 1.3 = $0.91). For the 70 cents to return to $1.00 in total value in Year 2, it would have needed to increase by 42%.

Try an easier example: If you have 1 dollar and it loses half of its value in the first year, it is now worth $0.50. For the 50 cents to return to 1 dollar, it needs to double in value. In other words, the increase in the second year needs to be +100% to return to its original value.

What is the conclusion? Gains and losses of similar or identical measures do not have the same impact on a portfolio. Losses are more impactful over the long term because gains and losses occur in a sequence. Every 1% of value lost requires an increase of more than 1% just to get back to even. The power of compounding comes into play. Compounding is the "Superman" of investing, and high volatility is the kryptonite.

Let's continue our study. Look at the two new portfolios shown in Table 8.2. Both portfolios have the same gain and loss profile, but Portfolio A changes the order of its gains and losses.

Table 8.2 Test #2

Portfolio A		Portfolio B	
Period	Performance	Period	Performance
Year 1	+30%	Year 1	–10%
Year 2	–30%	Year 2	+10%
Year 3	+30%	Year 3	–10%
Year 4	–30%	Year 4	+10%

Amazingly, many investors change their vote when presented with this data. More than a handful believed that Portfolio A now outperforms Portfolio B. When asked why, they explained that Portfolio A started with a gain instead of a loss. (Portfolio B started with a loss.) These investors concluded that starting with a gain gave the portfolio more potential to weather the losses that followed.

Of course, you know this is wrong. The overall portfolio performance did not change. Both portfolios ended with the same value as they had in Test #1. Again, this is just straightforward math. A portfolio that starts with a gain in Year 1 simply has more assets that suffer a loss in Year 2. The math is the same. Starting with $1.00 and a 30% gain, the result is $1.30. With a subsequent 30% loss in the next year, the loss is 49 cents, resulting in $0.91—the same result as Test #1.

So, the order of the sequence doesn't matter. What matters is the volatility in the performance returns and whether any of those returns were negative. Avoiding volatility—particularly losses—preserves your capital. More important, it sets you up to take advantage of the impact of compounding growth through positive returns.

Our study wasn't done yet. In a third data set presented to our friends, a fifth year of performance was added to the data, as shown in Table 8.3.

Table 8.3 Test #3

Portfolio A		Portfolio B	
Period	**Performance**	**Period**	**Performance**
Year 1	–30%	Year 1	–10%
Year 2	+30%	Year 2	+10%
Year 3	–30%	Year 3	–10%
Year 4	+30%	Year 4	+10%
Year 5	+15%	Year 4	+0%

The fifth year added a powerful boost to the performance of Portfolio A. As a result, most investors now definitively picked Portfolio A over Portfolio B. They reasoned that the performance percentages totaled to a positive 15% in Portfolio A while remaining at 0% in Portfolio B.

From what you learned in Test #1, you know that this logic doesn't work. Simply adding up these geometric return percentages will not tell you what your end return on investment equals. But does the 15% improvement in Portfolio A make up for the disastrous effects of volatility in the first four years? In this case, the answer is no.

Here are the portfolio values at the end of Year 5:

Portfolio A: $95,231

Portfolio B: $98,010

In other words, a 15% spike for Portfolio A could not overcome the negative impact of volatility on the portfolio.

More recently, we have added a fourth test to our informal study. Our intent is to highlight the impact that volatility has on a portfolio even when all the performance returns are positive. Table 8.4 shows two test portfolios.

Table 8.4 Test #4

Portfolio C		Portfolio D	
Period	**Performance**	**Period**	**Performance**
Year 1	+10%	Year 1	+20%
Year 2	+10%	Year 2	+0%
Year 3	+10%	Year 3	+20%
Year 4	+10%	Year 4	+0%

As in Tests #1 and #2, the totals of all the percentage gains and losses are equal in each portfolio (40%). But does the fact that one portfolio is more volatile than the other have an impact on performance even when all the returns are positive? Of course it does!

Portfolio C is worth $146,410 at the end of Year 4, and Portfolio D is worth $144,000. The difference is only about 2.5% over four years, or less than six-tenths of 1% per year. So, volatility has an impact even when all the returns are positive.

You might think the authors are advocating the "slow and steady wins the race" approach. Nothing could be further from the truth. We want you to run with the market when the market is running well, and we want you to deflect losses when the market is falling. This might sound like timing the market. It isn't. We would never advocate that, because we've seen thousands of former clients try to do so, with mixed results. Instead, we advise that you build a hedged portfolio that automatically runs with the market when the market runs and plays defense when the market runs scared. This kind of portfolio can be built. This book teaches you how in Part III, "The Five Iron Rules of Buy and Hedge."

Volatility erodes investor returns in several more ways. We can think of three in particular: mathematically, psychologically, and logistically. We've already covered the mathematical impact. Let's now look at the psychological and logistical.

The Psychological Impact of Volatility

When volatility in the market is high, market prices change quickly and often. The higher the volatility, the greater the price dispersion for your investments. These swings in the market cause many changes in the value of any portfolio that is invested in the market. Most portfolios have high exposure to market forces.

All this portfolio fluctuation will make your stomach churn, so there goes your good night's sleep. When your portfolio suffers wild swings in value, you spend more time thinking about it. And you know from the preceding chapter that all investors suffer from loss aversion. So, when these swings in portfolio value include losses, you can't help but be influenced by loss aversion. The result is poor investment decisions driven by loss aversion.

The Logistical Impact of Volatility

The investor who hedges a portfolio has built downside protection into his or her investments. This downside protection is obviously not free, just as purchasing insurance for your home isn't free. There is a premium involved in owning a hedge. In other words, hedging comes at a cost.

This book teaches you how to identity, price, and build these hedges. And the factor that influences the price of this hedge more than any other is the volatility of the investment you are trying to hedge. Earlier, you learned that volatility is the dispersion of prices around some average price. An investment with a high expected volatility has a wide expected dispersion of prices. To hedge an investment, another investor must want to sell you the hedge. The person selling that hedge must consider the expected price dispersion. The wider the expected price dispersion, the more premium the seller must collect.

Insurance underwriters act the same way. When an insurance company quotes a health insurance premium, it considers the applicant's medical history. The insurer uses that history to make an informed decision about the likelihood that the applicant will need future care. The more care the applicant has needed in the past, the more likely it is that he or she will need future care. Suppose the applicant's history of care is spread around more than just a few distinct maladies or problems. The insurance company will quote a higher premium to this person. Why? Because of the volatility of the applicant's past care.

So, higher volatility makes buying hedges more expensive. The higher cost of the hedge detracts from the portfolio performance overall. Your Buy and Hedge strategy needs to take into account the costs of the hedge in every investment you consider. This is the logistical impact of volatility on your portfolio.

Chapter Lessons

- Performance returns are measured as percentage gains and losses.
- Investment volatility is measured using percentage returns.
- Excess volatility erodes the overall returns of your portfolio.
- Compounding can be a powerful positive force for your portfolio, but volatility weakens the positive impact of compounding.
- Volatility in your portfolio value will cause you to experience emotions that can harm your portfolio.
- Higher volatility in an investment drives a higher cost to hedge that investment.

9

The Taxman Cometh

The Dude: *"By the way, do you think that you could give me that $20,000 in cash? My concern is, and I have to, uh, check with my accountant, that this might bump me into a higher, uh, tax...."*

The Big Lebowski: *"Brandt, give him the envelope."*

The Dude: *"Oh, you've already got the check made out; that's great."*

—From the cult hit *The Big Lebowski* (1998)

The next Immutable Law of Investing is that only after-tax returns matter. After all, even "The Dude" is planning for his tax situation.

Everyone knows the joke about death and taxes. Taxes are inevitable. Roads don't pave themselves, and teachers don't work for free. Without taxes, the government wouldn't have any revenue, and without revenue, there would be no public services. Paying taxes is our duty as citizens of this great country. Everyone uses public services such as roads and schools, so everyone has an obligation to pay his or her fair share. In fact, as a self-directed investor, you invest in the markets that your government spends billions to regulate on your behalf.

But don't mistake your patriotic duty for more than it is. There is no need to pay one dollar more than your fair share. And the tax laws are set up to incentivize certain behaviors. These are the behaviors that the government has deemed to be beneficial for the common good of all people. Incentives exist that encourage you to hold investments for longer than one year. Incentives also encourage saving for retirement and education. All smart investors need to take the time to understand these tax opportunities to maximize overall return.

Remember, you invest for a long-term life goal that you must fund sometime in the future (occasionally sooner rather than later). These goals will be paid for with funds that the government has already taxed. In other words, these are after-tax dollars. So, ultimately, to achieve your goals, your investment returns must be measured in after-tax returns.

Why is this elevated to a Law of Investing? Because Uncle Sam takes a healthy chunk of your investment gains, and because hedging requires regular maintenance transactions—and these are taxable events.

The first reason is simple enough. The government taxes investment gains at a high enough level to materially detract from your returns. Short-term capital gains are taxed at the same rate as your regular income. In 2011, long-term capital gains are taxed as high as 15%—about half the typical investor's regular federal income tax rate. Ordinary dividends are taxed at the same rate as your regular income tax rate, whereas qualified dividends enjoy a lower rate of 15% through 2012.

Now think about these tax rates in light of the actual investment performance in the market over the last ten years. Ouch! The last ten years have been flat. Maybe an investor had a breakout year mixed in and did a little better. But with typical investor tax rates between 25% and 33%, these returns would have been challenged by the tax bill. After-tax gains would have been materially lower. The result is less capital available to grow through compounding returns.

The second reason that taxes matter so much is specific to the Buy and Hedge strategy. Hedging requires regular and periodic transactions to maintain the proper position or portfolio protection. These regular transactions usually result in short-term gains or losses. As a result, these gains or losses are taxed at your regular income tax rate—in other words, a typically higher tax rate. To be an effective Buy and Hedge investor, you must consider these tax consequences when structuring a portfolio.

It would be irresponsible to invest using the Buy and Hedge approach without understanding the tax strategies that can reduce your overall tax obligation. This book includes an entire chapter on taxes that explains the many factors that go into designing a portfolio to maximize after-tax returns. From the type of account to the type of investment product to the type of hedge to build, these tax consequences can differ. But we'll take the time to teach you these considerations—at least according to the current tax code!

Chapter Lessons

- After-tax returns matter, because your life goals will be funded with after-tax dollars.
- Uncle Sam's tax rates are high enough to materially affect your returns.
- Hedging creates regular taxable transactions.
- The smart investor plans for tax efficiency knowing these factors.

Part III
The Five Iron Rules of Buy and Hedge

The authors have spent their corporate careers building financial products for clients. This includes more than 20 combined years building web products for do-it-yourself retail investors. We agree that there is no better feeling than seeing a well-designed product succeed after being launched in the marketplace. The satisfaction is tremendous.

While we were building those products, we learned many lessons about the markets and investing. After all, both of us were strong believers in "eating the dog food." In other words, we were avid users of the same products and tools that our clients used. We also tried many investing strategies along the way. All this experience served us well because it is now included in this book.

By now, you know that this book is organized into five parts. Part I, "Introduction to Hedging and the Markets," introduced the market forces that drive the need for a Buy and Hedge strategy. Part II covered the investing lessons that have most impacted us in our experience as senior executives in the online brokerage industry. The investor lessons described in Part II, "The Immutable Laws of Investing," are critical to the Buy and Hedge strategy. We could have presented more than 100 investor lessons in this book. The focus on the Immutable Laws we selected is key. These laws are the basis that truly informs the Five Iron Rules of Buy and Hedge described in Part III. These five rules were derived from these lessons. You must follow these rules to be a Buy and Hedge investor and successfully manage a hedged portfolio that is designed to outperform. Part III is the most important part of the book, because it is the heart of the Buy and Hedge strategy.

The rules appear one to a chapter. They are presented along with corollary rules to help you construct and maintain a Buy and Hedge portfolio:

Chapter 10   Rule #1: Hedge every investment.

Chapter 11   Rule #2: Know your risk metrics.

Chapter 12   Rule #3: A smart portfolio = long-term outlook + diversification.

Chapter 13   Rule #4: Unleash your inner guru.

Chapter 14   Rule #5: Harvest your gains and losses.

10

Hedge Every Investment

"Welcome to Fight Club. The first rule of Fight Club is: You do not talk about Fight Club. The second rule of Fight Club is: You DO NOT talk about Fight Club! Third rule of Fight Club: Someone yells "Stop!", goes limp, taps out, the fight is over. Fourth rule: Only two guys to a fight. Fifth rule: One fight at a time, fellas. Sixth rule: No shirts, no shoes. Seventh rule: Fights will go on as long as they have to. And the eighth and final rule: If this is your first time at Fight Club, you have to fight."

—Tyler Durden (played by Brad Pitt) in *Fight Club* (1999)

The good news: We only have five rules! The bad news: Our rules are going take longer to explain.

The first Iron Rule of Buy and Hedge is to hedge every investment.

If only one rule could encapsulate the heart of the Buy and Hedge strategy, this would be the one. If you remember only one of the Five Iron Rules, remember this one. It is the only rule that contains the word "hedge," like the book's title.

The rule is simple: Hedge every investment. A portfolio is a collection of investment positions. The investor must pick positions that offer suitable hedges—or otherwise, pick a different position. But what is a suitable hedge? Actually, what is a hedge?

For the purposes of Buy and Hedge, an investment is considered hedged if the investor has reduced or capped the total downside loss that he or she could incur on the position(s) that make up that investment. In other words, if the investor makes an investment and it declines in value, the loss incurred is reduced by some gain from the hedge. In this case, it is reduced when compared to not having any hedge in place.

Most often, an investment is hedged by combining two or more positions. In other words, the investor owns an investment position and specifically purchases another investment position to create the hedge. When taken together, the collective investment position is considered hedged. Some positions can be purchased and come with a built-in hedge. In the end, what matters is whether the client has achieved an "effective hedge" for each investment.

Figures 10.1 and 10.2 illustrate the concept of an effective hedge. Figure 10.1 shows the profit/loss (P/L) characteristics of owning any investment. As the price of the investment goes up or down, the P/L moves coincident to the price. A hedge changes the P/L line in at least one of two ways. It builds in a floor for the total loss the client might suffer. Or it changes the slope of the P/L line, causing the loss to be less than owning the investment outright.

But what makes a hedge suitable? An investor should use a checklist to build hedges that are suitable to his or her specific needs. We present that checklist and the tactics for building hedges in Part IV, "The How-To and Basic Tactics of Hedging." But here's a quick acid test for your hedge. Is the hedge predictable in its price behavior? Is it one of the approved hedge tactics described in Part IV?

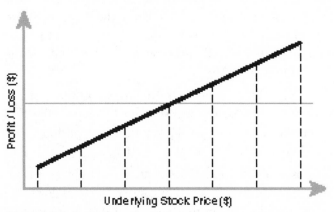

Figure 10.1 Profit/loss chart for stock

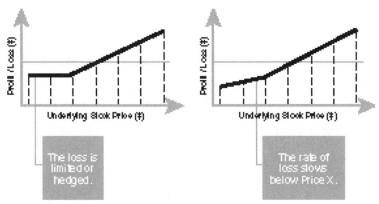

Figure 10.2 Profit/loss chart adjusted for hedging

Finding the right hedge is important. Ultimately, we recommend that investors use only investments that have highly predictable hedging alternatives. Ninety-nine times out of 100, this means picking investments that have derivatives that trade on that investment. The most reliable hedges are ones that include derivatives. Specifically, we recommend investing in stocks and ETFs that have Options that trade on the same underlying symbol of the stock or ETF.

When you can build a hedged position with an Option, you know that the Option derives its price from the underlying stock or ETF. Only then can you have complete confidence that the hedge will have predictable price behavior. Options for underlying investments are reliably correlated to the underlying investment, because they share the same underlying symbol. When the price of that underlying symbol moves, the price of the Option moves.

The second acid test for whether a position is hedged is fairly straightforward. Does the position use one of the hedge tactics we recommend in Part IV? If you are using the tactics described in Part IV, you are well on your way to becoming a Buy and Hedge investor.

We recommend three basic hedging tactics for your positions. And Part IV explains how to choose from these three tactics. These tactics are often called Option "strategies" in Wall Street lingo. Don't let the terminology fool you. These are the *tactics* for constructing hedged investments in your portfolio. Your *strategy* is what guides you to make investment decisions such as what to invest in or when to sell an investment.

Here are the three basic tactics that we recommend that use Options:

- Married put (or the inverse for short positions, married call)
- Collar
- In-the-money Options (also known as ITM calls or ITM puts)

These tactics are all explained in detail later in this book.

This book also recommends a series of advanced tactics for investors with Options experience or for Buy and Hedge investors who are ready to graduate to more-advanced techniques. We use both basic and advanced tactics. As you gain experience, you will learn that each investment has a hedge tactic that works best based on the current pricing in the Options market.

The advanced tactics for hedging are vertical and diagonal spreads. Advanced tactics require more analysis and typically more monitoring compared to the basic tactics.

Building a Portfolio Hedge Instead of Position Hedges

We recommend building a hedge for every investment. When this is done successfully, you know that the overall portfolio is hedged because all the individual components are hedged. But the investor can also build one hedge for the entire portfolio instead of a hedge for each individual investment. This is the corollary to Rule #1.

Corollary to Rule #1: An Alternative to Hedging Every Position Is Building a Portfolio Hedge

The portfolio hedge is the fourth basic hedging tactic taught in this book. The process of selecting a good hedging investment for an entire portfolio is explained in detail in Chapter 24, "Portfolio Puts." Here's a simplified explanation of building a portfolio hedge:

1. Calculate your overall portfolio value, and determine the net long or net short value.

2. Find an investment that is an index product (such as an ETF) that has a high correlation to your portfolio and that has Options that trade on it. (Typically this is a broad market index for most investors, such as an S&P 500 ETF.)

3. Buy the put protection (for net long portfolios) or the call protection (for net short portfolios) that provides the downside protection the investor wants. Calculating the protection amounts is explained in Chapter 24.

So, for an investor who wants to just focus on buying the stocks and ETFs he or she likes at the moment, the portfolio hedge can be an effective approach. It permits the investor to manage a less complicated portfolio, because there would be only one Option position in the portfolio, coupled with a group of ETFs and equities.

Some investors have shown a tendency to use this strategy for two other reasons. First, this technique is less time-consuming to manage, because it requires only a single Option to be bought and rolled forward periodically.

Second, the investor prefers a market hedge. In other words, the investor just wants protection from a market crash. Therefore, he or she is willing to take the risk that the individual investments he or she makes might deviate significantly in performance from the market. This investor assumes that market tumult is the most important risk to manage, and that the idiosyncratic risk associated with each individual stock does not need regular attention. We sometimes call this approach managing for "9/11 risk." In other words, managing for the potential market crash that is completely unforeseen. We can understand this approach, but we recommend hedging every individual position for the most effective Buy and Hedge portfolio.

Using Greeks to Design Your Hedge

Options traders often rely on Options analysis that uses metrics commonly called "the Greeks"—measurements used to assess risk inherent within Options positions. The Greek called delta measures the sensitivity of an Option's price to a change in the price of the underlying security. Put more simply and specifically, if the underlying security moves up by $1, the delta is the prediction of how much the value of the Option will move with the aforementioned $1 move up.

To calculate the total delta of an investment, add together the delta of all the positions you own for that investment (the Options and the underlying security if you own that also). The underlying security, when owned, has a delta of 1. If you are short the underlying security, it has a delta of –1. Owning a put Option results in a negative delta of some amount, because it decreases in value when the underlying security increases. A call Option is the opposite.

So, when you add together all the deltas for each position for the investment, a number results that is ideally less than 1. For example, if the delta is 0.7, this implies that a $1 increase or decrease in the underlying security results in an increase or decrease of 70 cents. The delta gives the investor an idea of how hedged the investment is. Put simply, the lower the delta's absolute value, the more hedged the investment.

Building and maintaining a position with a delta of less than 1 is a great litmus test for whether the investor has appropriately built an effective hedge.

Advanced Concept

There's an easy litmus test for whether your position is hedged. For bullish exposure, if the delta of the position is less than 1.0 but more than 0, the position is hedged. For bearish exposure, if the delta of the position is more than –1.0 but less than 0, the position is hedged.

Chapter Lessons

- Rule #1 is to hedge every investment.
- Rule #1 has a corollary: If necessary, build a portfolio hedge as an alternative to hedging every investment.

- An investment is considered hedged if the investor has reduced or capped the total downside loss that he or she could incur on the position(s) that make up that investment.
- Using Options is the most effective hedging technique.
- You can use delta to assess the extent to which you have hedged a position.

11 ———————————

Know Your Risk Metrics

Judge Smails: *"Ty, what did you shoot today?"*

Ty Webb: *"Oh, Judge, I don't keep score."*

Judge Smails: *"Then how do you measure yourself with other golfers?"*

Ty Webb: *"By height."*

—Ty Webb (played by Chevy Chase) in conversation with the snooty Judge Smails (Ted Knight) in the hilarious movie *Caddyshack* (1980)

There is a popular management axiom that says you can't manage what you can't measure. Our second Iron Rule pays homage to that axiom.

Iron Rule #2 is know your risk metrics.

Recalling the first chapter, you should remember that the retail investor has a singular focus on his investment returns. Typically, this same investor lacks the appropriate appreciation for his portfolio's risk. Ultimately, the investor can appreciate his returns only when considered in the context of the risk of his portfolio. The Buy and Hedge investor would never fall into that trap. Risk-adjusted returns are the measurement of success for the Buy and Hedge investor.

This is where the second Iron Rule comes into play. The Buy and Hedge approach requires you to understand risk and to use it to add context to your performance returns. But risk is not as well understood as returns, so you need a framework for risk that you can use to successfully manage a portfolio.

The Buy and Hedge risk framework uses four risk metrics. And as a Buy and Hedge investor, you calculate these risk metrics at both the portfolio level and the individual investment level. These metrics provide insight and context for you to make better investment decisions. Often, additional context comes from comparison to a relevant benchmark for the risk metric.

The Four Key Risk Metrics

The word "metric" is just another term for "measurement." Four key metrics matter to the Buy and Hedge investor:

- Capital at risk (CaR)
- Volatility
- Implied leverage
- Correlation

Let's examine each of these measurements and determine how they provide the Buy and Hedge investor with context on risk.

Capital at Risk

This first risk metric is a custom-made metric from Buy and Hedge. Capital at risk (CaR) is a term we created. But the measurement concept already existed, and it's simple. CaR is the maximum loss an investor could incur on an investment given the hedges put in place. In other words, if the underlying investment were to make the worst possible price move relative to the investment bias, CaR is the total loss you would incur on that investment.

For example, suppose you buy $10,000 worth of Microsoft stock. You have a CaR of $10,000 if it has no hedge, meaning that you own only the stock. You could lose the full value of the stock in the worst-case scenario. Now assume that you own that same stock but buy a hedge that costs $500. Also assume that the hedge kicks in and protects the downside of the stock after a 10% move down in the price of Microsoft stock. In other words, the loss on Microsoft stops at $1,000. In this example, the CaR would be $1,500. Why $1,500 and not $1,000? It is the potential loss before the hedge kicks in ($1,000) plus the cost of the hedge ($500). The CaR assumes the worst-case scenario for every investment.

The way to think of the overall portfolio CaR is to consider it the worst-case scenario given the hedges the investor has built into the portfolio. It is the loss that results if every investment in the investor's portfolio moves against the investor in a very short time frame. These events are rare. But as you know, the markets can spiral downward with dizzying speed, such as in the fall of 2008 and September 2001. Luckily, even when the markets move downward quickly, the investments often have more salvage value than the CaR indicates. That is because a hedge rarely loses its value overnight. Hedges, when built with Options in particular, usually retain some value even when the market is moving against you.

As a Buy and Hedge investor, you need to track the CaR for every investment. As your investments change in value, the CaR changes. The total CaR for your portfolio is the sum of each CaR for each investment in your portfolio. This is your overall portfolio CaR.

Have you seen the commercials for the Sleep Number bed? This special adjustable bed offers a customizable level of firmness or softness for each side of the bed. The commercial asks, "What's your Sleep Number?" The Sleep Number is the firmness setting for your side of the bed. Well, think of the CaR as your portfolio Sleep Number. It is the money you could lose if you wake up tomorrow and the markets have been turned on their head by some unforeseen event overnight. So, it needs to be a number that allows you to sleep comfortably, knowing that the worst-case scenario could happen.

Volatility

Volatility is the most commonly used measure of risk on Wall Street. It is the most talked-about risk metric by experts. Volatility is a statistical measure. Every investment that has a regularly changing price can have a measure of volatility. Basically, volatility looks at the price changes for an investment and reports on the dispersion of those prices. The higher the volatility metric, the higher the dispersion of the prices. And hence, typically the wider the potential range for the prices at which that investment might trade. In other words, the wider the potential change in value for that security. The change in value can be up or down. So, higher volatility is considered riskier because of the wider range for potential changes in the value of the investment.

Volatility is measured using the recent prices for the security being measured. If the recent prices had very large changes in value (up or down or both), the volatility metric for that security will likely increase—as long as the large changes were larger than normal for the security. The time period observed to measure volatility is relevant to the measurement. Most commonly, the prices for the last 12 months are used, and it is called the one-year volatility. We recommend that you use that measure, along with the 90-day measurement. The one-year measurement is helpful. But when an investor can compare the 90-day metric with the one-year metric, he or she gets directional context. In other words, you start to understand whether the most recent price changes are causing the investment to become more or less volatile.

Understanding volatility at the portfolio level is probably the most important lesson for the investor. When Wall Street talks about risk-adjusted returns, it is often referring to the percentage portfolio returns juxtaposed against the volatility metric for the same time period. In fact, these two metrics (performance return and volatility) are most commonly charted on the x- and y-axis to provide context about the overall returns compared to the overall risk taken, as shown in Figure 11.1.

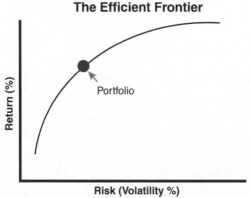

Figure 11.1 Risk versus return chart: portfolio efficiency

Calculating your overall portfolio percentage return and charting it against your portfolio volatility is an effective way to understand whether your investment strategy is or isn't yielding excess returns. You need to know your portfolio volatility to be able to add that context.

Portfolio volatility is easy to calculate:

1. Gather the closing portfolio liquidation value for every day the market was open in the trailing 12 months. (This should be about 252 data points.)

2. Calculate the percentage change in your portfolio each day. (Remember to adjust for any deposits or withdrawals each day.)

3. Of the resulting 252 percentage changes calculated, determine the standard deviation of these percentage changes. (All spreadsheets offer this calculation.)

4. Multiply the standard deviation by the square root of 252 (15.87).

Now you have the portfolio volatility for the last year, and you can compare it to your portfolio returns.

The volatility metric can help the Buy and Hedge investor in two ways when it comes to managing your portfolio. First, you can use volatility to estimate the impact of any new investment on the portfolio's overall volatility. If the overall portfolio volatility is X, adding a new investment with a historical volatility that is higher than X implies that the portfolio volatility will increase. And the inverse is also true. If you add an investment with a historical volatility that is lower than X, then your overall portfolio volatility will likely decrease.

Second, the volatility metric provides a good basis for understanding risk-adjusted return. As shown in Figure 11.1, returns and risk are often charted on the y- and x-axis, in which volatility is used for the risk axis.

In this second lesson about using volatility, let's take a closer look at the risk/return chart. Ideally, the investor always wants his portfolio to be plotted above the efficient frontier on the chart. Being above this line means that the portfolio generated excess returns. In other words, the investor made excellent risk-adjusted decisions. Of course, the investor wants increased returns—but ideally the risk does not increase as fast as the returns increase. On this chart, the farther your portfolio moves upward and to the left, the more excess returns are being generated on a risk-adjusted basis. Ultimately, for many investors, just being able to compare your portfolio volatility to the market's volatility helps you manage risk in your investments.

Many experts criticize volatility as a metric. But the most resounding criticism tends to focus on the fact that volatility is overutilized by many on Wall Street. The metric by itself is insufficient to manage risk. We agree with this critique. By itself, volatility tells a limited story. But in the construct of all the risk measures being taught in this chapter, it works well—especially when used with the other three measures.

Implied Leverage

Leverage has become a popular buzzword on Wall Street in the last decade. Many more people now understand the risk associated with leverage after the stock market crash of 2008. Leverage was the key culprit in the financial services collapse of 2008—and it's the key driver of financial reform being led by regulators now. Hopefully, the markets will never again see the kind of leverage that occurred on Wall Street in 2008.

The leverage deployed on Wall Street was achieved with borrowed money—and that is the traditional measure of leverage. Leverage has always really been a measure of how much of the portfolio was funded by borrowed money. The simple equation was as follows:

$$\frac{\text{total portfolio value}}{\text{total portfolio value} - \text{borrowed money}}$$

A measure of 1.0 meant that no leverage existed in the portfolio, because it contained no borrowed money. Anything above 1.0 meant that some borrowed money must exist in the portfolio.

Retail investors can borrow from their broker; this is called borrowing on margin. The broker uses the portfolio's investments as collateral against the loan amount. If the portfolio value declines by a significant amount, the broker can sell the portfolio's investments to protect its collateral. The broker is just protecting its loan collateral. The average retail investor typically cannot achieve a leverage score of greater than 2.0 without getting a margin call. A margin call is when the broker instructs the investor to add capital to the account or face the possibility that the broker will sell investments to protect the collateral.

Leverage has a different context in Buy and Hedge. We have created a slightly different measurement to understand portfolio leverage. First of all, we do not recommend borrowing money to make investments in your portfolio. In other words, Buy and Hedge recommends a leverage measure of 1.0. There may be times when your leverage may temporarily go above 1.0 because of timing issues, but these should be short-lived. So don't focus on the traditional measure of leverage. Instead, focus on a metric we created called implied leverage.

Options, by their very nature, create leverage for a portfolio. Buy and Hedge recommends using Options to create the most efficient and effective hedges for your investments. But Buy and Hedge recommends avoiding excess leverage in your portfolio. For this reason, the investor needs to track implied leverage, which encapsulates the power of leverage from Options. To understand our new metric of implied leverage, you need to understand the power of leverage from Options.

You will learn how to create exposure to equities and ETFs using Options—in many cases without having to own the underlying equity or ETF. Not every recommended tactic works that way, but several do. So, when the investor uses this kind of tactic, he likely uses less capital to create the bullish/bearish exposure than if he bought/ shorted the equity directly. Let's look at an example.

Suppose an S&P 500 ETF is trading at exactly $100 per share. You open an account with $100,000 in cash. Then you purchase ten Options contracts that are calls with a $90 strike price that expire six months from today. This is a common hedging tactic that we recommend. The price of these Options is $11 per share ($10 of intrinsic in-the-money value plus $1 extrinsic or time value). Because a contract has 100 shares, the total price is $11,000. And with these ten contracts, you control 1,000 shares through your call Option. If you owned 1,000 shares of the ETF, you would own $100,000 worth of the ETF. So, effectively, using the Option, you control $100,000 worth of S&P ETF, which is called the implied equity controlled. For every investment that uses Options to create bullish or bearish exposure, you need to calculate the implied equity controlled.

Our portfolio in this example looks like this:

$11,000	S&P 500 ETF call Option @ $90 strike
+ $89,000	Cash
$100,000	Total portfolio value

The implied equity controlled in the portfolio is $100,000—the ETF value of the 1,000 shares controlled using the Option.

When you calculate the portfolio's implied leverage, be sure to factor in the leverage that comes from Options positions. But do so only when Options positions are used to create bullish/bearish exposure in place of an equity or ETF. The formula for the implied leverage is similar to the leverage formula mentioned earlier:

$$\frac{\text{total market value of nonderivative securities + implied equity value for each derivatives position}}{\text{total portfolio value - borrowed money}}$$

Nonderivative securities are primarily stocks, ETFs, mutual funds, and fixed income. They do not include cash or cash equivalent securities.

Derivative securities are Options, futures, and index Options.

Using this formula, the implied leverage metric would be 1.0 in our example. The implied equity value for the Options position is $100,000. No other investments except for cash exist in the portfolio. The total portfolio value is $100,000, and no money was borrowed. So, the numerator is $100,000, and the denominator is $100,000. Hence, the implied leverage is 1.0.

So, for this portfolio, let's add more securities and see how this impacts the implied leverage calculation.

Let's add $50,000 worth of Microsoft stock. Assume that it is trading at $25 a share, so you purchase 2,000 shares. Your portfolio now looks like this:

$11,000	S&P 500 ETF call Option @ $90 strike
$50,000	2,000 shares of Microsoft
+ $39,000	Cash
$100,000	Total portfolio value

Although the total portfolio value has not changed, the portfolio now controls more stock and ETFs than in the first portfolio. The portfolio now controls the $100,000 of implied equity value, in the S&P 500 ETF and $50,000 worth of Microsoft. These two amounts total $150,000, which yields a numerator for our implied leverage calculation. The denominator didn't change, however. The portfolio is still worth $100,000 total, with no borrowed money. So, the implied leverage is now 1.5. This portfolio has more implied leverage than it did before.

So you understand that the leverage has increased. But has the risk in that portfolio increased? The higher the implied leverage, the higher the portfolio's risk. And the reason is that leverage causes portfolios to gain or lose ground faster than when the portfolio lacks leverage. Although an investor would love leverage in an up-moving market, the smart investor knows that he is never guaranteed an up-moving market all the time. So, creating a portfolio that has accelerating loss potential is more risky than a portfolio without that same potential.

Let's examine the two portfolios just described and examine the gain/loss scenario for each one to understand why we use leverage as a risk measure—particularly implied leverage. Table 11.1 shows the first portfolio.

Table 11.1 Scenario #1: the S&P 500 and Microsoft Both Increase by 10%

	First Portfolio (Started with an Implied Leverage Metric of 1.0)	**Second Portfolio (Started with an Implied Leverage Metric of 1.5)**
S&P 500 Position (S&P 500 ETF Increases from $100 Per Share to $110 Per Share)	The Option position would appreciate by about $9.50 to $10 per share, or $9,750 (the midpoint).	The Option position would appreciate by about $9.50 to $10 per share, or $9,750 (the midpoint).
Microsoft Stock (Increases from $25 Per Share to $27.50 Per Share)	None.	Increases by $2.50 per share, or $5,000.
Total Portfolio Value	$109,750	$114,750

Note

The Option position does not increase by the full $10 increase in the S&P 500 ETF because the time value in the Option likely declined by somewhere between 0 and 50 cents as the Option moved further into the money. In other words, the hedge was worth less now, and that is reflected in the price.

Both portfolio examples share a traditional leverage metric of 1.0. In other words, neither portfolio uses any borrowed money. And the first portfolio has an implied leverage of 1.0 also. However, the portfolio that added the Microsoft stock has higher implied leverage, because it controls more equity when you consider the Options leverage. The implied leverage of the second portfolio prior to the market move was 1.5. And the result when the market moves up is a bigger move up for the second portfolio. It increases by roughly 50% more than the first portfolio increased. This is the impact of the higher implied leverage.

Table 11.2 shows an example in which the portfolio decreases so that you can get a feel for the impact of leverage.

Table 11.2 Scenario #2: the S&P 500 and Microsoft Both Decrease by 10%

	First Portfolio (Started with an Implied Leverage Metric of 1.0)	Second Portfolio (Started with an Implied Leverage Metric of 1.5)
S&P 500 Options Position	The Option position would decline by about $8 to $10 per share, or $9,000 (the midpoint).	The Option position would decline by about $8 to $10 per share, or $9,000 (the midpoint).
Microsoft Stock	None.	Decreases by $2.50 per share, or $5,000.
Total Portfolio Value	$91,000	$86,000

Note

The Option position does not decrease by the full $10 decrease in the S&P 500 ETF because the time value in the Option likely increased by somewhere between $0 and $2 as the Option moved out of the money. An Option so close to the at-the-money position tends to have the most time value. In other words, the hedge increased in value due to the decline.

The first portfolio suffered a decrease, but this was somewhat muted because the sole position in the portfolio was hedged (the S&P 500 ITM call Option). The second portfolio suffered a materially higher decrease because it had an extra position—the Microsoft stock. So, despite both portfolios having a value of $100,000 prior to the decline and a traditional leverage ratio of 1.0, the portfolio with the extra position in Microsoft lost more value. This happened because its implied leverage was 1.5 compared to the 1.0 implied leverage of the first portfolio.

Options create leverage by their very nature. The Buy and Hedge investor must consider this leverage when determining the appropriate portfolio construction. Too much leverage increases your portfolio's volatility by increasing the portfolio's rate of change. The recommendation from Buy and Hedge is to avoid all excess leverage. Your implied leverage should always be 1.0 or lower. Your traditional leverage should always be 1.0 also.

The Buy and Hedge investor can build a diversified portfolio that delivers superior risk-adjusted performance without using leverage, implied or otherwise. A handful of advanced tactics in Part V, "Advanced Tactics," of this book will drive your implied leverage well past 1.0. But these are advanced topics and are best suited to investors who are looking for the specific risk trades described in those chapters.

Correlation

The word "correlation" gets its root from "relation." It is a helpful word for understanding the meaning of correlation. Everyone understands the word relation, because everyone has relatives. All family relationships have specific labels that connote the "closeness" of that relation. Fathers, mothers, brothers, and sisters all have a closer relation than cousins, aunts, or uncles. Often, the closer the relation, the more similar the family members. Brothers and sisters often share many traits, physical and behavioral. Twins often have the closest similarities of all—especially identical twins.

Correlation attempts to measure the degree of "sameness" between two items. In the world of finance, the correlation metric analyzes price movements of two different investments. Specifically, it measures the degree to which the prices of the two different investments show a tendency to change together. In other words, when the price of one investment moves up or down, what happens to the price of the other investment? Does it move in the same direction (up or down)? Does it tend to move to a similar degree or scale (such as size)?

The more highly correlated two investments are, the more their prices have historically moved together. The lower the correlation, the less likely they are to move together. A high negative correlation is when the two investments are very likely to move to the same or a similar degree, but in opposite directions. In investing, correlation between two investments is measured between 1.0 and –1.0.

Let's look at two firms that most investors would agree are closely related—or, at least, close cousins: United Airlines (UAL) and Delta Airlines (DAL). They are the two largest airlines and operate both domestically at most major U.S. airports and internationally. Both have stopped offering meals on flights. And both now charge passengers to check their luggage. Very similar, indeed.

The historical correlation between these two stocks is fairly high. The correlation measured over the three years ending in April 2011 is 0.84. Any positive correlation between 0.75 and 1.0 is considered high. The six-month correlation measure was 0.87. Interestingly, the one-year correlation for these two stocks is only 0.4, which is low. This means that the price movement of these two stocks must have varied quite a lot in the time period between six months and one year from April 2011. Especially since the correlation for the last six months was so high and is included in the one-year measure.

So, how does a Buy and Hedge investor use the correlation metric to manage risk in his portfolio? Well, the correlation metric is not really a traditional risk metric. It measures the past tendency of two prices to move together. It explains how two investments tend to move in price in relation to each other. By itself, that is not a risk measurement. However, the data about correlation among your positions will greatly inform your decisions about risk and hedging. Understanding your portfolio's overall correlation to the market also is helpful.

Here are the steps for using correlation to inform your risk decisions:

- Know the correlation of each underlying investment in your portfolio to each other.
- When adding a new investment to your portfolio, know the correlation of that investment to each investment already in your portfolio.
- Know the correlation of each position to the broader market. We recommend the S&P 500 Index.

Buy and Hedge further recommends that investors use the six-month, one-year, and three-year correlation measures. The one-year and three-year measures obviously paint a picture for a longer window. On the website for SPDR ETFs, there is an excellent correlation tool that calculates six-month, one-year, and three-year correlation between any two ETFs or stocks. It can be found at http://www.sectorspdr.com/correlation.

When these longer measures are close in measurement and the six-month correlation is materially different, keep in mind that a correction in the price of the stock is possible. But for a long-term investor, the one- and three-year correlations deserve the most attention. Additionally, knowing the correlation of our investments to the broad market can help manage your risk. An investor who believes in indexing (an approach that Buy and Hedge endorses) would want a close correlation to the broader market.

So, is a high correlation between positions in a portfolio good or bad? Actually, it's neither. The higher the positive correlation between the investments in your portfolio, the less diversification you have achieved in that portfolio. You will learn in the next chapter that diversification is an important part of limiting the risk in your portfolio. So, the more your investments share a high positive correlation, the more important it is for you to structure the proper hedges.

Ultimately, the correlation informs the investor about the level of diversification achieved in the portfolio. The level of diversification is a measure of risk. The more diversified, the less risk—and vice versa.

If the portfolio is not very diversified, you should consider structuring more conservative hedges to make up for the risk. The inverse is also true. A portfolio that is more diversified can be more aggressive in setting the hedges because some of the risk has been managed through the diversification.

Chapter Lessons

- The four key risk metrics must be used together. None of them stands on its own. When used together, they provide sufficient risk management information for solid portfolio management decisions.
- Capital at risk is the most capital your portfolio could lose if all your investments moved against you to maximum effect.
- Volatility is the dispersion of prices for a given security or portfolio. It helps you understand the likely future potential price movement for your securities.

- Implied leverage is the total leverage you maintain in your portfolio given the use of Options to create bullish/bearish exposure.
- Higher correlation inside a portfolio means less diversification exists. This means that the hedges set for this portfolio need to be more conservative. The inverse is also true. A portfolio that is more diversified can have more aggressive hedges.

12

Constructing a Long-Term, Diversified Portfolio

"If I'm not back in five minutes...just wait longer."

—Ace Ventura (played by Jim Carey) in *Ace Ventura: Pet Detective* (1994)

As a Buy and Hedge investor, time is on your side. Your portfolio is built to out-perform over long stretches—not short ones. Be patient. Give your portfolio more than five minutes to succeed.

Rule #3 is that a smart portfolio equals long-term outlook plus diversification.

The first Iron Rule is investment-specific and goes to the heart of the Buy and Hedge strategy. Rule #2 is about the measurements that support both portfolio management and portfolio construction. Rule #3 is all about portfolio construction. To build an effective Buy and Hedge portfolio, you need to invest for the long term while maintaining a well-diversified portfolio. This third rule is a nod from the authors to a tried-and-true investment methodology. We are not too proud to borrow from others. In this case, the Nobel Prize for economics was given to Harry Max Markowitz in 1990 for his work on the benefits of diversification.

By now, you should have noticed a few themes in this book. The Buy and Hedge strategy puts a premium on managing for risk. Another theme is that sometimes psychology gets in the way of being a successful investor. One more theme is that while managing for risk, you must optimize for returns. This rule has two parts and each part impacts each of these two themes.

Having a Long-Term Outlook

Maintaining a long-term outlook for your investments is a key success factor in a Buy and Hedge portfolio. However, we could easily rewrite this rule as "Avoid having a short-term outlook." The reality is that the benefits of a long-term outlook are as powerful as the problems resulting from a short-term outlook. Let's start by examining the destructive powers of a short-term outlook and then return to the advantages of a long-term outlook.

Having a short-term outlook is what defines the active trader or active investor. A short-term outlook results in frequent trades because the portfolio must always find replacement investments. Here are the reasons why a short-term outlook typically spells disaster for most investor portfolios:

- **Higher expenses drag down returns.** A short-term outlook means that hold times typically are six months or less, and often just one month or less. This creates high portfolio turnover, because the investor needs to find a replacement for the last investment that was closed. And this must occur more often. As a result, fees and commissions get paid more frequently. These fees are a drag on your overall returns.

- **Excess portfolio monitoring leads to excess trades.** The psychology of a very active investor can work against him. Short-term outlooks require more frequent monitoring of the portfolio because the investor needs to continually look for a replacement investment. Studies show that excessive portfolio monitoring leads to too many trades that degrade performance. Why? This is human nature. The more the investor looks at something, the more he thinks he can improve it. So, the investor looks for reasons to change his portfolio. Too frequently the investor finds reasons to change it that are not good for the portfolio. But the changes still get made. This is often a curse for investors who really enjoy managing their own money.

- **It's too time-consuming.** The primary reason that active investors or active traders stop investing actively is time constraints. Contrary to popular belief, the primary reason is not losing money or lack of capital. Instead, frequent trading requires lots of time—time to decide when to sell current investments, time to determine the new investment to make, time to research, time to monitor prices. Everyone leads busy lives, and too often life gets in the way of active trading. And when these time constraints collide, the life constraints usually win out. Think about it: getting a promotion, a time-consuming project at work, your kids, your hobbies, home projects. All of these things create a time constraint. And this is why traders stop trading. The portfolio suffers as the time constraints from life creep in. The portfolio that needs regular monitoring and turnover doesn't get those things from its owner and therefore suffers from neglect.

The lifestyle of the short-term investor is undesirable to the authors. Instead, we believe in the benefits of a long-term outlook. Our preference for the long-term outlook includes many supporting features, but ultimately the two we care about the most:

- **Long-term portfolios are less time-consuming.** The math is irrefutable. If the investor intends to hold an investment for a long time (one to three years or more), he doesn't have to find a replacement investment very soon. Hence, the portfolio requires less monitoring, because the intent is to hold every investment for the long term. Add the fact that every investment is hedged, and the Buy and Hedge investor can sleep comfortably, logging into his portfolio only once a week (or less) to see how it is performing.

- **The longer a hedge is given time to perform, the better it performs.** History tells us that hedged portfolios tend to outperform the broad market. These portfolios generate excess returns. Furthermore, the same data tells us that the longer the period of time measured, the higher the excess returns. Here's another way to think about this: Every long time period for the modern-day market has produced a window of high volatility that destroyed returns considerably. Hedging counteracts volatility, and the performance gains more than make up for the cost of hedging. Hence, excess returns are generated.

Really, the long-term portfolio is the natural partner to a hedging strategy. And that is why the authors believe so strongly in the long-term outlook endorsed in this book.

So far, this chapter has focused on the benefits of a long-term outlook. Now we need to tie the long-term approach back to portfolio construction. In other words, let's get prescriptive. Here are the short rules for constructing a long-term portfolio:

- New investments should have an expected hold time of more than one year.
- The portfolio should regularly have investments that have been held for two years or more. These are often your broad market index investments.
- Never invest with an intended hold time of less than six months. Intentionally designing a portfolio with short-term investments will only lead to problems.

These rules are key to investing with a long-term horizon. If you are considering adding a new investment to your portfolio, make sure you are comfortable holding on to it for a long time period. If you don't have the confidence in the investment to hold it for the long-term, then do not make the investment.

The next section discusses diversification. Part of being diversified in a Buy and Hedge portfolio includes using broad market indexes. Luckily, these indexes are easier to invest in for the long term. Investing in these indexes creates logical market exposure for a large part of your portfolio. Let's examine why that is important.

Building a Diversified Portfolio

The authors believe in hedging because it is a foundational way to manage risk. What does foundational mean? A foundation provides stability, and hedging gives your portfolio stability. That stability reduces risk in the portfolio. Diversification is another key technique for managing risk. It is also foundational in its importance to the investor. When the two techniques of hedging and diversification are combined, the portfolio has managed for risk in two material and distinct ways. In other words, the portfolio is truly set up for success.

But what does it mean to be diversified? Later, this chapter will get prescriptive in building a diversified portfolio. For now, let's be sure you understand the concept and how it reduces portfolio risk.

Let's look an example. Suppose you have retired to Hawaii. Life is good. Your house is on the water on a remote part of the island. You are tan and enjoy the sun. You swim every day and eat fresh, delicious fish for dinner.

But to eat that fish, you need to catch it every day. In the morning, you cast a line and come back in the late afternoon to check it for fish. If you cast only one line, you give yourself only one chance to catch fish that day. The potential negative outcome is no fresh fish for dinner. That risk exists for every line you cast. Maybe the line gets caught or the bait falls off. Any line can fail for any reason. But when you cast only one line, that risk looms large.

But if you cast a second line with the same bait, and a third line with a new type of bait, and a fourth line with a different lure and hook, you have four different chances to catch fish for dinner. And maybe you even drop a crab trap in the water for good measure.

Each line still has a risk of coming up empty. The risk of each individual line failing does not change. But the risk of going hungry is much lower now. Only one line has to succeed for you to be able to eat fresh fish for dinner. Of course, you now have more lines to maintain, which is more work. You might snap two lines, lose an extra lure, or even lose the trap. Or you might catch fish on multiple lines and end up with enough dinner for two or three nights. But by investing in extra fishing gear and casting those lines, you end up with more opportunities for dinner—and reduce the risk of going hungry.

Take the analogy further. Extra lines and traps may cost you a little, just like wasted bait or damaged equipment may cost you more. Alternatively, you may get more than you expected by way of extra food, which you could store for future meals or sell to others. You might even use the extra fish you caught as bait the next day—an attempt to compound your returns.

Diversifying your investment portfolio has the same effect. A portfolio invested in only one stock carries significant risk. If that one stock were to fail and lose most or all of its value, the entire portfolio would also lose most or all of its value. Think about it. What if that stock were Enron in 2001?!

But even a diversified portfolio that includes Enron has potential to overcome the Enron failure when surrounded by other stocks. A portfolio that had GE, Cisco, Caterpillar, Apple, and five to ten other individual stocks would have helped overcome the Enron loss in your portfolio. And the investment in multiple stocks and ETFs would change your portfolio's overall risk profile. Adding investments doesn't change the risk of any existing individual stock in your portfolio. Instead, it changes the risk measured at the portfolio level. What are the odds that all 10 to 20 of these stocks decline in tandem? That all sectors perform badly at the same time? Or that all of these stocks file for bankruptcy like Enron? The odds are low.

The technical definition of a diversified portfolio is a portfolio whose investments, when measured in dollars, are spread across asset classes and investment sectors that are noncorrelated. Remember that you learned about measuring correlation in the preceding chapter. Two noncorrelated assets would be two assets whose prices have not historically moved in tandem. To be truly diversified, your portfolio must meet this technical definition—it must have many investments that are noncorrelated.

But how do you achieve that? It sounds very technical. Well, it's time to get prescriptive. With Buy and Hedge, we have identified some shortcuts to help the investor build a diversified portfolio without spending hours filling in a spreadsheet.

In the preceding chapter, you learned that you always need to know the relative correlation of all the different investments in your portfolio. But to truly build a broadly diversified portfolio of stocks and bonds, you would need to invest in somewhere between 30 and 50 specific stocks. This would be unwieldy. Just looking up the correlation between all these different investments would involve over 1,000 data points. It just won't work.

Luckily, the industry has created a great new tool to achieve diversification across many sectors while providing significant exposure to the asset classes desired. This tool is called an exchange traded fund (ETF). ETFs trade like stocks but work like mutual funds. In fact, ETFs are legally organized like mutual funds. The ETF holds many individual investments that are representative of the asset class it is trying to mimic. The ETF, by itself, is broadly diversified, just like mutual funds. The ETF is organized to provide the returns of a specific index. The index is often a broad index but can also be a more specific index such as a sector within an asset class (such as a technology sector within the stocks asset class or treasuries within the bonds asset class).

So, instead of needing to pick more than 30 stocks to achieve diversification, the investor can invest in ETFs (discussed in Chapter 23, "ETFs Will Look Great in Your Portfolio) that represent broad indexes of stocks or bonds. These ETFs often hold 100 different stocks or more. The portfolio can achieve diversification just by buying a handful of these ETFs—and have exposure to hundreds of stocks. And you can pick ETFs that have Options that trade on them so that you can hedge them.

So, you know you want to use ETFs to create broad diversification in your portfolio. But how much of your portfolio should be in ETFs? To figure this out, you need to unleash your inner investment guru, as discussed in the next chapter. *Buy and Hedge* recommends setting aside some of your portfolio for idiosyncratic investment ideas you want to make. Don't ignore these investment ideas. Test them. Hedge them. See the results.

We want to recommend an asset allocation that can help you achieve a well-diversified portfolio while leaving room for your individual stock/ETF selections. To help you do that, let's discuss the asset classes for building our portfolio.

For our purposes, we recommend three asset classes: stocks, bonds, and cash.

Stocks fall into three categories: broad market, sector indexes, and inner guru picks. We'll help you decide how to allocate among these three categories.

For bonds, the authors recommend using them only within your asset allocation when nearing or during retirement. Bonds historically have been used to reduce the overall risk in a portfolio, because bonds typically have a noncorrelated relationship to stocks. Bonds can counter-balance the risk of your stock positions. However, with Buy and Hedge, the recommendation is to use *hedges* to reduce your risk. As a result, bonds are not as critical to counterbalancing the risk of stocks in your portfolio. But bonds still play a role—they become a tool for *income only*.

As for cash, Buy and Hedge recommends that you put only 10% of your allocation in cash and cash equivalents—just enough for new investment ideas or for that cash you might need for unexpected expenses.

Putting It All Together in Your Portfolio

Let's examine how you get to an asset allocation when constructing your portfolio. First, recognize that your allocation is fluid and can be adjusted according to several factors.

The base portfolio looks like Figure 12.1.

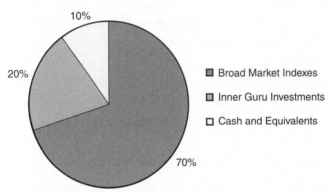

Figure 12.1 Target asset allocation: a core Buy and Hedge portfolio

To adjust this portfolio, answer these basic questions:

1. Do you want to invest more or less of your assets in individual investments (your inner guru ideas)? Adjust this to as low as 10% or as high as 40%, as shown in Figure 12.2. Reduce the broad market index allocation percentage accordingly.

2. Do you prefer to follow a strict regimen of index investing? If you don't want to make any individual investment decisions (using your inner guru), you can drop this weight to 0%. This means that a full 90% of your allocation is invested in broad indexes and 10% in cash, as shown in Figure 12.3.

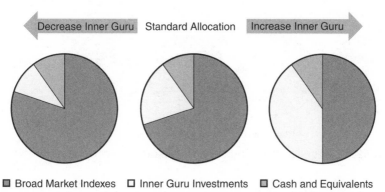

☐ Broad Market Indexes ☐ Inner Guru Investments ☐ Cash and Equivalents

Figure 12.2 Target asset allocation: adjustable inner guru

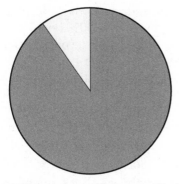

☐ Broad Market Indexes ☐ Cash and Equivalents

Figure 12.3 Target asset allocation: full indexing strategy and no inner guru

3. Are you at or near retirement? If you are within ten years of retirement, we recommend allocating 10% of your portfolio to bond ETFs, as shown in Figure 12.4. If you are within five years, adjust the bond ETFs to 25%. After retirement starts, you should increase your bond ETF allocation by 5% for every year of retirement, until you max out at 50% allocation in bond ETFs. Every 1% increase in bond ETFs should result in even reductions in index allocation and individual investment allocation (a .5% reduction to each). Do not permit the inner guru allocation to decline below 10%. At the point where your inner guru can go no lower, adjust only the index allocation downward: 1% for each 1% increase in the bond allocation.

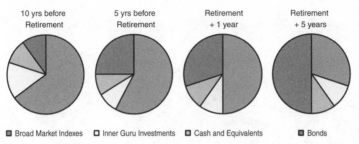

Figure 12.4 Target asset allocation: adjustable for retirement

4. Corollary rule: If you are investing toward a lump-sum-based goal (not retirement, but a dream home or college education), adjust your allocation to include a higher use of bond ETFs when you get close to your finish date. In the case of a lump sum due at one time, start to move to a 30% bond allocation with two or three years to go. If the goal is a college education paid over four years, steadily increase the bond exposure by 10% each year of the college window after the payments start.

It is important to note that this is not a traditional asset allocation. It assumes that the investor is following our Five Iron Rules of Buy and Hedge. It assumes that every investment is hedged (Rule #1). As a result, these recommended allocations do not look like the traditional allocations presented in textbooks. But remember that those textbook allocations manage risk solely through diversification and they don't take advantage of hedging to control for risk. Buy and Hedge investors use the power of ETFs to create material diversification. And then you use the power of Options to further manage your risk. A portfolio can be overmanaged for risk, so the portfolio allocation is adjusted to take both factors into account.

Warning

If you do not hedge every position (Rule #1), this allocation recommendation adds substantial risk and has a good chance of not working.

Within the index allocation percentages for each asset class, you need to decide how to allocate across multiple ETFs within that category. The authors recommend using broad index ETFs such as the S&P 500; NASDAQ; or the Russell 1000, 2000, or 5000. Chapter 23 highlights many of these ETFs. They are well diversified and highly liquid. Even more important, we have identified some ETFs that include Options.

Deciding to have your entire allocation in indexes is not an uncommon strategy. Passive investing strategies are very popular. This approach can work for the investor who cannot find time to make individual investing/inner guru decisions for his or her portfolio. This is even common among professional traders. Listen to market experts who give commentary on financial TV networks. These pundits usually include some kind of ETF or index in their discussion to create some broad exposure for a particular investment hypothesis.

Wrap-Up

When it comes to portfolio construction, you have learned three key lessons about managing for risk: hedge every investment, invest with a long-term outlook, and diversify your portfolio. Each of these techniques reduces risk and will help you create excess returns over the long term. These techniques are tried and true Wall Street lessons.

Chapter Lessons

- Target investments to hold for more than one year; avoid short-term investments.
- You can achieve diversification by investing in broad-market and sector ETFs for the majority of your portfolio.
- Use bonds in your portfolio allocation only as your investment goal time horizon comes near. Use them sparingly, because hedging already has protected your downside.
- Follow the asset allocation advice in this chapter when designing your portfolio.

13

Unleash Your Inner Guru

"Rule #76: No excuses. Play like a champion!"

—Jeremy Grey (played by Vince Vaughn) to best friend John Beckwith (played by Owen Wilson) in the hit movie *Wedding Crashers* (2005)

The hardest thing about investing your own money is picking investments that out-perform the market. But I can tell you for sure that unless you take the time to execute your individual investment ideas, you will never know if you are any good at it. No excuses. Play like a champion.

Rule #4 is unleash your inner guru.

If you've made it this far in the book, clearly you're committed to being a do-it-yourself (DIY) investor. Whether new to investing or experienced, each investor develops a style of investing that suits him or her over time. Mostly, this style describes the types of investments the investor makes—fast-moving, risky stocks versus blue-chip stocks; sector rotation approaches; stock picker versus indexing; value versus growth. The many investment books that are available promote a number of investment styles. And those just scratch the surface.

Most investors tend to gravitate toward the types of investments that make them the most money—the investments that have led to the most success. Which investments were those? For each investor, the answer is different. Each do-it-yourself investor has built a base of knowledge and experience that is unique to him or her. The investments you excel at making are specific to your background. Plus, your experience in making the investments plays a key role. An investor could be very good at picking stocks that are poised to be winners but could be very poor at the discipline of determining the right exit points after setting up the trade. This could cause the investor to think his strengths lie elsewhere.

The investor who can perform self-analysis and determine his investing specialty has a real advantage. Focus equals power. Focusing on your strengths should lead to success. To put it another way, do what you are good at! The challenge is the self-analysis. Are you self-aware enough to determine which investments you are good at making? When you can pull this off, you have unleashed your inner guru. The authors believe that everyone has one; you just need to find it.

Unleashing your inner guru introduces two significant challenges. The first is to identify your investing strengths.

Challenge #1: Identifying Your Investing Strengths

Ultimately, every year a great number of do-it-yourself investors wash out and stop investing on their own. By "wash out," we mean their portfolio performs very badly, and that performance drives them to quit. We don't know exactly how many people suffer from this problem, but our experience tells us that about one-fourth of all DIY investors stop investing. Given the annual turnover in the industry, this could be as many as half a million households per year. That's a lot!

In many of these cases, the investor just never figured out what his investing strength was. More than likely, he had some winning investments, but the losing ones wiped out the winning ones. Identifying your strengths as an investor is not as easy as it sounds. So many factors can influence your success and failure that isolating those factors is difficult.

Our solution for challenge #1 is to keep an investment journal. In that journal, every time you make a new investment or sell an existing one, write down some notes about your investment rationale. In particular, note the investment name, your investment bias (bullish or bearish), your market bias (bull or bear), your reason for liking this investment, the sector of the investment, the target price for the investment, and your expected hold time for the investment. Also include an honest assessment of whether any emotional thinking went into your buy/sell decision.

Regularly return to your journal, and update it after you sell the investment. Indicate its overall success, including the gain/loss, the actual hold time, and whether the investment reached its target price.

Regularly review your investment history, and look for trends. Look to see if certain sectors tend to dominate your success or failures. Look to see if certain hold times were more successful than others. Look to see if you frequently closed your investment at or near your expected target price.

Go to http://www.BuyAndHedge.com to print a blank journal page that you can use for your investment tracking.

Challenge #2: Being Overconcentrated in One Sector

The investor who is lucky enough to discover his investing strengths is a step ahead of other investors. Discovering your strengths usually coincides with discovering your weaknesses. This makes the investor even more self-aware. The reality is that many investors tend to find strengths in specific investment sectors. Often, these sectors are the ones the investor follows closely or a sector he or she works in. Having that kind of insight is great and can make the investor much more effective.

So why does that create a challenge? The investor often over-concentrates his portfolio in a sector he knows. Buy and Hedge can support a slight overweighting toward the sectors the investor knows best. But the smallest bit of success can often breed overconfidence in the investor. And many investors create a dramatic overweighting in the portfolio toward one or two sectors. This overweighting can be bad for the portfolio.

As discussed in the preceding chapter, a portfolio that has a large percentage of its assets in one sector will have multiple investments with very high correlation to each other. The result is less diversification. The investor needs to monitor for this risk and be sure not to overconcentrate in one sector. Sometimes a whole sector can go down—including the best companies in that sector. So, even an investor who has picked the best companies in that sector will suffer in his portfolio when that happens.

Our solution to Challenge #2 is not to let one specific stock sector exceed 10% of the total assets in your portfolio—*ever!* Be sure to invest at least 50% of your portfolio in broad market indexes. (If you are following the rules of diversification discussed in the preceding chapter, you already have at least 50% of your portfolio in broad market indexes.) These two rules are simple and easy to follow. They will ensure that your portfolio does not end up overconcentrated and underdiversified.

Implementing Rule #4

We don't want to belabor or complicate this rule. Our readers are DIY investors, so making individual investment decisions should feel right to you. But let's put a nice bow on how this rule gets implemented.

Buy and Hedge recommends that 20% of your portfolio's assets be committed to individual investment ideas. In other words, commit 20% of your portfolio to unleashing your inner guru. You can invest as much as 40% of your portfolio in individual investment ideas, but we recommend no more than that. And you can go as low as 10%. You should always have at least 10% to ensure that you are engaged in your portfolio.

Why do we recommend that you make these kinds of investments? If you don't try to make these kinds of individual moves, you will never find out what your investing strengths are.

Remember that every investment is hedged (Rule #1). Therefore, the Buy and Hedge investor can make individual investment decisions with confidence, because the downside of the investment is protected. The risk is not as high as just buying the stock or the ETF, because the investor hedged the investment.

So, don't be nervous about your investment ideas. Trust your instincts. Make some investments just because your instinct tells you to. With the hedge in place, the downside is under control. Just don't forget to follow Rule #1! And don't forget to mark down your investment rationale in your investment journal!

Chapter Lessons

- Unleash your inner guru by making individual investment decisions.
- Keep a journal for your investments. This is the only way to determine your investor strengths and weaknesses.
- After you discover your strengths, focus your individual investment ideas on those strengths.
- When you follow Rule #1, you can trust your instincts and make trades knowing that your downside is protected.
- Keep between 10% and 40% of your investment portfolio in individual investment ideas.
- Keep 50% of your portfolio in broad market indexes.
- Make sure that no more than 10% of your portfolio is ever concentrated in one sector.

14

Harvest Your Gains and Losses

"A, B, C. A. Always. B. Be. C. Closing. Always Be Closing. Always Be Closing."

—From the 15-minute motivational speech delivered by Blake (played by Alec Baldwin) in *Glengarry Glen Ross* (1992)

Alec Baldwin delivers what is most likely the best fifteen minutes of acting in his career. His speech is legendary in sales offices everywhere. Although his speech was about sales, we want you to apply it to harvesting your investment gains and losses. To take gains and losses, you must be closing positions. So, always be closing.

Rule #5 is harvest your gains and losses.

Harvesting sounds agricultural—and indeed it should. Harvesting means to cut and gather a crop after it has matured. Farmers need to harvest crops before taking them to market and realizing some profit from the work involved in planting and caring for the crops. We chose the wording of Rule #5 carefully. The similarity to closing and changing positions in your investment portfolio is uncanny.

Every farmer wants the most successful crop possible. He wants a large yield and very little waste. He wants to deliver the freshest, healthiest, and largest possible crop. And the investor wants the same thing for his investments: the best possible gain. After all, the investor nurtures and cares for his investments, just like a farmer nurtures and cares for his crop.

But investors experience losses sometimes, just like farmers experience crop loss. Even a crop that fails and dies must still be harvested. The farmer needs to remove the dead crop from the field so that the next crop can be planted. The waste needs to be removed to make room for new opportunity. The same is true in your portfolio. Sometimes, an investment results in a loss, and it is necessary to move on from the bad investment and find a new opportunity.

The Three Times We Harvest Gains or Losses

With Buy and Hedge, we advocate three scenarios in which you harvest your gains and losses. These scenarios are straightforward but require you to regularly monitor your portfolio to identify the harvesting opportunities. You need to consider harvesting gains or losses when

- The investment has reached its target price, or your investment hypothesis no longer holds up.
- The investment has a large embedded gain, but you want to stay exposed to the investment.
- Tax opportunities present themselves near the end of the calendar year.

The Investment Has Reached Its Target Price, or the Investment Hypothesis No Longer Holds Up

At any given time, your portfolio will have several investments that represent your inner guru investments. Remember the preceding chapter. Your investment ideas need to see the light of day in your portfolio. And when you have these ideas, your investment journal will include your investment hypothesis for each investment.

Closing these investments and opening new ones is a regular part of managing your portfolio. Your portfolio will have regular turnover. You should close one of your investments for one of two reasons: either the investment hypothesis is no longer true, or your target price for the investment has been reached.

The investment hypothesis should be straightforward. When you set a hypothesis for each investment, at least once a month you must question whether the hypothesis still holds true. And although the hypothesis may change somewhat, your standard for closing the investment is materiality. The breakdown in the hypothesis must be material, meaning that it no longer holds true, and you cannot stomach holding onto the investment. When this occurs, close all the positions associated with the investment.

The second reason to exit an investment is that the target price has been reached. You learned in the preceding chapter to record your target price for each investment you make. The target price is actually two prices: the price you expect the investment to reach that would result in a gain, and the price that results in a loss that would cause you to abandon the investment. Every month, when you examine your investment hypothesis, consider whether you need to adjust the two target prices also.

The rule is simple: If either target price is reached, close the investment in full. In other words, harvest the resulting gain or loss.

The Investment Has a Large Embedded Gain, but the Investor Wants to Stay Exposed to the Investment

Sometimes, your investments will run like the wind and achieve significant gains in a short amount of time. But the investment might still be short of your target price. When this occurs, you are in a real bind. The investment has a very attractive gain embedded in it, but the investment still meets its original hypothesis for ownership. What is an investor to do?

Buy and Hedge knows exactly what to do. We don't pull any punches on this topic. Failing to follow this advice means failing your portfolio! The advice in this section describes one of the true advantages of hedging: reset your hedge to reset the protection level for your investment, hence locking in the gain while staying invested.

When an existing investment has a gain but hasn't been closed yet, the investment is said to have an "unrealized gain." That unrealized gain is, of course, measured in dollars. There is a very effective way to identify opportunities to reset your hedges using the unrealized gain (in dollars) and a concept you learned in Chapter 11, "Know

Your Risk Metrics,": capital at risk (CaR). Remember that CaR is a risk measure that is also measured in dollars.

The simple test to see if your investment is a candidate to have its hedge reset to lock in your gain is to compare the unrealized gain (in dollars) to the CaR (in dollars). Once a new investment is opened and hedged, it has no gain or loss but has CaR, as shown in Figure 14.1.

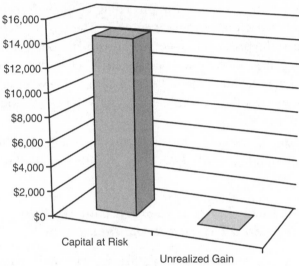

Figure 14.1 Charting CaR and unrealized gains

Every week, review your investments that have unrealized gains, and compare them to your CaR for that position. Over time, the gain will grow to become some percentage of the total CaR for that position. Once the unrealized gain is at least 50% of the total CaR for the same investment, you should consider it for resetting the hedge. Figure 14.2 is an example.

When you reset the hedge to create a new level of exposure in the investment, the new hedge results in a new CaR and potentially a new unrealized gain or loss. The new comparison of CaR to unrealized gain should look like Figure 14.3 or Figure 14.4.

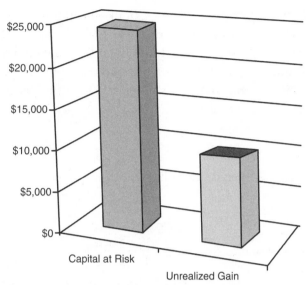

Figure 14.2 Unrealized gains exceed 50% of CaR

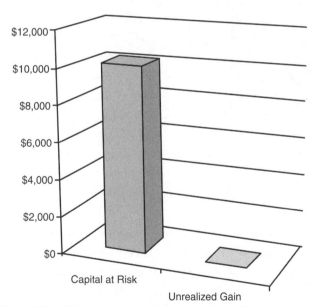

Figure 14.3 Harvesting the gains and resetting CaR

Figure 14.3 shows a new unrealized gain of $0 and a new CaR. In this case, the client reset the hedge to a new, higher price for the underlying investment. More important, the client has converted the unrealized gain into a realized gain. To reset a hedge but still stay invested in the investment, sometimes the gain has to be realized. Two kinds of tactics require the investor to realize the gain and reset the hedge:

- Basic tactics: ITM calls and puts
- Advanced tactics: spreads, including calendar spreads

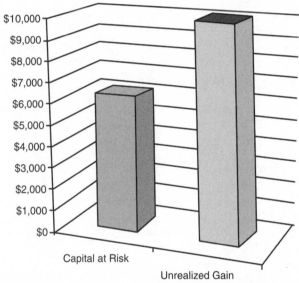

Figure 14.4 Retaining the unrealized gains and resetting CaR

In Figure 14.4, the client retains the unrealized gain but resets the hedge, resulting in a new CaR. Buy and Hedge recommends that the client reset the hedge so that the unrealized gain is now larger than the new CaR. In fact, ideally, the hedge can be reset such that the unrealized gain will now equal 150% or more of the new CaR. Effectively, when this can be accomplished, all the unrealized gain that is above the new CaR amount is the gain that has been "locked in" or protected. The investor can use tactics that result in a profile like the one shown in Figure 14.4:

- Basic tactics: married puts (and calls)
- Basic tactics: collars

In addition, with certain spread tactics, the investor can reset the "protective" side of the spread without changing the other leg of the spread. In these cases, when the other leg of the spread contains the unrealized gain, the investor has kept the unrealized gain in place. In other words, sometimes the investor can retain an unrealized gain using spreads—an advanced tactic.

Tax Opportunities Present Themselves Near the End of the Calendar Year

Taxes can be an intimidating concept for some people, so we will keep this simple. When the end of the calendar year (the U.S. tax year) approaches, the investor needs to think about optimizing his tax liabilities, which come due April 15 of the following year. Buy and Hedge teaches three conditions that the investor should start watching for in October through December:

- The investor has unrealized losses that can offset already realized gains from earlier that year.
- The investor has unrealized gains that can offset already realized losses from earlier that year.
- The investor wants to close a position with a large unrealized gain but delay the tax consequence until the next tax year.

Condition #1: Taking a Loss to Offset a Gain

Again, let's not make this more complicated than it has to be. Do you have realized gains from earlier in the year? Great. Do you have some unrealized losses in your current investments that could offset some or all of the gains? If so, you have a chance to optimize next year's tax bill.

To take the unrealized losses off the table, close the existing positions with the loss. Then use one of the other tactics we recommended in Chapter 10 to create the same or similar exposure to the underlying investment. Just remember that to avoid IRS wash sale rules, you must avoid owning the same position again for at least 30 days after closing the position. Make sure to use a new tactic that doesn't use the same position to create the exposure you want. You have kept yourself exposed to the investments you wanted—with the hedge protection you wanted—while creating a loss that can make you more tax-efficient.

Condition #2: Taking a Gain to Offset a Loss

This is the inverse of condition #1, with a slight twist. The IRS lets the investor use only $3,000 in losses to offset personal income in any tax year. The IRS makes you carry that loss forward to use in future years. So the test is similar. Do you have more than $3,000 in losses when you combine all your realized gains and losses for the tax year to date? If so, do you also have some unrealized gains in your current investments? If so, you have a chance to harvest those gains for tax efficiency.

To take the unrealized gains off the table, close the existing positions with the gain. Then use one of the other tactics we recommended in Chapter 10 to create the same or similar exposure to the underlying investment. If you can do so, you should convert enough unrealized gains into realized gains until you are back to only a $3,000 total realized loss—the amount by which you can offset personal income. You have kept yourself exposed to the investments you wanted—with the hedge protection you wanted—while creating a gain that can make you more tax-efficient.

Condition #3: Pushing a Tax Gain into the Next Tax Year

When you have a very large gain and are ready to close the investment, you should consider whether to delay the realization of the gain until the next tax year. You can use some advanced tactics to achieve that aim. This is recommended only when it is late in the tax year—and obviously you don't have losses to offset against the gain.

The basic approach is simple. Keep the investment that has the large unrealized gain, and find a suitable investment that has the opposite or negative correlation to the investment with the large unrealized gain. In other words, create a neutral investment outlook for the investment instead of the bullish or bearish outlook you have maintained until now.

After picking the right positions to make the investment neutral, you have effectively locked in your gain up until that point. When January comes, you can close out the investment and realize the total gain. You have now effectively pushed the gain into the next tax year.

This tactic also works well if an investment has a large unrealized gain and the specific position with the gain is 10 or 11 months old. In this case, the gain is short-term but is only one or two months from changing to long-term in the eyes of the tax collector. Long-term capital gains have a materially lower tax rate—almost half the tax rate of the average upper-middle-income family. So, if you have an opportunity to hold onto a position for one or two more months to convert a gain from short-term to long-term, you should also consider using this tactic.

Wrap-Up

Ultimately, harvesting gains and losses is about managing the turnover in your portfolio. But being successful requires a smart logistical approach to taking gains and losses off the table. Be sure to use the techniques described in this chapter to most effectively optimize your returns.

Chapter Lessons

- Portfolio turnover is normal, but make sure that it occurs because you have entry and exit points for your individual investment decisions.
- Hedging provides several tactics for locking in gains while staying invested in a specific position. This is an advantage that just owning stocks does not provide.
- Several tax opportunities drive decisions to harvest gains and losses. Because Buy and Hedge teaches multiple tactics to deliver similar investment exposure, you can use these tactics to optimize your near-term tax bill.

Part IV
The How-To and Basic Tactics of Hedging

This book has taught you about the theoretical aspects of hedging. You know why it's important, you know what it's designed to do, and you know how to assess it. Now it's time to learn how to do it.

In the Buy and Hedge approach, the discussion is specifically about defensive hedging. Defensive hedging is designed to protect against losses and define risk. Options are the single most effective method of hedging available to the individual retail investor. Part IV describes what it means to be hedged, the reasons why Options are the best vehicle for hedging, and some basic Option hedging strategies.

Here's a review of some of what you've learned so far about hedging. First, you learned that hedging is a technique that limits your downside losses. Additionally, it helps you limit your bad decisions influenced by loss aversion and emotion. You also learned that although hedging isn't new to the world of investing, the real power comes from combining it with indexing and asset allocation strategies. When reading about risk, you learned that risk is the input and return is the output. If hedging is designed to define risk, it will be the means by which you control risk. Last but not least, you learned that hedging comes at a cost.

15

Hedging with Options

Sy Spector: *"Bill said you used to be with the Secret Service."*

Frank Farmer: *"That's right."*

Sy Spector: *"Ever guard the main man?"*

Frank Farmer: *"I was two years with Carter, four with Reagan."*

Sy Spector: *"Reagan got shot!"*

Frank Farmer: *"Not on my shift."*

—From *The Bodyguard* (1992)

As mentioned earlier, hedges are designed for protection, and the degree of protection can be customized to the investor's preference. Defensive hedging means that some kind of negatively correlated position will reduce or completely offset losses if the market moves opposite of your investment bias. Many times we talk about absolute hedges. These are investments where, after a specific price point, your losses stop accumulating. This is not a stop loss or stop limit order. These are popular order types used by retail investors that exit a position after it declines to a certain price. Mechanically, the hedge is an investment with specific positions that appreciates in equal value as the underlying position depreciates.

Think of an absolute hedge as a counterbalance. Have you seen Chinese finger cuffs? You put a finger in each side, and when you try to pull them out, the cuffs tighten. The harder you pull, the tighter the cuffs get. That is what an effective hedge is like: The worse one position gets, the better the hedge offsets it.

Hedges don't always have to be absolute; they can partially reduce the impact of adverse market movements. Putting on a hedge that will reduce downside risk by 50%, for example, is still a good way to reduce volatility in a portfolio. When you read about risk graphs in Chapter 19, "Risk Graphs: A Picture Is Worth a Thousand Dollars," this point is illustrated visually.

The bottom line is you want to use defensive hedging to stop or reduce your losses and, in turn, reduce your overall volatility. Remember the "investor taste test" introduced in Chapter 8, "Volatility Is Krtyptonite"—up/down 10% versus up/down 30%? Portfolios perform better when the swings are reduced, especially swings to the downside.

Hedging can be done in a number of ways. Someone on TV always seems to be talking about how to hedge a current market trend by entering or exiting a certain sector to reduce risk. They may talk about gaining exposure to something that might offset potential losses or provide an advantage based on market conditions. Maybe you've heard about a popular hedge of buying an oil company such as Exxon Mobil (XOM) to offset the price increases at the pump experienced in everyday life. It's a hedge, yes, but there are plenty of times when those two expenditures are out of alignment.

Recommendations like this are standard practice among institutions that have lots of time and money to spend on research and analysis. We know you don't have the time or money to do this. So this book teaches you how to create correlated hedges by using Options on the positions that are to be protected. "Correlated" may be a bit of an understatement. More directly said, Options as hedges can define with a very high degree of certainty the exact risk profile of an investment. It turns out to be very mathematical and predictable. Remember, risk is what you want to control; it is what you *can* control. The results are less in your control, but the potential range of outcomes is defined up front when you hedge with Options.

The second reason that Options offer so much utility is that they can control the market value of what you want to hedge without requiring that much cash. Options provide leverage because they represent the buy/sell action for a certain number of shares versus actually doing the buy or sell ahead of time. The next three chapters discuss this topic in more detail. The bottom line is that Options let you control many shares at a significantly reduced cost.

Think about it this way. If you wanted to insure your house, it wouldn't make much sense to pay the full value of the house in insurance. That's like taking out a loan and putting up 100% of its value in collateral in cash.

Options let you provide highly correlated protection with a significantly lower capital commitment.

The third and final advantage of using Options is that they can be used to help fund the protection you seek. You can use combinations of buying and selling Options to create a defined downside risk at the cost of selling some upside. Another way of thinking about this is that Options give you the flexibility to sell a portion of the potential stock appreciation as a means of funding the reduction of risk. For example, if you own IBM at $150, you may have an outlook that it will rise steadily and predictably to your target price of $200 over the next year. If that is your belief and outlook, why not sell any appreciation over $200 to generate income in the current month? Options allow the investor to sell profit at any level to generate premium. This strategy will be explained more in Chapter 21, "Collars," but it is a good example of how you can generate income with Options.

Chapter Lessons

- Options are the preferred method of creating defensive hedges.
- Options allow investors to define risk levels with a high degree of certainty (a married put).
- Options are leveraged vehicles that allow hedges to be set without requiring a large amount of capital.
- Options can be sold for income to help fund the cost of hedges (a collar).

16

What Is an Option?

"We've never lost an American in space; we're sure as hell not gonna lose one on my watch! Failure is not an option."

—Gene Kranz (played by Ed Harris) in *Apollo 13* (1995)

Often it is said that Options are risky investment instruments, and that is true. However, it is less frequently said, but even more true, that Options are the single most versatile instrument to limit and define risk. When used as a hedge, Options provide more protection and are better at stopping losses in a portfolio than any other investment vehicle. If you've ever traded an Option, you know they are no longer considered obscure derivatives used only by the most sophisticated traders. The volume of Option contracts is growing at an astronomical rate. Both individual and professional traders use Options regularly to manage assets. Currently, nine different Option exchanges handle nearly 14 million contracts a day.

What are Options?

Options are contracts to take some buy/sell action at a predetermined price by a predetermined time on a defined asset. Anyone familiar with the term "optionality" knows that it provides a choice to take some future action. This is exactly what Options are, but they occur in the financial markets. Believe it or not, you use the basics of Options in everyday life with things such as shopping at sales or buying insurance as protection.

Consider a coupon to buy a pizza for $10 from Tony's Pizzeria. A former coworker of ours used this example to help describe how a call Option works, and it's worth repeating here. As the holder of the coupon, you have the right to buy a pizza regardless of what Tony is selling it for over the counter (pun intended). On the other side of the coupon is Tony, who is obligated to sell you the pizza for $10. This is exactly how an Option works. It gives the holder the right to buy stock (or some other asset) for a certain price regardless of what it is trading for in the market. Like coupons, Options have an expiration date. This is an example of what happens with a *call Option.*

Another example is buying a warranty on a new appliance such as a dishwasher. Suppose the retail store sells you a warranty. It gives the holder the right to have defects repaired or maybe even get your money back if you're dissatisfied. It can be said that the warranty starts to become more valuable if your new dishwasher stops working. If the dishwasher needs a minor repair such as a new handle, the warranty provides an offset for that problem. You call the store and order a replacement. After all, you bought the warranty, so why not use it? You will feel like you even made a little money back from the investment in the warranty.

If the dishwasher starts making loud noises and leaking water all over the kitchen and needs a new motor, now you'll really feel smart about buying the warranty. As the dirty dishes begin piling up, you start to value the money you spent on the warranty. For you, the warranty has a value equal to the replacement cost of the dishwasher. This is similar to what a *put Option* does. This will become more clear as the book gets into the definition of an Option.

Let's break that definition into its parts to give you a better understanding.

"Options are *contracts*...." In this case, we mean a contract as an agreement. Later we will expand on what that agreement is when describing the buy/sell action. Options are traded in the open market and can be bought or sold like any other investment. Your broker will require you to affirm your Options knowledge before approving you to trade Options. When you trade Options, there isn't any specific paperwork to sign, like a legal contract, but it is certainly binding in the most fundamental of ways—the monetary impact it has on a portfolio. There's no renegotiating this kind of contract. If it's in a portfolio, the holder of the contract is bound by its terms. So although the terms are absolute, the great thing is that the holder of the Option contract can trade out of it the same way he or she traded into it—as long as it hasn't expired, of course.

Let's dig into the next part of the definition.

"Options are contracts *to take some buy/sell action....*" There are two kinds of contracts: a put and a call. A call gives the owner the right to buy stock at a specific price, and a put gives the owner the right to sell stock at a specific price. It's easy to confuse the two, so here are two easy definitions that might help you remember.

A call allows the owner to *call* the stock away from someone (buy stock), and the put allows the owner to *put* the stock to someone (sell stock).

Here's another way to remember in everyday terms. When someone *calls* his dog, he usually wants it to come to him because it is somewhere else. You call your dog, and now it's with you. You call stock, and now it's in your portfolio.

When someone *puts* something away, he leaves it and doesn't have it anymore. You put away the groceries so you don't have to carry them anymore. You put stock to someone, and it is no longer carried in your portfolio.

Calls = buy action

Puts = sell action

The owner of a call Option has the right to call away stock (buy stock) from the writer of the contract. That means that the seller/writer of the contract is obligated to deliver the stock the owner calls. In the earlier pizza example, the holder of the coupon has the right to buy a pizza for $10. And Tony is obligated to sell it for $10.

The owner of a put Option has the right to put the stock (sell stock) to the writer of the contract. This means that the seller/writer is obligated to take the stock that is put to him or her—in other words, buy the stock from the put owner. In the dishwasher example, the holder of the warranty has the right to put the responsibility of the repairs on the store that sold the warranty. Effectively, the store is obligated to take on the liability associated with the broken appliance.

When an owner decides to use the rights granted by the Option, this is called *exercising*. When a writer has a contract exercised on him by the other side, this is called getting *assigned*. The owner exercises his or her contract rights, and the owner gets assigned to take the action the owner dictates.

It may appear that the owner of a call (the right to buy stock) looks very similar to the seller of a put (obligated to take stock) or that the owner of a put (the right to sell stock) looks similar to the writer of a call (obligated to deliver stock). From an investment bias perspective, this is true. The owner of a call is bullish, just like the seller of a put. Similarly, the owner of a put is bearish, just like the seller of a call.

However, that is all they have in common. There are many differences in the risk and reward profiles of buyers and sellers of Options, as you'll learn in later chapters.

Here's the next part of the definition:

"Options are contracts to take some buy/sell action *at a predetermined price....*"

The predetermined price is known as the *strike price*. This is the price at which the buy/sell action occurs if and when the owner decides to exercise his rights. This strike price is actually included as one of the components of the *Option symbol*. This is helpful because multiple Options with multiple strike prices are always available on the same underlying symbol.

For a call owner, the strike price is the price paid when he wants to exercise and buy stock. For the put owner, the strike is the price he sells the stock for when delivering. As defined by the terms of the Option contract, an Option's strike price doesn't change. It is locked in no matter how the asset performs in the market.

It's worth noting that sometimes a strike price can be adjusted due to a corporate action such as a stock split or a large dividend. Mathematically, the markets handle these changes at parity, so the Option holders aren't disadvantaged. You won't encounter this situation very often, but you should know it exists.

For a call, the Option is valuable when the strike price is lower than the stock's current market price.

For example, imagine GE is trading at $20 in the open market. A call with a $15 strike would allow the owner of the call to buy the stock at $15 versus the $20 market price. Yes, the call owner actually gets to buy the stock for $5 less than the market price. This is a good position to be in if you own the Option. Buying for less than the market is always a good thing, because you can turn around and sell it for a $5 profit right away.

For puts, Options have more value when the strike price is greater than the stock's current market price.

Here's a put example: Suppose that GE stock is still trading at $20 in the open market. A put with a $30 strike will allow the holder of the put to sell GE for $30—$10 more than what the open market would give for the stock. The long put Option holder can sell for an instant profit above fair market value because of the rights the put gives him. A $10 instant profit is a good thing for the owner of the put. The next chapter contains more details on values, but these examples should help you understand why the strike price matters.

Back to the description of Options:

"Options are contracts to take some buy/sell action at a predetermined price *by a predetermined time....*"

Options have an *expiration,* meaning that they aren't valid forever. Once the expiration arrives, the Option is worth nothing. This is very different from stocks, which can be held in an account as long as the company still trades publicly. There are many different Option expiration periods—weekly, monthly, quarterly, and annually. However, the most widely used Options are the ones that expire monthly.

Monthly Options expire on the Saturday following the third Friday of the month. Yes, this is as convoluted as figuring out what Sunday will be Easter or what week Election Tuesday falls on. Options don't trade on Saturday, so the last day to trade these before expiration is the Friday before the Saturday expiration date. And there are exceptions to this rule (as with all things on Wall Street), such as index Options. As strange as all this seems, brokers make this rule easy to figure out by noting how many days are left before expiration in the quotes or positions list. Figure 16.1 illustrates this timing.

The time of expiration is clearly stated in the Option symbol. For the monthly Options it is usually denoted as the month and year. For example, an Option with a SEP11 designation for expiration means that the Option will expire on the Saturday following the third Friday of September 2011. SEP11 is certainly easier to say.

The monthly Option periods begin as soon as the previous month ends. If the SEP11 Option period ends on the Saturday following the third Friday of the month, the OCT11 period begins the following

Monday. Yes, that is in September, but it is considered the October Option period because that is when the Options will expire.

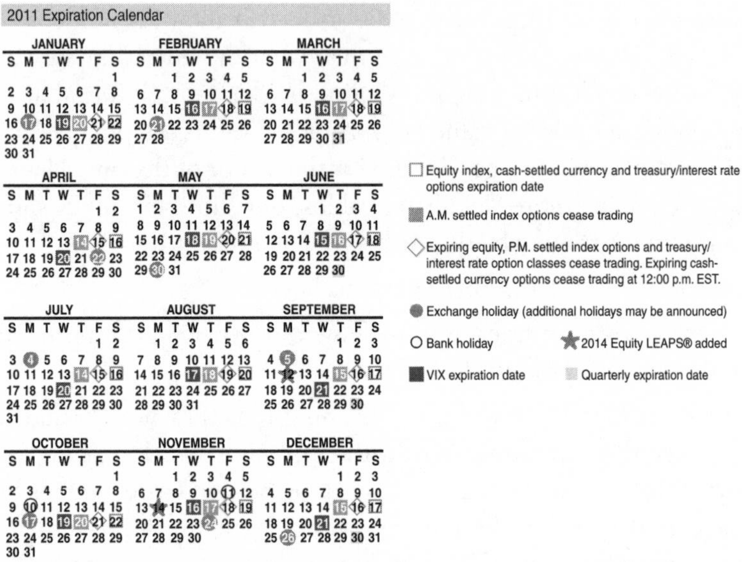

Figure 16.1 2011 expiration calendar

Monthly Options usually exist for at least two months: the current month and the following one. So as soon as a month ends, the Options two months out are created. For example, when the SEP11 Options expire, the Monday that begins the OCT11 period will be when the NOV11 Options start trading.

Adding to the confusion, weekly Options stop trading on the Thursday of the week and are denoted by the week in which they expire during the Option period. So SEP2 11 means that the Option expires on the Thursday of the second week of September 2011. Because Buy and Hedge recommends investing for the long term, you will rarely use the weekly Options, but you need to recognize them in the Option chain to avoid confusion. The other thing about weekly Options is that they come out only in the weeks in which they trade. This prevents you from accidentally using them most of the time, but you still need to recognize that they are there.

Long dated Options include quarterly and annual Options known as *LEAPS*, which stands for Long-term Equity AnticiPation Security Options. Expect the LEAPS to be in the January Option expiration period of every year. Quarterly Options expiration is indicated in the quote in the same way as the weeklies if it doesn't fall on the normal monthly week. Different symbols have different quarterly Options expirations, but they are always three months apart. For example, quarterlies may expire during the months of DEC, MAR, JUN, and SEP, although this can vary.

The good news is that the methodology of how these dates are set isn't that important. The most important thing to watch for is the number of days until the Option expires.

Here's the last part of the description:

"Options are contracts to take some buy/sell action at a predetermined price by a predetermined time *on a defined asset.*"

Options don't exist on every single asset type. They are predominantly used for stocks, indexes, and ETF's, but Options do exist on other vehicles, such as futures and forex. (This book doesn't discuss those asset classes.) The Option description includes the underlying asset and is usually the same letters as that asset symbol. Standard Options denote 100 shares per contract. Nonstandard Options may use a different number of shares, multiple symbols, and even cash. However, brokers usually note in their quote when an Option is considered nonstandard. There is no standard way to denote nonstandard Options. (This is not meant as a joke, but it's fun to say nonetheless.)

Usually called the *multiplier*, the 100 shares per contract ratio is used throughout this book. This means that one contract controls 100 shares. For example, one call with a strike price of $15 means that the owner has the right to buy 100 shares for $15 each.

Not all stocks, indexes, or ETFs have Options available to trade on them. Typically they are restricted to larger volume or very popular symbols. But don't worry. You'll have thousands of choices when you decide it's time to invest.

Before you move on to the next chapter, let's examine a couple of Option symbols and break down their parts.

GE SEP11 20 call

- GE is the underlying stock symbol (the defined asset).
- SEP11 is the expiration date. In this case it is the monthly Option, because no week is indicated.
- 20 is the call's strike price.
- Call is the type of Option. Remember that a call gives the owner the right to buy stock.

Put into everyday language, this Option means that the owner has the right to buy shares of GE at $20 by the September 2011 expiration.

Here is a put example position:

IBM OCT2 11 205 put

- IBM is the underlying company.
- These Options expire in the second week of the October 2011 period, which could be in September.
- The strike price is 205.
- This is a put Option. As a reminder, a put gives the owner the right to sell shares at the strike price before expiration.

In plain English, an IBM OCT2 11 205 put means that this contract is for the right to sell shares of IBM at $205 up until the second week of the October 2011 monthly Options period.

Chapter Lessons

- Options are contracts to take a buy/sell action at a predetermined price by a predetermined time on a defined asset.
- An Option has four parts:
  - What underlying asset the Option is on
  - When the Option expires
  - The strike price
  - Whether it is a call or put

17

Option Positions

"Listen, I'm a politician, which means I'm a cheat and a liar, and when I'm not kissing babies I'm stealing their lollipops. But it also means I keep my options open."

—Jeffrey Pelt (played by Richard Jordan) in *The Hunt for Red October* (1990)

We picked this quote not to claim using options means you have to be a liar or a cheat but to get to the root of the word. Choice, Options give you the ability to choose how you want to manage your portfolio.

In the preceding chapter you learned that Options are a contract to take a buy/sell action at a predetermined price by a predetermined time on a defined asset. In this chapter you'll learn about Option positions, how to read an Option chain, and why the strike price really matters.

Every Option contract has two parties: a buyer and a seller. This matters because each party has a different role in the contract, and each role needs to be identified. As a review, the buyer (also known as the owner) of the Option contract has all the rights and decision power. Meanwhile, the seller (also known as the writer) is obligated to meet the terms of the agreement whenever the buyer decides to exercise the contract. This seems fairly lopsided in favor of the buyer. But don't worry about the seller, because he gets paid in advance for this obligation. Often, the seller is on the better side of the trade.

Investors are *long* when they are the owner or buyer of the Option, and they are *short* if they are the seller or writer of the contract. This is just like being long or short stock; the same terms apply to Options. In addition, just like stocks, the way to tell if the holder of the Option is long or short is a minus sign or no sign, respectively, in front of the number of contracts. A negative Option position means that the holder is short. When the number of contracts has no sign or a plus sign in front of it, that holder is long.

Here's a summary of these terms:

owner = buyer = being long

writer = seller = being short

It's worth noting that the owner doesn't have to exercise the rights of the agreement. The decision is completely up to him. The seller, however, has no say and is obligated whenever the owner decides to exercise his rights. However, both sides always can trade out of the position in the open market if they feel it's time to exit the contract.

As stated before, Options are agreements. These agreements include a number of contracts and can be structured in just about any size. Contracts are created based on the demand to enter into the terms of the agreement. This means that as soon as an investor wants to enter into an agreement, the Options can be created to trade. This differs from stocks, because stocks have a limited number of shares, and that share count can't change without some kind of corporate action. With Options, as long as the terms of the agreement exist in the market, there will always be contracts to trade.

Here is an example of an Option position:

5 GE SEP11 20 calls
- Five contracts of 100 shares each, meaning 500 shares
- The position is a long position.
- The underlying is GE.
- The expiration is in the September 2011 period.
- The strike price is $20.
- This Option is a call.

Expressed in plain English, this Option position grants the holder the right to buy 500 shares of GE at $20 before expiration in September 2011.

Option Chains

One stock can have many different Options. The fact that there are many different strikes and expirations can create multiple Options on the same underlying stock. This list of Options quotes is known as an Option chain. Figure 17.1 shows an example.

CALLS | PUTS | In-the-money

Symbol	Last	Change	Vol	Bid	Ask	Open Int.	Strike	Symbol	Last	Change	Vol	Bid	Ask	Open Int.
JUNE, 2011 OPTIONS														Hide
quote	0.00	0.00	0.00	10.85	11.05	406.00	7.50	quote	0.00	0.00	0.00	0.00	0.01	541.00
quote	0.00	0.00	0.00	8.35	8.55	250.00	10.00	quote	0.00	0.00	0.00	0.00	0.01	3,125
quote	6.40	-0.10	2,000	6.35	6.55	1,035	12.00	quote	0.00	0.00	0.00	0.00	0.01	11,577
quote	0.00	0.00	0.00	5.35	5.55	1,245	13.00	quote	0.00	0.00	0.00	0.01	0.01	3,696
quote	0.00	0.00	0.00	4.35	4.55	1,547	14.00	quote	0.00	0.00	0.00	0.00	0.01	49,834
quote	3.40	-0.25	12,015	3.35	3.55	3,986	15.00	quote	0.00	0.00	0.00	0.01	0.01	23,254
quote	2.52	-0.18	20.00	2.35	2.40	15,996	16.00	quote	0.00	0.00	0.00	0.01	0.02	26,023
quote	1.35	-0.29	90.00	1.38	1.42	9,911	17.00	quote	0.02	0.01	349.00	0.01	0.02	23,005
quote	0.39	-0.22	2,074	0.37	0.40	15,399	18.00	quote	0.08	0.04	2,946	0.08	0.09	43,130
							18.36	Current price as of 6/15/2011 01:36:44 PM						
quote	0.02	-0.01	459.00	0.01	0.02	44,162	19.00	quote	0.77	0.19	1,819	0.74	0.78	55,224
quote	0.01	0.00	2,432	0.01	0.01	80,685	20.00	quote	1.75	0.21	2,908	1.73	1.76	61,200
quote	0.00	-0.01	0.00	0.01	0.01	101,751	21.00	quote	2.74	0.21	190.00	2.74	2.79	29,253
quote	0.01	-0.01	11.00	0.01	0.01	54,011	22.50	quote	4.24	0.14	73.00	4.20	4.30	7,627
quote	0.01	0.00	10.00	0.00	0.01	10,838	24.00	quote	5.75	0.05	12.00	5.65	5.80	1,720
quote	0.01	0.00	20.00	0.00	0.00	236.00	26.00	quote	0.00	0.00	0.00	7.55	7.80	782.00
JULY, 2011 OPTIONS														Hide
Symbol	Last	Change	Vol	Bid	Ask	Open Int.	Strike	Symbol	Last	Change	Vol	Bid	Ask	Open Int.
quote	0.00	-0.20	0.00	5.30	5.60	2.00	13.00	quote	0.00	0.00	0.00	0.01	0.02	165.00
quote	0.00	0.00	0.00	4.35	4.60		14.00	quote	0.00	0.00	0.00	0.01	0.03	105.00
quote	0.00	0.15	0.00	3.35	3.55	15.00	15.00	quote	0.03	-0.01	251.00	0.02	0.04	15,479
quote	0.00	0.00	0.00	2.33	2.42	363.00	16.00	quote	0.07	0.02	2.00	0.05	0.07	2,851
quote	1.42	-0.31	245.00	1.40	1.43	2,079	17.00	quote	0.15	0.06	274.00	0.14	0.16	9,849
quote	0.65	-0.12	1,028	0.63	0.66	5,303	18.00	quote	0.40	0.10	482.00	0.41	0.42	20,813
							18.36	Current price as of 6/15/2011 01:36:44 PM						
quote	0.23	-0.03	17,425	0.21	0.22	24,509		quote	0.97	0.17	1,622	0.97	0.99	26,308
quote	0.06	-0.01	2,607	0.05	0.06	24,107		quote	1.77	0.18	366.00	1.78	1.82	17,642
quote	0.02	0.00	99.00	0.01	0.02	23,497		quote	2.54	0.04	9.00	2.76	2.81	2,520
quote	0.01	0.00	1.00	0.01	0.01	9,324		quote	0.00	0.00	0.00	3.60	3.80	1,878
quote	0.00	0.00	0.00	0.01	0.01	3,399		quote	0.00	0.40	0.00	4.55	4.80	1,182
quote	0.00	0.00	0.00	0.00	0.02	1,451		quote	5.50	-0.04	10.00	5.55	5.90	116.00
quote	0.04	25.00	25.00	0.00	0.02	603.00		quote	0.00	0.55	0.00	6.55	6.90	22.00
AUGUST, 2011 OPTIONS														Show
SEPTEMBER, 2011 OPTIONS														Show
DECEMBER, 2011 OPTIONS														Show
JANUARY, 2012 OPTIONS														Show
MARCH, 2012 OPTIONS														Show
JANUARY, 2013 OPTIONS														Show

Figure 17.1 Option chain for General Electric

To use Options to hedge, you need to learn to read this chain.

First, note the strike prices that run down the middle of the list. You'll find the calls on the left and the puts on the right. This is always the case when you look at both types of Options simultaneously. Calls or puts can be viewed independently. This varies by whatever interface is being used.

Next is the expiration period. The grouping of Options is broken up by the expiration period. This makes it easier to show how the Option prices move with the strike price, leaving the date constant.

Finally, notice the price of the Option. This is represented by the bid, ask, and last. Just like stocks, the last is the last price at which the Option traded, the bid is what the Option can be sold for at the market price, and the ask is what the Option can be bought for at the market price. The difference between those last two price points is known as the bid/ask spread. For stocks traders, the last, bid, and ask are usually pretty close in price. The small difference in the bid/ask spread isn't worth worrying about unless you're talking about a large number of shares. But with Options, the bid/ask spread can be much wider. The disparity in price is because the Option may be less frequently traded, regardless of how much volume the underlying stock has. The last may also be very far from the Option's bid/ask price, because it might not have traded in days or even weeks. Yet the Option bid/ask will update as the market moves.

Many platforms and brokers will calculate the middle of the bid/ask spread, known as the *mark*, as the market value of the Option. However, this practice varies, so be sure to ask your broker about the impact of Option pricing on a portfolio. In general limit orders should be placed at the mark or slightly away from it to expect your order to get filled. Don't expect a buy order to fill at the bid or a sell to fill at the ask with Options. This is unlike stock trades, in which buys placed at the bid or sells placed at the ask are frequently filled. This doesn't happen with Options.

The Option chain shows some other data points. Option volume and option open interest are just as standard as the bid/ask. Volume is similar to stock volume and represents how many contracts have traded that day. Open interest represents the cumulative amount of how many Option contracts were outstanding as of the previous day's close. Open interest increases as new opening positions are taken and held overnight. Opening a new position can mean opening a long or short position. Open interest decreases as Option contracts are closed out. Open interest can be used in conjunction with other Options data to get an idea of the market's bias about the underlying position. For hedging purposes, we don't use open interest or volume very often, but it's good to be familiar with this concept.

ITM, OTM, ATM

Before we move on to how Options premiums are valued, it's worth exploring a little what the Option position means to the holder. As a review, you learned in the preceding chapter about strike prices. For a call owner, the strike price is the price he pays when he wants to exercise and buy stock. For the put owner, the strike is the price he sells the stock for when delivering.

Let's return to the GE example when it is trading at $20 in the open market. A call with a $15 strike would allow the call's owner to buy the stock at $15 versus the $20 market price. As a smart investor, you know that buying GE for less than the market is a good thing, because you can turn around and sell it at the $5 profit right away.

For puts, Options have more value when the strike price is greater than the current market price.

Here is a put example: GE stock is still trading at $20 in the open market. A put with a $30 strike allows the holder of the put to sell GE for $30. This yields a $10 instant profit for the owner of the put.

These two examples of Options are referred to as *in-the-money* (ITM). ITM Options have a strike price that is advantageous to the owner of the Option. For calls, this means that ITM Options have a strike price lower than the market price of the underlying symbol. Meanwhile, ITM puts have a strike price higher than the market price of the underlying symbol.

The arithmetic value of these Options is known as intrinsic value. It's the simple mathematical value that the Option is worth when it is in the money. This is calculated by simply taking the difference of the strike and the stock's price in the open market. So in the call example, the intrinsic value is $5 ($20 to $15), and in the put example, the intrinsic value is $10 ($30 to $20).

If the owner is getting the benefit of these ITM contract examples, who is on the other side of the trade? The seller. In both of these examples, the writer (seller) of the contract is obligated to deliver or take the stock at the strike price. So in the call example, the writer of the call is forced to sell the stock at a lower price than what the market is selling it for. In the put example, the writer of the put is forced to buy it from the long put contract holder for more than the market price.

This mathematical value and simple calculation of intrinsic value make it easier for investors to use Options as a viable hedging tool. The price of the ITM contracts is highly correlated to the underlying symbol. It is known mathematically, with a very high degree of certainty, what an Option will be worth relative to its underlying. Said another way, an ITM option is expected to move one point when its stock or index moves one point. This feature of Options enables the creation of defensive hedges.

The term *out-of-the-money* (OTM) refers to Options that are in the exact opposite situation of ITM Options with regard to the strike price. An OTM call Option has a strike price that is higher than the market price, and an OTM put has a strike price that is lower than the market price. In these circumstances, the owner of the Option would not have an advantage of exercising, because he would be paying too much or selling for too little versus what the market will pay.

Suppose GE is trading at $10 instead of $20, and you own a $15 strike call. If you wanted to buy the stock, would you exercise the Option to buy at $15, or would you just go to the open market and pay $10? Clearly it is to your advantage to pay $10 in the open market versus $15 by exercising the call. Yes, this is a silly question, but this is how you must think about Options. Always compare them to the open market to get an idea of the Option value.

Now suppose you own the $30 strike put when GE trades at $35. Again, ask yourself if you would exercise the put Option that gives you the right to sell at $30 or just sell stock in the open market for $35. Another obvious answer, right? You'd sell it at $35, because you can get $5 more per share. In both of these situations, the long Option holder would not exercise, and the short holder wouldn't have to meet any obligation.

OTM Options have no intrinsic value. You can derive no value from just the mathematical value of the Options, because the owner will most likely never benefit from exercising them. So all OTM Options have zero intrinsic value. This doesn't mean that the Option has no value; it does have something called extrinsic value. We will cover that topic when we dig more into premiums. The writer of the Options should not expect to get assigned when holding OTM Options, because there just isn't a reason for the owner to exercise.

The term *at-the-money* (ATM) refers to Options that have a strike price right at the price of the stock. Rarely does an Option expire exactly ATM, but this reference is used for Options that have strike prices closest to the current market value. ATM Options also have no or very little intrinsic value, but they usually have the highest extrinsic value. This is because the Option has the highest probability of change. This concept is covered in the next chapter, which explains extrinsic value in more detail.

Chapter Lessons

- Option holders can be long or short.
- Option chains are used to access price quotes for Options contracts.
- ITM calls have a strike price below the current market, and ITM puts have a strike price above the current market.
- OTM calls have a strike price above the market, and OTM puts have a strike price below the market.

18

Understanding and Using Options

"I guess that was your accomplice in the wood chipper."

—Marge Gunderson (played by Frances McDormand) in
Fargo (1996)

Just a gentle reminder that there are two sides to every option trade. The value that options command isn't as unpredictable as a staged kidnapping like Fargo, but nonetheless, there are winners and losers in every trade. Being aware of how options are valued is important to know before using them as a hedging vehicle and keeping you out of the wood chipper.

As discussed in Chapter 16, "What Is an Option?," the investor can use Options in many ways to create an investment bias. This flexibility allows you to fine-tune your approach and create the most cost-effective set of positions. To understand how this is done, you must understand where Option valuations come from and what they mean.

Option Valuation

We find it easiest to describe Option values from the buyer's perspective. We'll start with the easiest one to grasp—the call. If you have ever worked for a large publicly traded company, you have probably heard of stock Options. Corporate stock Options used to be a popular form of compensation offered to employees. They allowed the employee to benefit from the growth of company stock. If you were one of those people, like we were, the Options were granted around bonus time and came with a strike price that was usually some strange number, such as $9.37. These were private Options that could not be traded in the open market but that had real value to the holder. The value came as the stock price went up because the employee would have the right to buy the stock at the Option strike price. If this sounds familiar, you already understand how a call Option works.

But if you never had this kind of compensation, you have missed the joy of seeing your company stock go up from a great earnings report and knowing those Options went up in value. You also have missed out on the vastly larger disappointment when some terrible news crushed the company's value in the marketplace. When stock Options were popular, employees would watch the company stock price all day long. Swings in the price of the stock would swing the mood in the office, both good and bad. Each employee had his own rooting interest: get the stock price up over his own stock Option strike price. The worst part was that when the stock fell below the strike price, the Options had no value. Zero. You now know this as intrinsic value, and those Options were out of the money.

This book focuses on Options that are open market instruments. These types of Options can be traded at the investor's discretion and are not restricted to the terms of a compensation plan.

As a quick review, a call Option gives the owner the right to buy the stock at a given price by a certain time. This right costs something called the premium. As the stock price of the underlying moves prior to the expiration time, the value (premium) also moves.

The Pizza Coupon

You got a taste of this mental model a few chapters ago, but it works so well, we will use it again and build on it. In the pizza coupon example, you had a coupon to buy a $10 pizza good for a year from Tony's Pizzeria. This coupon is very much like a call Option. The holder of the coupon has the right to buy a pizza from Tony within the next year for $10, regardless how much he is selling pizzas for at the time. Let's look at its parts. The coupon is in reference to a pizza (the underlying asset), the coupon lists a price for the pizza ($10), and the coupon has an expiration date (one year). If at the time Tony is selling a pizza over the counter to anyone without a coupon for $15, this coupon will save $5 ($15 – $10). This is pretty easy math. It can be said that the coupon has at least a $5 value. Said another way, the coupon has an intrinsic value of $5 or is ITM by $5.

Theoretically, you could stand outside Tony's shop selling these coupons for $5. However, if you did that, Tony would probably come out and break your legs. To be on the safe side, we'll keep it theoretical for now.

A coupon with a different pizza price will have a different value. A coupon to buy a pizza at $12 would save only $3 on a $15 pie. The same math applies: $15 – $12 is $3 in intrinsic value.

But what if Tony was having a one-time special this week and was selling pizzas for only $8? Would this coupon have any value? Of course not. Why would anyone pay $10 for a pizza with a coupon when he could walk into Tony's and buy one for $8 over the counter? Here, the coupon has no intrinsic value, and you now know that it is OTM. This helps illustrate how the intrinsic value is derived for both ITM and OTM Options.

Let's imagine that Tony's generosity has limits, so the price of pizza returns to $15. Perhaps your research leads you to anticipate that the price of Tony's pizza will go up due to an increase in the cost of cheese. You project that the price will move from $15 to $20. Of course, it's worth doing research on pizza; doesn't everyone? Anyway, you now believe that the coupon has a chance of being worth more than $5 at some time in the future—even as high as $10 ($20 – $10).

If other pizza lovers agreed that this change in pizza price was likely, they would be willing to pay for this coupon as well. However, since the price change hasn't happened yet, you are all speculating that it will go up. You can't know for sure that the price will go up; it is your educated pizza hypothesis. Therefore, it's unlikely that someone is willing to pay the full anticipated future value of $10 for a coupon. But if you tried to auction those coupons for $7, a similar pizza-loving speculator may be willing to put up the money. That buyer would be able to buy a coupon that he anticipates being worth $10 for $7. The pizza still costs the same $10 because of the coupon. But if the over-the-counter pizza price is $20, the buyer of your coupon would have paid only $17 in total, saving $3.

Let's review the data again. Over-the-counter pizzas are going for $15, you have a coupon that allows the holder to buy a pizza for $10, and you sell that coupon for $7. The intrinsic value of the coupon is still $5, because the pizza price hasn't moved yet. That is the market price minus the coupon price ($15 − $10). The extra $2 you're able to get is the speculative value based on the anticipated rising price of the pizza over the next year. This $2 is the Option's extrinsic or time value. It is calculated by subtracting the coupon sell price (total premium) from the intrinsic value ($7 − $5). This helps illustrate how time value is calculated.

With a year to go, it's easy to sell the coupon with $2 of time value. There is lots of time for pizza prices to go up. However, suppose only one week is left until the coupon expires. It will be much harder to get the extra $2 in time value, because the probability of Tony's changing his prices in the next seven days is much lower than a full year. Unless a sign in Tony's window tells everyone that prices are increasing, you won't get that extra $2, so you'll be forced to lower the coupon's asking price. Maybe you can get someone to buy it for $5.25 or $5.30 in the hopes of a fast price change.

It is also important to remember that once the coupon expires, it cannot be used. Tony probably won't honor that coupon, and it becomes worthless.

This helps illustrate how, as time to expiration gets closer, the coupon price has less and less time value, but the intrinsic price remains.

Now imagine that you are the person purchasing that $10 pizza coupon that has a year until expiration from someone else for $7. You do this based on anticipation that Tony will raise the price to $20 before the coupon expires. Paying $7 for a coupon that gives you the right to buy a pizza at $10 means you break even if the pizza price is at least $17. That break-even math is calculated by adding the coupon cost of the pizza plus the premium you paid for the right to use it ($10 + $7).

At this point, you believe that the price of pizza will go up, and it can be said that you are bullish on Tony's pizza. In other words, the more the price on Tony's pizza increases, the more valuable your coupon becomes. If the price of pizza were to go up to $25, your coupon would be ITM by $15. You could turn around and sell your coupon for an $8 profit if you wanted ($15 – $7 = $8). Your profit is restricted only by how high Tony can spike the price of his pizza.

Of course, your downside risk is linked to the price of the pizza. What if the price of the pizza doesn't change or even decreases? Remember, you paid $7 for the coupon, but that amount included $5 of savings you would get either way. If the price of the pizza never changes from $15, you could still use the coupon and buy a pie for $10. The coupon still carries a $5 value. All you did was put an extra $2 out of pocket and pay $17 for a $15 pie. You wouldn't throw away the coupon, because it is still cheaper to buy the pie for $10 versus $15. The $7 you paid to buy the coupon in the first place is money already out of pocket, so why not use what you bought? Put another way, if you didn't use the coupon and you wanted to buy a pizza, you would now have wasted the $7 you paid for the coupon and have to pay $15 for the over-the-counter price, essentially paying $22 for the pizza. Using the coupon at least reduces your total out-of-pocket expense to $17.

The worst-case scenario is that Tony decides to lower the price of pizza to a price below your coupon price. Maybe his one-week-a-year special for $8 pizzas is so good for business that he makes that price permanent. Now your coupon has no value at expiration. As before, it would make no sense to use a $10 coupon for an $8 product. The $7 you initially spent on the coupon is now gone; it was a total bust of an investment. (Yes, we consider pizza an investment.) The coupon that once had a value of $7 is now worthless. It would be better to just walk in and buy an $8 pizza than to spend the $10 that the coupon gives you the right to do. The silver lining here is that you can't lose more than the $7 you paid for the coupon, no matter how low the price of pizza gets.

Are you hungry yet?

What we just outlined is exactly how a call works, except that we usually don't eat the shares of stock purchased.

The Impact of Volatility on Option Pricing

Here's a little more information about volatility and its impact on Options. The more volatile the price action is for the underlying stock or index, the higher the extrinsic value. This is because the probability and risk of a stock jumping in or out of the money are higher.

Table 18.1 shows an example of two different stocks with similar prices but different volatility factors. At the time this book was written, Monsanto (MON) was trading at $65.25, and Johnson and Johnson (JNJ) was trading at $65.50. Monsanto had a volatility of 27.8%, and JNJ's volatility was 16.5%. Choosing the same month of expiration, OCT11, a look at the ATM call Options shows how that impacts the premium and break-even levels.

Table 18.1 Two Different Stocks with Similar Prices but Different Volatility Factors

JNJ OCT11 Call	Premium	Extrinsic Value	MON OCT11 Call	Premium	Extrinsic Value	Extrinsic Difference
60 strike price	$6.25	$0.75	60 strike price	$8.25	$3.00	$2.25
65 strike price	$2.65	$2.15	65 strike price	$5.40	$5.15	$3.00
70 strike price	$0.75	$0.75	70 strike price	$3.30	$3.30	$2.55

The first point to notice is that the extrinsic value for the same strikes is higher for MON than for JNJ, with a difference ranging from $3.00 to $2.25. Many factors can account for this fact, but it is mostly explained by the volatility difference between these two stocks.

It should be clear by now that as the price of the underlying stock goes up, so does the premium value of the call. But if this isn't clear yet, here is an example using the preceding data to illustrate.

If you bought the $60 strike calls on both of these stocks, and both stocks appreciated to $75 by the October expiration, your calls would be worth $15. We know this because the intrinsic value of a $60 call on a $75 stock is the difference between the price and the strike ($75 – $60).

For the JNJ calls, you spent $6.25, giving you a profit of $8.75 ($15 – $6.25). For the MON calls, you spent $8.25, resulting in a profit of $6.75 ($15 – $8.25). Both are winners, but you made more on the JNJ trade. Why? Because you paid more time value for the MON call Option. And you paid more time value because MON's volatility was higher. Another way to think about it is that JNJ was less likely to move to $75 than MON was because it had lower volatility. So, when JNJ moved to $75, your reward was larger.

The upside value of a call is limited only to the amount by which the underlying stock can rise. If JNJ appreciated to $200, the call would continue to appreciate. If JNJ shot up to $1,000 a share, the call would continue to go up in value. This is because the intrinsic value moves in lockstep with every dollar move in the stock. Because theoretically there is no limit to the value of a stock, there is no limit to the value of a call either.

In this example you controlled 100 shares of JNJ, a $65 stock, for $6.25 a share. If you were to buy the stock outright, you would need to put up $6,500. But with the call you needed to put up only $625. Seems too good to be true, right? Remember, as with the pizza example, that if the stock doesn't appreciate by the expiration, the calls will become worthless. Zero dollars. A coupon has no value once it expires; neither does an Option.

Here is a summary of principles to remember with a long call:

- Being long a call means that you want the underlying stock or index to go up.
- The breakeven is the cost of the call plus the strike price.
- The call has no intrinsic value if it is OTM.
- The most you can lose is the premium paid for the call.
- The call has intrinsic value—the amount it is ITM.
- The value of a call has no upside limit and can appreciate as far as the underlying stock can go.
- The further away the expiration, the more extrinsic value a call has.

The Flood Insurance Example

When describing a put, we like to use insurance as a metaphor to help put things in perspective. Here's a refresher on the definition of a put. A put gives the owner the right to sell an underlying asset for a specific price by a specific date. This right comes at the cost of paying a premium.

Assume you own a $500,000 home and, for simplicity, that it is fully paid off. It's OK to skip the complication of adding borrowing to the equation for this example. The home is your asset. You want to protect your asset in case it suffers some kind of damage. One of the ways to protect your home is to purchase flood insurance. Now imagine that you live in a 100-year floodplain and there is some risk of a flood to the property. A 100-year floodplain is an area that has a chance of flooding once every 100 years. Said another way, it has a 1% chance of flooding every year. Getting back to the insurance, you purchase a policy that has a $5,000 deductible and that will cost $300 a quarter. You can feel comfortable that as long as you pay the quarterly premium, you've just protected the home for $495,000 worth of flood-related damage ($500,000 value – $5,000 deductible).

This is just like owning a put. In this example the underlying asset is your home. Your strike price is $495,000, and the cost of the Option premium (not coincidentally named) is $300 per quarter. These rates and terms are defined by multiple factors, including the time the policy covers (quarterly in this case) and the chance or risk of a flood (considered to be the volatility).

When no flood occurs, you probably view the insurance policy as just another bill you have to pay to sleep better at night. But imagine a flood occurs, and your home suffers $150,000 worth of damage. It was just your luck that the 100-year flood happened while you owned the house. That kind of luck happens all the time to investors. (More than one talking head on financial television referred to the 2008 market crisis as the "100-year flood.") You are now loving the fact that you have flood insurance.

The terms of the policy insure you for $145,000 worth of repairs. Remember, you must pay the $5,000 deductible out of pocket. Right now that seems like nothing compared to all the damage. You can now think of this policy as having value—$145,000 worth of value, to be exact.

The same thing happens with a put. When you own a put, you have the right to sell stock regardless of what it is trading for in the open market. The put actually goes up in value as the underlying asset declines in value. Imagine if your home had $300,000 worth of damage from the flood; you could say that the insurance policy is now worth $295,000. The worse the damage, the more the policy is worth to you. It's the same with a put. As the underlying asset depreciates, the more the put is worth.

Taking this example to its endgame, you can see that the maximum value the insurance policy can be worth is when the full home loss occurs: $495,000. The same applies to puts. The most a put can be worth is when the underlying stock goes to zero. At that point the put is worth the strike price. This is different from calls that have no maximum value.

Just like a call, the intrinsic value of the put is calculated by taking the difference between the strike price of the Option and the current stock price when the Option is ITM. But for puts, remember that ITM means that the current stock price is lower than the strike price. If an Option is OTM, it has no intrinsic value.

Table 18.2 is a reference to help you remember when calls and puts are in- or out-of-the-money.

Table 18.2 When Calls and Puts Are ITM and OTM

	Call	**Put**
Strike Is Above Market Price	Out-of-the-money	In-the money
Strike Is Below Market Price	In-the-money	Out-of-the-money

Breakeven for puts is calculated as the strike price minus the premium paid for the put. Think about the insurance example again. If your home suffered $2,000 worth of flood damage within the first three months of your buying the policy, it wouldn't help offset the damage, because you have a $5,000 deductible. We mention the first quarter specifically because it means you've paid only $300 in premiums so far. For the policy to break even, you would need to have $5,300 worth of damage in the first quarter, or $5,600 worth of damage by the second quarter, or $5,900 worth of damage by the third quarter, and so on. For the policy to break even, you need the home's damage to offset all the money you paid for the policy.

By the way, it is worth noting that puts can be bought without owning the underlying asset. The put itself is not a hedged investment; but unlike everyday life, speculators can hold insurance on assets they don't own.

Looking at a real put may make this more clear. Using JNJ trading at $65.50 as an example again, the JNJ OCT11 60 put is trading at $1.35. This means that for the $60 strike to break even, JNJ will have to drop to $58.65 ($60 – $1.35). Think of the drop from $65.50 to $60 as the deductible, the current price to the strike price, and the $1.35 as the premium paid for the right to sell JNJ at $60. This Option is considered OTM and has zero intrinsic value. If it expires while JNJ trades above $60, you can kiss this Option good-bye. However, if JNJ were to drop by $10 to $55, now the Option has $5 of intrinsic value. If you hold this Option, you need that drop to happen before the expiration. In addition, some extrinsic value probably will remain in the premium.

Extrinsic value for a put is the same as it is with a call. It is based predominantly on time to expiration and volatility. It can be calculated by deducting the intrinsic value from the total premium.

Returning to the insurance example, when you insure the $500,000 home for each three-month period, you pay $300. This premium covers you for that amount of time, and then you have to pay it again. But what if you wanted to insure this home for only one week? The probability of the 100-year flood coming during that week is significantly less than the probability for an entire quarter. Therefore, the less time to expiration, the lower the risk—and the lower the risk, the lower the premium.

For one-week insurance, expect the premium to be significantly less than $300. We have never heard of flood insurance for just one week, but there is such a thing as gap insurance. That is the insurance people buy for a new car to cover any damage that may occur from the time the car is driven off the lot until natural depreciation catches up to the true value. The point is that time is a factor in calculating the value of any insurance policy.

Now say that your home is in a ten-year floodplain instead of the 100-year floodplain. The risk of a flood is ten times higher, and the cost of the insurance goes up dramatically. It stands to reason that the riskier the asset being insured, the more expensive the insurance. Have you ever received a traffic ticket and had your car insurance bill go up? That's because the accepted practice is to assume that drivers who speed are at a greater risk of having an accident and therefore are a greater risk to the insurance company.

The same concept applies to the stock market. If you want to buy a put on a volatile stock, the premium will be much higher, because there is a greater chance of a decrease in value.

Table 18.3 shows the puts for the MON and JNJ stock example again to compare premiums and break-even prices for stocks with two different volatilities.

Table 18.3 Puts for MON and JNJ

JNJ OCT11 Put	Premium	Break-Even Price	MON OCT11 Put	Premium	Break-Even Price
60 strike price	$1.35	$58.65	60 strike price	$3.45	$56.55
65 strike price	$3.00	$62.00	65 strike price	$5.65	$59.35
70 strike price	$6.25	$63.75	70 strike price	$8.50	$61.50

Again, MON with its higher volatility commands a higher premium and causes the break-even prices for MON to be much lower than those of JNJ. Remember that MON and JNJ are both trading around $65 and change.

Just like a call, the only money out of pocket you have with a put is the cost of the premium. You cannot lose more than this premium, because no matter how high the stock rises, you will never have to pay anything else. In other words, your maximum loss is the premium. That loss occurs only if the underlying stock price stays higher than the strike of the put.

Here is a summary of principles to remember with a long put:

- Being long a put means that you want the underlying stock or index to go down.
- Breakeven is when the underlying stock drops to the level of the strike price minus the cost of the put premium.
- The most the owner can lose is the premium paid for the put.
- The put has no intrinsic value if it is OTM.
- The put has intrinsic value equal to the amount it is ITM.
- The maximum gain for a put is realized when the underlying goes to 0 and the put is valued at the strike price.
- The further away the expiration, the more extrinsic value a put has.

The Other Side of the Trade

There are two sides to every story, and as you know from the definition, it takes two parties to trade Option contracts. For every buyer, there is a seller. It stands to reason that when the long side of the call Option is bullish, the short side is bearish, and vice versa for puts. As mentioned before, shorting an Option can be done just like shorting stock. Actually, it is easier than shorting stock, because Options can always be created to meet demand; with stocks, shorting depends on the availability of stock to be lent out. You don't have to worry about this for Options.

The writer of a call takes in the premium that the long side pays. This is the maximum gain for the seller of an Option. So although the owner of a call or put has the potential to make many times his investment, the writer can make only the premium paid to him. The writer of an Option maximizes his gain when the Option expires OTM. At that point, he can keep the premium paid to him at the opening of the transaction and have no obligation to the long side of the contract.

If the maximum gain for the call's buyer is limitless, the maximum loss for the seller of that Option is also limitless. This means that if a stock makes a huge run-up on the holder of a short call position, he stands to lose just as much as the long side stands to make.

So why sell Options when the maximum loss potential is so high and is offset only by the premium brought in from the buyer? The answer is that time is on the side of the seller. If there is one thing you can count on in the market, it is that time moves forward. In other words, every day that passes pays the Option seller. If time is against the long Option holder, it is on the side of the Option seller. There are many strategies in which sellers of Options benefit from the higher premium they can generate from volatile stocks. All they need to count on is the Options expiring OTM. If that happens, they keep all of the premium. Shorting Options is less risky than it appears when done with the right tactic and approach. Those structures will be outlined in later chapters when we discuss hedging tactics.

Maintenance Requirements

Placing the actual trade with Options requires some logistical consideration by the investor. Luckily, every broker treats Options in a similar manner. Typically, Options are not instruments that can be traded by borrowing money, like buying stock on margin. However, many recommended tactics in this book will require margin approval and Option approval from your broker.

As a rule of thumb, most brokers require upfront money equal to the maximum potential loss associated with the position. This means that for long Option positions, the full amount of the premium is required up front to avoid being bought on margin. In Part V, you will learn about spreads and how to calculate the requirement necessary for those. But the same theory applies: the maximum loss is required up front to create the position. The exception is naked calls and naked puts. But because we don't consider those hedged positions, we won't discuss them.

Chapter Lessons

- Option premium is determined by intrinsic and extrinsic value.
- Intrinsic value is the amount an Option is ITM.
- Extrinsic value comes from time to expiration and volatility.
- Long calls are bullish with unlimited upside.
- Long puts are bearish with the potential upside of the total value of the underlying.
- The maximum loss possible on long Options is the cost of the premium.
- Short Options maximum gain is the premium taken in.
- Time decay benefits short Option positions.

19

Risk Graphs: A Picture Is Worth a Thousand Dollars

"You're gonna need a bigger boat."

—Police Chief Martin Brody (played by Roy Scheider) in *Jaws* (1975)

Sometimes it's easier to understand your risk exposure if you can visualize it. When Chief Martin Brody, played by Roy Scheider, saw the size of the shark they were up against in *Jaws*, he immediately knew that they'd underestimated the risk they took. Visualizing your exposure through risk graphs will provide an easy way to understand your risk levels.

It's worth repeating that Options are the single most effective hedging technique available to the average individual investor. Options enable the creation of effective counterbalances while leaving room for the original asset to appreciate as expected. Remember that Options can be used to create bullish or bearish exposure. So, the Options investor needs to think carefully about how to use them, because it can get confusing.

In particular, when Options are bought or sold in tandem with stock or with other Options, the overall effect on an investment or portfolio may be confusing. These kinds of tactics are common and are recommended in this book. A simple tool can make this easier to track. A risk graph allows the Option investor to see a position's impact and bias through a graphical representation. Risk graphs help illustrate what happens to the value of an investment as the underlying stock or index moves.

Many stock traders track exposure in their head most of the time because it is relatively simple math. If you own 200 shares of a stock and it goes up 2 points, you know the value increases by $400. If the stock drops $3, you lose $600. The breakeven is always the shares' purchase price. There is unlimited upside for long stock positions, and the most you can lose is the entire investment. This "simple math" is what goes into creating a risk graph. The graph is the simple juxtaposition of profit/loss (P/L) against the price movement in the underlying stock. For additional context, many charts also include breakeven, maximum loss, and maximum gain.

As shown in Figure 19.1, a risk graph has two axes. The x-axis (horizontal) represents the market price of the underlying stock trading in the market, and the y-axis represents the profit or loss in the investment in dollars.

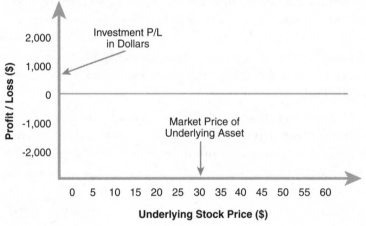

Figure 19.1 Risk graph

Table 19.1 is an example for a long position of 100 shares of Exxon Mobile (XOM). In this case, assume you bought XOM at $83 per share. The pricing table shows the calculations, and Figure 19.2 illustrates the position's profit or loss based on the movement of the underlying stock.

Table 19.1 100 Shares of XOM

Original Price	Shares	Cost
$83	100	$8,300
Price	**Value**	**P/L**
$74	$7,400	($900)
$77	$7,700	($600)
$80	$8,000	($300)
$83	$8,300	$0
$86	$8,600	$300
$89	$8,900	$600
$92	$9,200	$900

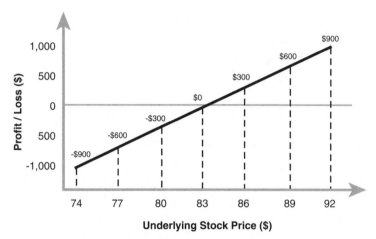

Figure 19.2 100 shares of XOM

It's easy to see that as the stock price goes up, so does the profit/loss, and as the stock price decreases, the profit/loss decreases too. The line simply connects the dots and helps illustrate the position's general bias.

When long 100 shares of stock, the stock has the potential to decline all the way to $0. If the graph were expanded to the left, it would show XOM dropping to $0, and the P/L would be –$8,300. The upside is unlimited, because the x-axis extends to the right; envision the line continuing to climb at the same angle. The break-even point (where the P/L is $0) is where the line crosses the $0 P/L value at the $83 price. Of course, if you bought the stock at $83, the breakeven is at $83. Yes, this is obvious, but it needs to be stated to establish a frame of reference for later.

Risk graphs for short stock look the exact opposite. Table 19.2 is a pricing table and a risk graph for a position of short 150 shares of General Electric (GE) at $20. This time we'll expand to a wider price range, as shown in Figure 19.3.

Table 19.2 150 Shares of GE

Original Price	Shares	Cost
$20	–150	–$3,000
Price	**Value**	**P/L**
$0	$0	$3,000
$10	($1,500)	$1,500
$20	($3,000)	$0
$30	($4,500)	($1,500)
$40	($6,000)	($3,000)
$50	($7,500)	($4,500)
$60	($9,000)	($6,000)

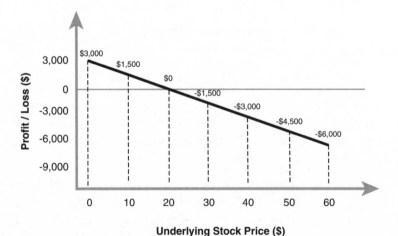

Figure 19.3 150 shares of GE

In a short position, the maximum gain that can be made is when the stock goes to $0. In this case the maximum profit is $3,000, as shown at the $0 mark in Figure 19.3. However, the maximum loss has no limits, and it's easy to see that as GE rises in price, the short position will continue to lose value. At a $60 GE price, the position loses $6,000. The graph again helps illustrate the investment bias. In this case, as the stock goes down, the position makes money.

Absolute Hedge Risk Graphs

Risk graphs are an important tool that you can use as you weigh and consider different choices of what position or hedge to create. The following sections describe risk graphs for some common Option positions.

Long Call

In Figure 19.4, the left side of the P/L line is horizontal. The horizontal portion represents a price range where, no matter the stock price along it, there is no difference in the P/L. Said another way, the change in P/L levels out in this price range, and in the case of the long call, the decline in value subsides. This is what an absolute hedge looks like.

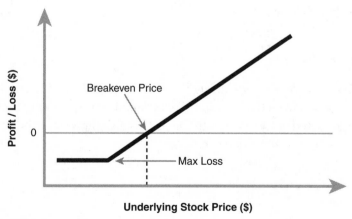

Figure 19.4 Long call

As discussed before, the maximum loss is the premium paid for the call Option. The graph also illustrates that the upside is unlimited as the stock rises. The inflection point, or elbow, in the P/L line is the strike price. This is because once an Option goes OTM, for calls whose level is below the strike, it no longer has intrinsic value.

Long Put

The risk graph shown in Figure 19.5 shows that there is a defined loss no matter how high the stock rises. By now you know that this is the premium paid for the put Option. This also illustrates that as the underlying stock price declines, the P/L increases for the long put and will continue to rise to its maximum value if the stock goes to $0.

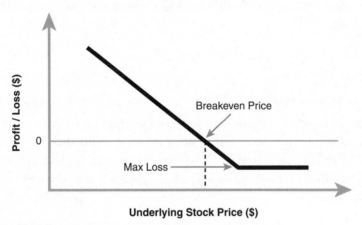

Figure 19.5 Long put

Short Call

The risk graph shown in Figure 19.6 shows that a maximum profit can be gained from this position. This amount is the premium that the calls generated at the time of the sale. This also shows that there is an unlimited loss as the stock rises.

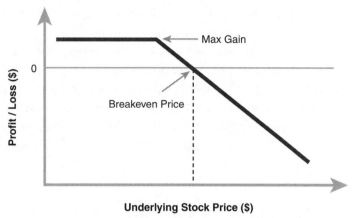

Figure 19.6 Short call

Short Put

Just like the short call, the risk graph shown in Figure 19.7 shows that a defined amount can be gained from this position. You know that this amount is the premium that the puts generate at the time of the sale. However, in the case of the short put, the loss is not unlimited, because the stock's decline stops at $0. The maximum loss is the value of the stock minus the premium generated.

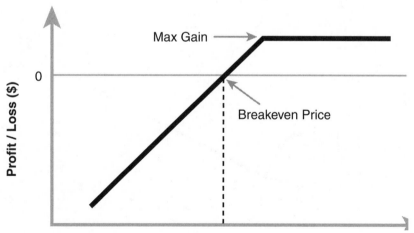

Figure 19.7 Short put

Combining positions is where risk graphs really begin to bring value. Buy and Hedge strategies include simple single-legged positions and some two-legged positions combining two Options or an Option with stock. This book recommends one strategy that includes three positions known as a collar that combines a call, a put, and stock into one investment, and hence onto the risk graph. It is worth noting that some strategies use three or four Options legs, known as butterflies and condors, but they are excluded from this book's discussion.

Partial Hedge Risk Graphs

Risk graphs can also display how partial hedges change the risk graph based on the movement of the underlying stock. Earlier in the book, we discussed the difference between partial and absolute hedges. Risk graphs are a great tool for visualizing the impact that partial hedges have on an overall investment.

Consider the following position, shown in Figure 19.8:

- Long 200 shares XOM @ 83
- Long one XOM 75 put @ $3

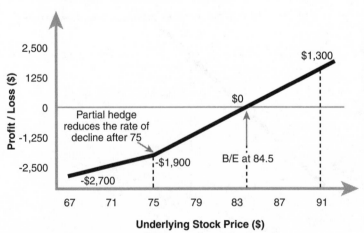

Figure 19.8 200 shares of XOM and one XOM 75 put

In this example, the angle (slope) of P/L decline lessens after the $75 mark but does not completely level out. This is because the long stock has two times the market exposure of the put. So although every point below $75 gives $100 in profit to the put, the stock decreases by twice the amount at $200. Also note that the breakeven in this case is not $86, where a perfect hedge would have it, but $84.50. This is because the gain in the stock needs to be only half as much due to the ratio of put exposure to long stock exposure.

Other Notes

Risk graphs don't take into consideration dividends or corporate actions. If a long holder of stock has received dividends, those must be considered separately when determining the overall investment gain/loss.

All the risk graphs shown here use only the intrinsic value of the Options. Intrinsic value is the mathematical value of the Option when it is ITM, and these P/Ls only reflect that. Essentially, these can be thought of as the risk graphs at expiration where there is no time value. However, when there is time value, these risk graphs look very different. Time adds a third dimension to risk graphing. This can be done in a few different ways. Typically an additional line or two are added to evaluate what the position will be worth at a certain time. We won't go into any detail about that. We just wanted to mention it so that you are aware of that usage of risk graphs.

Chapter Lessons

- Risk graphs chart the profit/loss (P/L) of a position against the value of the underlying stock.
- Risk graphs help illustrate the impact that a stock move has on a position value.

20

Married Puts

Evelyn Crouch: *"Hey! I was waiting for that spot!"*

Girl #1: *"Face it, lady, we're younger and faster!"*

(Evelyn rear-ends the other car six times.)

Girl #1: *"What are you *** doing?"*

Girl #2: *"Are you *** crazy?"*

Evelyn Crouch: *"Face it girls. I'm older and I have more insurance."*

—From *Fried Green Tomatoes* (1991)

Married puts are the closest thing an investor can get to insurance. As Kathy Bates's character, Evelyn, knows, you can take some risks when you have good insurance. Of course we aren't suggesting you ram your car into the stock exchange six times, but the point is when you're insured, you know the consequences of your investment actions in the event things don't go as planned.

Have you ever thought, "Wouldn't it be nice if a portfolio could come along with insurance?" Of course it would. You can purchase health insurance, homeowner's insurance, car insurance, and even travel insurance. So why wouldn't there be portfolio insurance? All investors have been well trained to know that investing in the market comes with risk, but no one seems to talk that much about how to insure against your risk. The good news is that it is fairly easy to do, and there is a very liquid and efficient market for it. This is exactly what put Options were designed to do: provide downside insurance by locking in a selling price over your expected investment horizon.

Buying a put in tandem with a long stock position is known as a *married put*. The benefits of the married put are that the owner has a defined downside with the put and can participate in the upside movement of the long stock. The negative about the married put is that there is an additional cost to the investment that the long stock alone would not have. That cost is the premium paid for the put. The investment of stock married to a put is considered to be bullish because profit is maximized when the stock appreciates, and the put protection expires worthless.

The married put is designed to help the investor define his risk. Because upside isn't capped or restricted, the structure of the investment won't be used to determine the potential reward of a married put. With this kind of hedging strategy, you will continue to use your own research to determine how much the stock will appreciate. The construction of the married put positions places no limits on upside potential.

Position Dynamics

Let's look at an example of a married put investment and its value dynamic with moving stock prices:

- Long 100 GE
- Long one GE 100 JAN12 17 put

One put contract of 100 shares at the 17 strike price protects the 100 shares of GE. This means that no matter what GE does, the owner of these investments will be able to sell the 100 shares of GE at 17 before the put expires, which in this case is January 2012 (JAN12). Essentially this put acts as insurance on the GE position. This is called a married put because the put is linked or "married" to the long stock position.

Table 20.1 shows the prices and values of each position.

The thing to notice here is that the investment is never worth less than $1,700, despite how low the stock goes because the put exactly offsets the decline in the 100 shares.

Table 20.1 Prices and Values of Positions

GE Price	100 Shares Value	1 GE JAN12 17 Put Value	Total Value
$20	$2,000	$0	$2,000
$19	$1,900	$0	$1,900
$18	$1,800	$0	$1,800
$17	$1,700	$0	$1,700
$16	$1,600	$100	$1,700
$15	$1,500	$200	$1,700
$14	$1,400	$300	$1,700

The married put is a great way to meet Buy and Hedge Iron Rule #1: Hedge every investment.

Like all insurance, protection comes at a price, and many days the hedged investor is more than happy to pay for it. That price comes in the form of the premium. When a put is bought, it comes with a price. As discussed in Chapters 15 through 18, that price is determined by a confluence of factors: time until expiration, volatility of the underlying stock, and how far the Option is in the money (the intrinsic value).

Think of that as the cost of the insurance. The put has some value when the position is established. If in the preceding example the put cost $1.00, that cost needs to be factored into the overall investment. Although value is important to know, it is even more important to know your risk and potential reward.

If GE were trading at $17.50 and the JAN12 17 put cost $1, the initial cost to establish is $1,850. This is calculated by adding the cost of the stock, $1,750 (100 shares × $17.50), to the cost of the put, $100 (one contract × 100 multiplier × $1.00).

The profit/loss (P/L) for the shares will be the current value of GE × 100 minus the cost to establish, which is $1,850. Table 20.2 and Figure 20.1 show the P/L for the investment.

Table 20.2 The Investment's P/L

GE Price	100 Shares Value	1 GE JAN12 17 Put Value	Total Value	Original Cost	Total P/L for the Married Put
$20	$2,000	$0	$2,000	$1,850	$150
$19	$1,900	$0	$1,900	$1,850	$50
$18	$1,800	$0	$1,800	$1,850	-$50
$17	$1,700	$0	$1,700	$1,850	-$150
$16	$1,600	$100	$1,700	$1,850	-$150
$15	$1,500	$200	$1,700	$1,850	-$150
$14	$1,400	$300	$1,700	$1,850	-$150

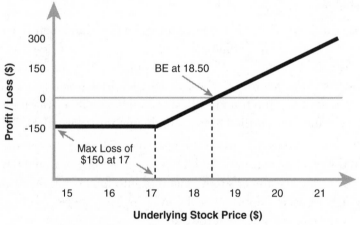

Figure 20.1 Long 100 GE and long 17 GE put

The thing to notice here is that the P/L of this investment will not lose more than $150 after the $17 level is breached. It is fair to say that this investment is effectively hedged.

The cost of the hedge was $100, and the total investment cost $1,850 to establish. This means that the protection cost 5.4% ($100 / $1,850) and the maximum loss is $150 or 8.1% ($150 / $1,850). So what is the downside of this tactic? The hedge has a cost—the $100 paid to buy the put (insurance). If you just bought the long unprotected stock position, you wouldn't have the cost of the hedge. To make a profit, you must now overcome the cost of the hedge.

Table 20.3 compares the married put and the unprotected long stock, and Figure 20.2 graphs the two investments on the same risk graph for a visual comparison.

Table 20.3 Comparison of the Married Put and the Unprotected Long Stock

GE Price	100 Shares Value	100 Shares Unprotected Original Cost	Unprotected Stock P/L	Married Put P/L	Difference
$20	$2,000	$1,750	$250	$150	−$100
$19	$1,900	$1,750	$150	$50	−$100
$18	$1,800	$1,750	$50	−$50	−$100
$17	$1,700	$1,750	−$50	−$150	−$100
$16	$1,600	$1,750	−$150	−$150	$0
$15	$1,500	$1,750	−$250	−$150	$100
$14	$1,400	$1,750	−$350	−$150	$200

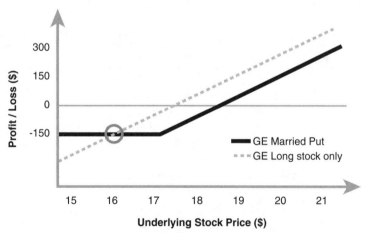

Figure 20.2 Long 100 GE and long 17 GE put versus long 100 GE

The thing to notice here is that the benefit of the insurance becomes evident at the $16 level when the loss of the married put equals the loss in the unprotected stock position. In this case each investment approach loses $150. It is also worth noting that the loss in the unprotected shares continues to decline below this level; meanwhile, the loss in the married put maxes out at $150.

From a holistic perspective, the drop in GE price from $17.50 to $16 can be viewed as an 8.6% decline in the stock. As stated before, the cost of the hedge is 5.4%. So is insuring against an 8.6% drop worth 5.4%? That is up to the individual to decide, but with unlimited upside and defined downside of 8.1%, this investment would attract many investors who are trying to reduce their exposure to volatility.

Risk Metrics: Married Put

As a reminder, the four key risk metrics are capital at risk, volatility, implied leverage, and correlation. Without a doubt, the biggest advantage that a married put gives the investor is the impact it has on the capital risk. Each of the four risk metrics for each of the main hedging tactics are considered and presented in a table in this and the following chapters. See Table 20.4.

Table 20.4 Considerations for the Four Risk Metrics

Risk Metric	Considerations for This Tactic
Capital at risk	CaR is dramatically reduced because this tactic defines with absolute certainty the most that can be lost.
	The CaR is calculated as the total cost paid to purchase the stock minus (the strike price of the married put multiplied by contracts multiplied by 100) plus the premium paid for the married put.
Volatility	Married puts will reduce your portfolio volatility, especially in a downward-moving market.
	In an upward-moving market, your volatility would also be slightly lowered, but not materially.
Implied leverage	The investor should treat a married put position as if it has an implied leverage measure of 1.0, because it includes a long stock or long ETF position.
	The put Option is bought out of the money, so it adds no implied leverage to the position.
	As usual, when entering any new investment, consider the overall impact of the new investment to the overall portfolio implied leverage.

Risk Metric	Considerations for This Tactic
Correlation	Correlation is a calculation that is not impacted by the hedge tactic chosen.
	When you structure your portfolio, you consider the correlation statistics of the underlying stock. That correlation is not directly impacted by your use of an Option tactic.

Choosing the Strike Price for a Married Put

Now that a married put has been defined and its financial impact illustrated, it is time to discuss how to establish the strike price to choose.

You should consider two major metrics when establishing a married put strike price:

- Downside percentage (DP)
- Cost percentage (CP)

Downside percentage is the amount by which you are willing to let the underlying asset decline before the hedge kicks in. Cost percentage is the percentage you are willing to pay for the downside protection.

These two percentages are inseparably linked; as one changes, so does the other. For example, as the downside percentage is reduced, the cost percentage increases. Or as the cost percentage is reduced, the downside percentage increases. It is impossible to separate these factors.

Downside percentage is the measure for controlling downside risk. It is the level at which the investor is willing to let his or her asset decline. Investors usually set this at either a dollar amount or a percentage of an investment. Think of DP as the level at which the insurance starts to kick in. In the GE example, that was $0.50 to the level of $17 because that is where the strike of the put was established. Anything lower than $17 on the GE price means the put starts to gain intrinsic value. Eventually that value will completely offset the loss in the stock dollar for dollar. At that point, the put stems the losses in the overall investment.

Generally, downside risk for index investments should range from 8% to 15%, and for individual stock picks, the range should be from 10% to 20%. This means that you will want to establish downside protection so that you do not lose more than these percentages on an investment. Think of how a car is insured, and consider the downside percentage the deductible. In other words, if you get into an accident and your car is damaged, you will have some out-of-pocket expense. In simple terms, if you have a policy with a $500 deductible, even if you have $2,000 in damages to your car, you still have to pay $500. If there is only $300 in damage to your car, the insurance doesn't provide any benefit. It was protection that didn't pay off because you simply pay $300 out of pocket for the repairs.

When applying this model to a married put, the strike price you choose establishes where your downside is capped. In the GE example, the $17 strike of the put meant that your losses on the GE stock stopped at the $17 level. If the stock dropped any more, the losses were offset by the put.

The downside percentage is calculated by dividing the reduction in stock price by the original purchase price of the underlying asset. DP = (stock cost – strike price) / stock cost. In the GE example, that number is calculated as follows: $0.50 / $17.50 = 2.9%. If a different protection level was chosen, the downside percentage would change based on the change in the strike price.

Cost percentage is how much you are willing to pay for insurance or protection. It stands to reason that the less you are willing to lose, the more costly your insurance is. This is true of all varieties of insurance. Returning to the car example, when you're deciding how low or high of a deductible to establish, cost becomes a factor. If you choose a low deductible, meaning lower out-of-pocket losses in the case of an accident, the price of the insurance goes up. The reverse is also true. If you choose a high deductible, meaning that the purchaser is willing to incur higher out-of-pocket losses, the price of the insurance goes down.

The same principle applies to establishing a married put. The lower the downside percentage, the higher the cost percentage of the put. Returning to the GE example, the cost of the put was $100. That was the cost of establishing the insurance at the $17 level. If the investor had chosen the $16 level, the cost of the put would be lower, because it is further from being in the money. However, that switch to $16 from $17 would increase the downside percentage. The investment with a $17 strike put would stop taking losses after the $17 mark, but now the protection kicks in at the $16 level. That is another dollar per share that is now at risk.

Cost percentage is calculated by taking the cost of the put (insurance) and dividing it by the total cost out of pocket to establish the investment. Cost percentage = put cost / (stock cost + put cost). In the GE example, the cost percentage = $1 / ($1 + $17.50) = 5.4%.

Is this a good level? It all depends on the DP. As a rule of thumb, the CP should be less than the DP. This is because if it costs more to insure than to be uninsured, why bother insuring at all? This hedge, however, does not meet that criterion. In market terms, this means that the volatility of the underlying warrants a higher premium, and more consideration should be given to the hedge level. Lowering the strike price to the $16 or $15 level should remedy this example's imbalance.

Table 20.5 illustrates how the two data points look.

Table 20.5 Two Data Points

The Two Percentages	GE
DP (downside percentage)	2.9%
CP (cost percentage)	5.4%

It is worth noting that the more volatile the asset being protected, the higher the cost of the protection. Let's return to the insurance example. A bad driving record or living in an area where many accidents occur will cause the insurance company to increase the policy's premium. This is done because the risk of a claim is increased. In other words, if a bad driver in a high traffic state wants insurance, he has to pay more.

Let's look at two similarly priced stocks and create a comparative married put investment. Think about owning a volatile stock such as Baidu (BIDU), a Chinese Internet stock, versus a U.S. blue chip tech stock such as IBM (IBM). When this book was being written, the two stocks were trading in a similar range. BIDU was at ~$146, and IBM was at ~$165. The data in this example is from the beginning of May 2011. The option expiration period was April 17, 2011.

BIDU data:

- BIDU last trade $146
- BIDU 100 JAN12 130 put @ ~$13
- DP = ($146 − $130) / $146 = 11%
- CP = $13 / ($13 + $146) = 8%

IBM data:

- IBM last trade $165
- IBM 100 JAN12 150 put @ $7
- DP = ($165 − $150) / $165 = 9%
- CP = $7 / ($7 + $165) = 4%

Table 20.6 organizes the factors to take into consideration.

Table 20.6 IBM and BIDU Data

The Two Percentages	IBM	BIDU
DP (downside)	9%	11%
CP (cost)	4%	8%

You can interpret the risk of these two investments as follows:

- The cost percentage for the BIDU married put is two times as much as the IBM married put.
- The downside percentages are similar, but IBM still prevails, with 2% less at risk.
- It can be assumed that BIDU is much more volatile based on the difference of the CP for similar DPs.

Summing it up, the IBM investment is cheaper to protect and has a lower downside percentage move before the hedge kicks in. So IBM is the better trade, right? Wrong. More accurately, the answer is, not necessarily. This is just one side of the story. Remember that the married put is just a tactic to create a hedge. Ultimately, to make money, you have to be right about your investment bias. The married put is a bullish strategy. As a reminder, for all investments, be sure to compare the risk and reward.

As mentioned at the beginning of the chapter, the reward associated with a married put isn't determined by the Option structure. Only risk is defined with the married put. Selecting between IBM and Baidu is primarily an investment decision that depends on your investment selection process.

Let's say you prefer the IBM investment due to your lower risk tolerance. Is this the right hedge? Are you willing to have a higher CP for a lower DP? Here is one more married put investment for comparison:

IBM data:

- IBM last trade $165
- IBM 100 JAN12 155 put @ $8.50
- DP = ($165 − $155) / $165 = 6%
- CP = $8.50 / ($8.50 + $165) = 5%

Table 20.7 compares the $150 level protection with the new $155 level protection.

Table 20.7 $150 Level Protection Versus $155 Level Protection

The Two Percentages	IBM with a 150 Put	IBM with a 155 Put
DP (downside)	9%	6%
CP (cost)	4%	5%

Here is what jumps out with this comparison. The $155 put provides 3% more protection for only 1% additional cost. Overall the $155 put strike seems to provide the better hedge, but it's up to the individual investor which one to choose.

Because the upside target for both investments is the same because both investments share IBM, it is now easy to compare apples to apples. One item to note is that the level where the trade breaks even is different. This is because the $150 Option costs less ($7) than the $155 Option ($8.50).

Figure 20.3 is a risk graph overlaying both of these married puts.

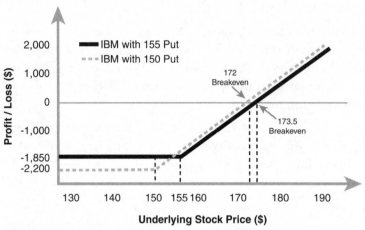

Figure 20.3 Comparing the 150 and 155 IBM married puts

Depending on your risk tolerance for this investment, you need to determine if that $1.50 difference per share makes a great enough impact to sway the decision of which investment to make. It is most likely that the $1.50 difference is negligible enough to not make a difference. It is less than 1% of either investment, but again, this is up to the individual. The Buy and Hedge investor with a long-term outlook is not hamstrung by the minutia of small changes in price levels. It simply isn't plausible to forecast nine months out to within 1%. The goal of these percentages is to give you, the investor, the means to make a metric-driven decision.

Choosing the Expiration Month

P/L charts are an easy way to visualize DP and CP when deciding which strike price to choose. But what about the time to expiration? How is that chosen? Again, we remind you that you are investing with a long-term outlook. This means that you should stay away from near-month expirations unless absolutely necessary. With a married put bought out of the money, all the cost is extrinsic value. This means that time and volatility make up the cost of the put. And if there is one thing you can be absolutely certain of, it is that time moves forward. In other words, time value erodes even if volatility increases. So time works against the long Option holder, and it is most against him or her in the last month before expiration. After all, at expiration, you can be certain that no time value will remain in your long put Option. Conversely, it decays more slowly the further away from expiration it is.

Combining these factors leads you to conclude that the further out you go, the more time decay you avoid. And you don't run afoul of our Iron Rules, either! The rule of thumb we like to use is to go out around six months. It makes the annual percentage easy to calculate (you just double the cost) and meets the long-term outlook rule.

Using long dated put Options has one more advantage, and it comes when you're deciding to harvest gains. Having Options that aren't close to expiration provides a more even swap from one Option to another when rolling up.

Said another way, if an investment has gained 80% of its target three months early, why not sell the put and use a little of the gains to buy one that is closer to the market price? This will move up the hedge, locking in some gains, and also allow the investor to extend the hedge if he wants to. The benefit of the original put being long dated is that it will still have some residual time value when traded in, reducing the cost of extending and rolling up the hedge.

The hedged investor must deal with one restriction in the Options market: it might be hard to find the six-month dated Option. Not every month has Options. Typically there are Options for the current month and the next month, as well as quarterly Options and annual Options (LEAPS). So although that would seem like enough, sometimes you may find yourself having to choose between four or six months out. When that happens, go longer. Going further out has many advantages for the married put strategy.

Remember to track your investments in your trade log. By reviewing your trade log, you can figure out what investments represent your "sweet spot." Knowing how well you perform based on your decision process is important. See our template trade logs at http://www.buyandhedge.com.

Bonus Strategy: Married Calls

The same principles of the married put can be used for a tactic called a married call. The married call is used to create protection for a short stock position with a long call, just like a long put can protect long stock. The married call is a bearish investment bias for the underlying stock. This works because the risk of a short stock position is an unlimited loss when the underlying stock goes up. A long call offsets that short stock because it appreciates at a dollar-for-dollar rate once the call is in-the-money.

The tactic is to buy a call that is above the price of the short stock position. You can still consider the DP and CP calculations. The only difference is that the DP in this case is an upside movement in the stock.

Many investors choose not to short stock because of the risk of unlimited loss and the margin requirements, but when hedged with a call, those risks no longer apply. Capital at risk is still the most important risk metric. It allows you to define your losses associated with the investment.

Believe it or not, two other tactics involve short stock combined with a long call. We mention this because we want you to become familiar with these tactics and not shy away from them if you find yourself in a position you don't understand.

Chapter Lessons

- The married put is a combination of a long stock and put for protection for a bullish outlook.
- The married put is used to define and limit the downside of a stock position.
- The biggest advantage of a married put is that it can significantly reduce the capital at risk—*the* key risk metric.
- Use the two percentages of downside and cost to define which strike to choose.
- Go at least six months out when choosing the expiration period.

21

Collars

"I have strong feelings about gun control. If there's a gun around, I want to be controlling it."

—Tommy Nowak (played by Clint Eastwood) in *Pink Cadillac* (1989)

This quote by Clint Eastwood's character reminds us that what we control is risk, not return. Although being able to forecast outcomes is unpredictable, being able to define potential results is well within the investor's control. Collars are strategies that "collar" a stock by defining the upper and lower price limits through options. As you're learning, Options can provide many different solutions for how investments are structured. In the preceding chapter you learned about a married put and that for a price, you can protect your long stock. Well, believe it or not, you also can sell Options to generate some income as an offset of the premium costs. You do so by writing calls with a strike price above the strike price of the married put. Usually this is done at a level at which you thought about selling the stock for in the first place. Many would consider this a way to bring in some cash by selling the upside you never planed on seeing. This in essence contains or "collars" the stock's total performance. As you may recall, being short a call means you have to deliver the shares if the stock price goes above the call's strike. Knowing this in combination with the right to sell stock at a certain price granted by the married put if it declines will define the range in which an investment will perform.

A collar is the combination of a long stock, a short call, and a married put. Typically the put strike is bought below the current stock price, and the call strike is written above. This means that both positions are out-of-the-money. An investor might prefer this tactic because he can use the revenue generated from writing the call to pay for the put that protects the long stock. Therefore, the investment is considered moderately bullish. The investment's maximum loss is defined by the protective put; meanwhile, the writing of the call pays for the cost of that insurance in part or in whole. The upside of the investment is capped by the call's strike price. If that price is reached, the stock can be called away or by rule force delivered at expiration.

Position Dynamics

Let's look at an example of a collar and its value dynamic as the stock price moves:

- Long 100 GE
- Long one GE 100 JAN12 17 put
- Short one GE 100 JAN12 20 call

You will notice that the first two parts of this investment are the married put from the preceding chapter. This tactic is similar to the married put tactic. Downside protection still exists in case the stock declines below 17. However, in the collar tactic, the short call generated some revenue to help raise the money to pay for the put. That income comes as an exchange for giving up some upside potential. If GE were to appreciate above $20, the profit of the investment would be maxed out. As a reminder, when short a call, the writer is obligated to deliver the stock at that strike price if the call is in-the-money and exercised by the holder. The writer gets paid a premium for taking on this obligation.

That value of "owing" the stock ends up being reflected as a negative for the call position value. For example, if GE is trading at 22, the short call has a value of –$200. This is calculated by subtracting the price of the stock from the strike price times the multiplier. In this case that value looks like ($20 – $22) × 100.

Table 21.1 shows prices and values of the collar positions as the price of GE fluctuates.

Table 21.1 Prices and Values of Positions

GE Price	100 Shares	1 GE JAN12 17 Put	–1 GE JAN12 20 Call	Total
$22	$2,200	$0	–$200	$2,000
$21	$2,100	$0	–$100	$2,000
$20	$2,000	$0	$0	$2,000
$19	$1,900	$0	$0	$1,900
$18	$1,800	$0	$0	$1,800
$17	$1,700	$0	$0	$1,700
$16	$1,600	$100	$0	$1,700

Notice that the total value stops gaining value once the underlying is greater than $20 a share. It is also worth noting that the put continues to protect the investment if the price drops below $17, effectively keeping it hedged.

You might wonder why an investor would cap his upside potential. Although a topside restriction exists, it should be at a level where you feel comfortable selling (exiting) the stock. And for that restriction, you are paid a premium. In the case of a collar, that premium helps pay for the hedge. Selling an upside you never planned to participate in makes sense. In other words, if your goal was to sell GE at $20 anyway, why not get paid some premium?

From the GE example, the upper limit of selling GE at $20 has already been established, so generating some premium for the $20 strike call will help pay for the $17 strike put. In this case, assume that GE is trading at $17.50, the GE JAN12 20 call has a $0.50 premium, and the GE JAN12 17 put is still trading at $1. The initial cost to establish this collar is $1,800. That is $1,750 for the stock (100 shares × $17.50 price) plus $100 for the put ($1 × 100 multiplier) minus $50 credit from the call ($0.50 × 100 multiplier).

Table 21.2 shows the value for each of the positions against the initial cost to establish, and the risk graph shown in Figure 21.1 illustrates the total P/L.

Table 21.2 Total P/L

GE Price	100 Shares	1 GE JAN12 17 Put	–1 GE JAN12 20 Call	Total Value	Original Cost	Total P/L for the Collar
$22	$2,200	$0	–$200	$2,000	$1,800	$200
$21	$2,100	$0	–$100	$2,000	$1,800	$200
$20	$2,000	$0	$0	$2,000	$1,800	$200
$19	$1,900	$0	$0	$1,900	$1,800	$100
$18	$1,800	$0	$0	$1,800	$1,800	$0
$17	$1,700	$0	$0	$1,700	$1,800	–$100
$16	$1,600	$100	$0	$1,700	$1,800	–$100

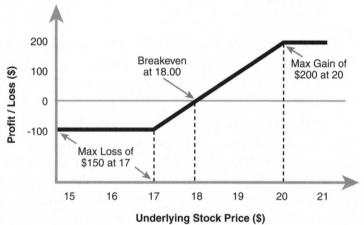

Figure 21.1 GE 17/20 collar

Note that the investment breaks even at the $18 level and will not lose more than $100—nor will it gain more than $200. This is a hedged investment that has a defined upside and a defined downside. This tactic is effective in lowering the volatility of the overall investment—and hence, your overall portfolio. Said another way, regardless of what GE does, you won't lose more than 5.5% ($100 / $1,800) or gain more than 11% ($200 / $1,800). This comes at a cost of $0.50 per share, and the break-even price for GE is $18 even though you bought it for $17.50. By now you know that the capital at risk of this investment is $100, which occurs at $17.

You may notice that the holder of this investment keeps the stock at expiration only as long as GE stays between $17 and $20. If the stock is below the $17 mark at expiration, your broker will autoexercise you and sell the stock at $17 for you. If the stock is above $20, your broker will automatically assign you and deliver your stock at $20. This means that if either of these scenarios happens, you no longer have the stock in your account.

When the call is in-the-money, the writer is forced to deliver the stock. When the put is in-the-money, the owner should exercise and sell the stock at a higher price than market to gain the benefit of the hedge, as shown in Table 21.3.

Table 21.3 Call and Put in- and out-of-the-Money

GE Price	GE 100 JAN12 20 Call	GE 100 JAN12 17 Put
GE > $20	In-the-money	Out-of-the-money
GE between $17 and $20	Out-of-the-money	Out-of-the-money
GE < $17	Out-of-the-money	In-the-money

The way to avoid any conflict is to make sure the strike of the call is higher than the strike of the put. By the way, there is no reason to worry about the out-of-the-money Options in the account. Your brokerage will remove them at expiration.

Mathematically, these numbers are accurate and make it easy to illustrate the dynamics of the collar.

Risk Metrics

Just like with the married put, a collar is effective at managing your capital at risk—our most important risk metric. Table 21.4 shows the key considerations for the four major risk metrics when using collars.

Table 21.4 Considerations for the Four Risk Metrics

Risk Metric	Considerations for This Tactic
Capital at risk	CaR is dramatically reduced because this tactic defines with absolute certainty the most that can be lost.
	The CaR is calculated as the total cost paid to purchase the stock minus (the strike price of the put multiplied by contracts multiplied by 100) plus the premium paid for the put Option minus the premium collected for selling the call Option.
Volatility	Collars are an effective tool for controlling the volatility of an investment.
	A collar is effective for creating a range-bound gain/loss scenario for your investment.
	As long as the investment is range-bound, the investment volatility can be well controlled.
Implied leverage	The investor should treat a collar investment as if it has an implied leverage measure of 1.0, because it includes a long stock or long ETF position.
	The put and call Option is bought out-of-the-money, so neither adds any implied leverage to the position.
	As usual, when entering any new investment, consider the overall impact of the new investment on the overall portfolio implied leverage.
Correlation	Correlation is a calculation that is not impacted by the hedge tactic chosen.
	When you structure your portfolio, you consider the correlation statistics of the underlying stock. That correlation is not directly impacted by your use of an Option tactic.

Choosing Strike Prices for Collars

Now that the collar has been defined as a married put with a short call, it's time to discuss how to establish what strikes to choose.

The two things to consider from the preceding chapter still exist in the collar. But there is one more percentage to consider:

- Upside percentage (UP)

As a refresher, here are the two percentages from the preceding chapter:

- Downside percentage (DP)
- Cost percentage (CP)

Upside percentage is the percentage above the current market price where the call strike is written. Downside percentage is how much the underlying stock will decline before the hedge begins to kick in. Cost percentage is how much you're willing to pay for the downside protection, but this time it includes the premium generated from writing the call.

This may seem like it's getting more complicated, but it really isn't. Throwing in the call premium essentially lowers the cost of the put protection and defines the upside in the process. The percentages are all still related to each other and help you better understand the risk exposure, what the reward will look like, and even the underlying asset's volatility.

Upside percentage is how much you are willing to let the stock price appreciate to before selling. In this case you are willing to let the stock go from $17.50 to $20.00. This is a $2.50 appreciation, and the percentage is 14.3% ($2.50 / $17.50). This provides the other half of the risk/reward equation now defined in the performance of the over-all investment. This is because when you write a call covered by stock, you are obligated to sell the stock at the call price if the other side of the contract exercises. That wish usually happens when the stock is trading above the strike of the call and usually at expiration or around dividend time. In other words, you have no chance of selling the stock higher than the call without going naked on the call. (We never recommend going naked on a call because it is a speculative unhedged position.) This means that you know for sure the highest price you will get for the stock, and that defines the upside level.

The range of how high a stock will go should be determined by your outlook for the stock, and this is based on whatever analysis you use. For stocks that can be a pretty wide range, but as a general rule, it should be at a level high enough to make the premium generated worthwhile. If not, there is little reason to cap the upside if it won't make a difference against the cost of the put. You should consider the call premium to be at least 50% of the cost of the protective put and at a high enough strike price to make the reward of delivering the stock attractive. This isn't a hard-and-fast rule, but it is a technique to make you consider your upside carefully.

The upside percentage is calculated by dividing the difference of the upper strike and the current stock price by the stock price:

UP = (strike – stock price) / stock price

In the GE example, UP = ($20 – $17.5) / $17.5 = $14.3%.

Downside percentage is calculated in the same fashion as the married put:

DP = (stock cost – put strike price) / stock cost

In the GE example, the DP = ($17.50 – $17) / $17.5 = 2.9%.

Cost percentage for a collar needs to take into consideration that the premium offsets some of the cost of the investment as well as the protection. The cost percentage is calculated by taking the cost of the put and subtracting the revenue of the call and dividing it by the overall out-of-pocket cost:

$$CP = (\text{put cost} - \text{call premium}) /$$
$$(\text{stock cost} + \text{put cost} - \text{call premium})$$

In the GE example, the CP = ($100 – $50) / ($1,750 + $100 – $50) = $50 / $1,800 = 2.7%.

Table 21.5 compares the collar to the married put from the preceding chapter.

Table 21.5 Comparing the Collar and the Married Put

The Three Percentages	GE Collar	GE Married Put
UP (upside percentage)	14.3%	Unlimited
DP (downside percentage)	2.9%	2.9%
CP (cost percentage)	2.7%	5.4%

The thing to notice here is that the DP is identical for the collar and the married put, but the CP is much lower for the collar.

As always, you need to be aware of your risk. In the case of the collar, CaR is the most important one to watch. In this case the CaR, or maximum loss, is $100.

Let's look at some real examples of where this applies by revisiting the IBM/BIDU example from the preceding chapter. As a reminder, the example showed how the volatility of BIDU made the cost of the put protection more expensive. That same volatility will actually increase the amount of money generated by writing calls to create the collar. Said another way, the challenge of spending more for protection on volatile stocks becomes a benefit when you write calls to generate income.

Let's compare the data on calls 10% above the stock price. Let's also keep the married put level the same from the preceding chapter, at approximately 10% below the stock.

BIDU data:

- BIDU last trade $146
- BIDU 100 JAN12 160 call @ ~$15.75
- BIDU 100 JAN12 130 put @ ~$13
- UP = (160 – 146) / 146 = 9.6%
- DP = (146 – 130) / 146 = 11%
- CP = (13 – 15.75) / (13 + 146 – 15.75) = –2.75 / 143.25 = –2%
- CaR = 100 × ($16 – $2.75) = $1,325

Note

In the next-to-last example, the CP is indeed negative. This means it actually generates a net positive cost because the money brought in from the call is more than the cost of the protective put.

IBM data:

- IBM last trade $165
- IBM 100 JAN12 180 calls @ ~$5.75
- IBM 100 JAN12 150 put @ $7
- UP = (180 – 165) / 165 = 9.1%
- DP = (165 – 150) / 165 = 9.1%
- CP = (7 – 5.75) / (7 + 165 – 5.75) = 1.25 / 166.25 = 1%
- CaR = 100 × ($15 + $1.25) = $1,625

Table 21.6 compares these two collar investments.

Table 21.6 IBM Versus BIDU Collar Investments

The Three Percentages	IBM Collar	BIDU Collar
UP (upside percentage)	9.1%	9.6%
DP (downside percentage)	9%	11%
CP (cost percentage)	1%	–2%

Here is how to interpret this data:

- The upside percentage for the two investments is nearly the same, with the edge going to BIDU.
- The downside percentages give the advantage to IBM by 2%.
- The cost percentages give the BIDU investment a 3% advantage.
- CaR is lower for BIDU by $300.

Figures 21.2 and 21.3 are P/L graphs for both of these collars.

In the preceding chapter it was difficult to say which was a better trade, IBM or BIDU because the potential upside was never identified. In the collar case, the upside is defined, so the BIDU trade looks much more attractive than it did before. This is because the premium generated from the call was significant enough to offset the price of protection and even generate an extra $2.75 per share of revenue.

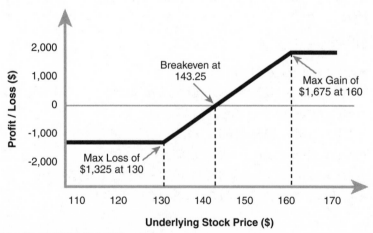

Figure 21.2 BIDU 130/160 collar

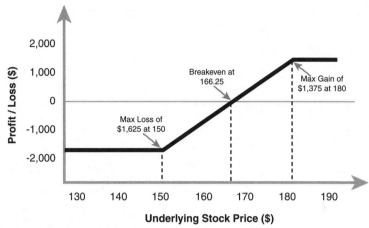

Figure 21.3 IBM 150/180 collar

Choosing between these two trades is up to the investor, but at least this structure helps you understand the risk as well as upside potential.

Selecting the Expiration Month

As with the married put, you want your put protection to be far out in the future—at least six months. That doesn't change for this tactic. However, when you write a call, time is actually on your side. The same forces of time decay that work against you when you go long a protective put work for you when you write a call. The time value of short-term Options erodes faster than the time value for longer-term Options. In this case, time erosion is good when you are short an Option. So why not write a call every month for six months instead of writing one call for six months?

For example, look at the calls discussed in the IBM/BIDU example that were 10% above the current market. The BIDU MAY11 160 call that is one month out is going for ~$3. The JAN12 calls are nine months out, going for $15.75. Writing the one-month-out calls nine times could potentially bring in $27 versus the $15.75 the JAN12 call does alone. Compare this to the IBM one-month calls that generate only 20 cents versus the nine-month call that would bring in $5.75.

In the case of IBM, the stock's lower volatility doesn't warrant much premium. Nine months at 0.20 won't even generate $2, so going with the JAN12 for $5.75 makes more sense.

Table 21.7 compares this data.

Table 21.7 IBM Data Versus BIDU Data

10% Above Market Price	IBM	BIDU
One-month call	$0.20	$3.00
9 times the one-month rate	$1.80	$27.00
Nine-month call	$5.75	$15.75

If IBM is the underlying the investor wants, he will have to choose the nine-month-out expiration period. Alternatively, the investor can look to see if writing the three-month-out call three times makes more sense. In fact, the investor can even try to change the call's strike price to get more premium. The investor should explore any combination of these factors to get the right risk/reward factors based on his outlook.

Deciding to write multiple monthly calls against a longer-term put has still more advantages. One advantage is the opportunity to move up the strike price as time goes by if the underlying stock appreciates. This can move up the upside percentage, allowing the investment to enjoy more of the gains in the stock position. The shorter time horizon gives the writer the advantage of not having to forecast nine months into the future. Although you will always keep your long-term outlook, forecasting one month should inherently be easier than nine months. This gives the investor the chance to adjust if his bias begins to change.

The chance that a stock grows 10% in one month is almost always less than the chance it goes up by 10% in nine months. Then again, it's not a bad thing to have the stock called away if it makes money. If this does happen, and the stock hits the upper limit earlier than expected, you don't need to wait around eight more months, hoping it stays up there. You can take your profits and go find some other investment.

The downside of writing multiple monthly calls is that you collect your premiums in installments by the month. The result is that your CaR will be higher. This is because until enough calls are written to equal the long-term call premium, there is always a risk that the stock will drop, and you will collect less premium. For instance, in the BIDU example, suppose you were to write the MAY11 call for $3 instead of the JAN12 call for $15.75, and the stock drops below the $130 protective put. You would miss out on the benefit of $12.75 in premium that would have eased the sting of the underlying stock dropping. This applies even if the stock doesn't go below the protective put strike, but it goes down only a little. If BIDU is $5 lower after one month and it's time to write calls again, the $160 call won't fetch as much premium as before. You will have to decide whether to lower the call strike or take less premium, or some combination of the two.

One way to mitigate the potential effects of a negative stock move is to write out two or three months instead of one. This approach should still generate enough premiums to make it worthwhile, and it will reduce the risk of having to immediately change the upside percentage the next month. Then, when enough premium is collected to pay for the put or equal the long-term call premium, switch to monthly call writing. This is done because now the risk of negative stock movement won't affect the original data, because the entire long-term premium has been realized. Think of this as being able to get a few free months of call writing without the negatives.

It is important to think about the option to write monthly calls against a long-term married put. You should consider it based on the circumstances of the trade and your investment outlook. And even though you must consider pros and cons either way, it is generally accepted that writing calls multiple times against one long-term put is the preferred method.

Chapter Lessons

- The collar is the combination of long stock, a protective put, and a short call. It is used for a mild bullish outlook.
- The collar uses premium generated from writing the call to help pay for the protective put.
- The collar defines a limited upside and limited downside of a stock position.

- Use the three percentages of upside, downside, and cost to define what strikes to choose.
- The protective put leg should be at least six months out when choosing the expiration period.
- Write calls at expirations of one to three months out when the opportunity presents itself. This can be an improved source of premium over the term of the protective put.

22

Stock Replacement Tactic That's Easy on Your Cash

"My philosophy: a hundred-dollar shine on a three-dollar pair of shoes."

—John Winger (played by Bill Murray) in *Stripes* (1981)

Bill Murray's character in *Stripes* just may have had the right idea. If your shoes look like they cost you $100, do they serve the same function as if they actually cost a $100? Maybe, but the point is do you need to buy outright stock if long calls will give you virtually the same exposure?

One of the most popular uses of Options is buying calls. Calls, as you are now well aware, give the long holder the right to buy shares of an underlying at a given price by a certain time. The owner puts up a premium that affords him this right. This is probably one of the most powerful and widely used strategies involving Options, mainly because it is the strategy investors can most easily relate to. Although this strategy can be used as a hedge or a speculative play on a stock, the one thing all Option investors can agree on, it is best suited as a stock replacement strategy.

In-the-money calls are used to control shares of stock when having a bullish bias. They allow the holder to use leverage to control the desired number of shares by not putting out all the money needed to buy the stock. More important, the ITM call offers a natural, built-in hedge. The strike price represents the floor for losing money on your investment. Of course, the ITM call does include a time premium—effectively, the cost of the hedge.

As described in Chapter 16, "What is an Option?," a call gives the owner the right to buy at a specific price by a specific point in time. The owner/buyer pays the writer a premium for this right of control. The term "control" is used because the owner of the call controls if and when the Option is exercised, which effectively controls the equivalent amount of stock. Calls can be classified as in-the-money (ITM), at-the-money (ATM), or out-of-the-money (OTM). In-the-money calls have a strike price lower than the current stock price. At-the-money calls have a strike price at the market price for the stock. Out-of-the-money calls have a strike price above the market price.

Buy and Hedge recommends the use of ITM calls in this chapter because it is the closest thing to actually owning the stock—and it includes a built-in hedge. In addition, you can control the stock equivalent for significantly less out-of-pocket expense. Last, ITM calls are considered the least speculative when compared to ATM and OTM calls.

Position Dynamics

With an ITM call, the strike price is significantly lower than the current market price. Let's use an ETF that represents the S&P 500 as an example. SPY is the symbol.

At the time this chapter was written, SPY was trading at $130. So purchasing 100 shares of SPY would cost $13,000. However, look at the price of the call Options that are six months out that are in-the-money by 10%. Said another way, you pick a strike price that is 10% below the current market price. That is the SPY SEP11 117 call, and it has a premium of ~$15.50. The 117 call is in-the-money by $13 points (130 to 117), and this is considered to be the intrinsic value. This is the mathematical value that the call is worth if the Option were to expire today, while the stock is trading at $130. The other $2.50 ($15.50 – $13) is called the extrinsic value (or time value) and is driven primarily by time to expiration and volatility.

If an investor wanted to control 100 shares of stock via the SPY SEP11 117 call, it would cost $1,550 ($15.50 premium × 100 multiplier)—essentially, buying one contract. This means that the investor has the choice to buy SPY at 117 before the SEP11 expiration period, regardless of what the market price of the ETF is at the time. The breakeven for this position is when SPY is at $132.50. This is because the time value (extrinsic value) of $2.50 needs to be offset.

Let's look at what happens as the price of SPY moves. Table 22.1 and Figure 22.1 show the potential profit and loss of the position compared to owning the ETF outright.

Table 22.1 Potential Profit and Loss with SPY

SPY Price	100 Shares of SPY Value	P/L for 100 Shares of SPY	One SPY SEP11 117 Call Value	P/L for One SPY SEP11 117 Call
100	$10,000	–$3,000 (-23%)	$0	–$1,550 (–100%)
110	$11,000	–$2,000 (–15%)	$0	–$1,550 (–100%)
117	$11,700	–$1,300 (–10%)	$0	–$1,550 (–100%)
120	$12,000	–$1,000 (–8%)	$300	–$1250 (–81%)
130	$13,000	$0 (0%)	$1,300	–$250 (–16%)
132.5	$13,250	+$250 (2%)	$1,550	$0
140	$14,000	+$1,000 (7%)	$2,300	+$750 (48%)
150	$15,000	+$2,000 (15%)	$3,300	+$1,750 (113%)

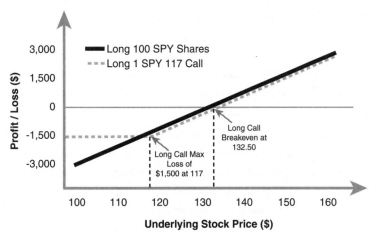

Figure 22.1 Comparing SPY long calls and long shares

The $117 and $132.50 marks are specifically called out to show some important levels that correspond to the call. When SPY is at $117, the call incurs its maximum loss and ceases to lose money. It will be worthless at expiration for any value under $117. This is because it will be cheaper to buy the stock at the market price than pay $117. Meanwhile, if you owned the ETF shares outright, the value of the investment continues to decline as SPY goes down. At the $132.50 level, the call position is at breakeven. This is the price that SPY needs to exceed for the call to become profitable. Hopefully in six months you should be able to get $2.50 growth in an ETF you are bullish on. This may seem obvious, but it needs to be mentioned anyway: the break-even price for owning stock is at the price it was purchased—in this case, $130.

The next thing to point out is that the P/L percentage of the 117 call ranges from –100% to +113%. This seems pretty volatile when compared to the long ETF position P/L, which ranges from –23% to +15%. The data would suggest that the long shares are a better choice here if you are trying to reduce volatility. However, that is not the whole picture. The calls have a higher return volatility because you use less capital to purchase the call. In other words, the call position has leverage built in. The maximum loss of the call is limited to $1,550—compared, for example, to the $3,000 loss observed at the $100 SPY price for the long ETF position. Dollar for dollar, the risk is twice as much if SPY were to drop to $100 per share. Losses for the call position are limited to the amount paid for the premium at the 117 level. The ETF position losses are not limited after 117 and can actually go all the way down to $0 in value. The CaR for the ETF long position is $13,000, and the CaR for the 117 call is only $1,550.

The call is still very efficient on the gain side of the P/L. The call can also participate in the same upside appreciation as the ETF, minus the $250 time value paid. Every dollar that the stock position goes up over $132.50, the call position increases dollar for dollar in intrinsic value. The call controls the same number of shares and as such can participate in the upside as SPY appreciates. Remember also that you had to put up only an initial cost of $1,550 for the call versus the $13,000 for the shares. It can be said that you were much more efficient with your cash, freeing it up to be invested somewhere else or to earn interest.

Another way to view this is that $1,550 can buy only 11 shares of the SPY ETF, but $1,550 spent on the call can control the upside gains of 100 shares. This extra control comes at the small cost of the premium. If SPY were to go up by $20 to $150, the 11 shares you might have bought with the $1,550 would make only $220 (11 shares × $20). However, the call makes $1,750. This illustrates the leverage benefit that is embedded in Options.

The deeper you go in-the-money, the more the call will cost over-all, because of the increase in the intrinsic value, but the cheaper the time value. This lowers the break-even price. This means that the amount the underlying stock or ETF needs to appreciate before you start making money is a smaller percentage. In the SPY example, you needed the stock to get above $132.50. This is $2.50 more than the current $130 price. That is a gain of ~2% ($2.50 / $130) to reach breakeven.

Table 22.2 lists some deep in-the-money calls to illustrate this dynamic.

Table 22.2 Deep ITM Calls

Strike Price	Premium	Intrinsic (from $130)	Time Value	Breakeven	Percentage to Breakeven
100	$31	$30	$1	$131	<1%
105	$26.30	$25	$1.30	$131.30	1%
110	$21.75	$20	$1.75	$131.75	1.3%
115	$17.30	$15	$2.30	$132.30	1.8%
120	$13.20	$10	$3.20	$133.20	2.4%
125	$9.40	$5	$4.40	$134.40	3.6%
130 (ATM)	$6.10	$0	$6.10	$136.10	4.7%

Risk Metrics

Table 22.3 shows the risk metrics for the ITM call tactic.

Table 22.3 Considerations for the Four Risk Metrics

Risk Metric	Considerations for This Tactic
Capital at risk	Calculated as the total premium (cost) paid to purchase the ITM call Option.
	Alternatively, this is always the current value of the ITM call.
Volatility	ITM calls have a natural downside built in and maintain some extrinsic value before expiration.
	Both of these factors reduce the volatility of your investment, and hence the volatility of your portfolio.
Implied leverage	This is the most important risk metric to watch when using ITM calls, because the implied leverage will always be greater than 1.0.
	ITM calls are inherently leveraged. The implied leverage for an ITM call is calculated as the total market value of the equity control implied through the call divided by the call's current total value.
	It is important when using ITM calls to keep your overall portfolio's implied leverage below 1.0. Be careful not to control so much "implied equity" that your overall portfolio controls more stock than you could purchase outright with your portfolio.
Correlation	Correlation is a calculation that is not impacted by the hedge tactic chosen.
	When you structure your portfolio, you consider the correlation statistics of the underlying stock. That correlation is not directly impacted by your use of an Option tactic.

Choosing the Strike Price

Now that we've reviewed the dynamics of how deep ITM calls work, it is time to figure out what strike prices to choose. The power of this strategy is that it locks in the hedge and reduces the number of dollars out of pocket—without giving up much of the upside. In fact, it has a similar risk profile to a married put, but with much less capital commitment.

All the percentages this book has taught you to use for married puts and collars don't apply. Why? Because the maximum loss will always be 100%, and the upside will be unlimited. Here are the numbers that are important to crunch for the deep in-the-money call:

- Capital at risk
- Break-even percentage
- Downside percentage

Capital at risk is one of your key risk metrics. It is the maximum amount the investor can possibly lose in the worst-case price scenario. This is not a percentage in the analysis, but an absolute number.

CaR is calculated by multiplying the call premium by the Option multiplier. Most of the time that is 100. In the SPY example, CaR = call premium × 100, or $15.50 × 100 = $1,550.

The *breakeven percentage* (BEP) is the amount by which the underlying asset needs to appreciate to offset the call's time value. Think of this as how much the stock needs to go up to offset your cost of getting the call leverage.

The BEP is calculated by dividing the time value by the cost of the underlying stock/ETF:

BEP = time value / stock price

In the SPY example, the BEP = $2.50 / $130 = ~2%. This means that after the stock goes up 2%, you can participate in the gains as if you actually owned 100 shares of the stock.

Downside percentage (DP) is how much the stock has to decline until it is below the call's strike price. As you saw in the SPY example, once the ETF got below 117, you took the full loss of the call that was $1,550. This is where you stop losing money and essentially are out of the investment. You accept that you were wrong about the stock's direction, and you take your lumps. Just be happy it's off your chest at a smaller loss than if you were long the stock. Think of the strike price on the ITM call as the price the stock must drop to before your hedge kicks in. This is synonymous with the intrinsic value.

Taking the difference between the strike price and current price and dividing it by the current price calculates the DP:

DP = (stock price − strike price) / stock price

In the SPY example, DP = (130 − 117) / 130 = 10%.

Let's look at the SPY example again, with the data points for multiple strike prices shown in Table 22.4.

Table 22.4 SPY Multiple Strike Prices

Strike Price	CaR	BEP	DP
100	$3,100	<1%	23%
105	$2,630	1%	19%
110	$2,175	1.3%	15%
115	$1,730	1.8%	12%
120	$1,320	2.4%	8%
125	$940	3.6%	4%

You can interpret this data as follows:

- The DP is fairly high for the lower three strike calls. This is a broad-based ETF that typically carries lower volatility; therefore, you should protect it with tighter strikes to the current price.
- The BEP is a little too steep at the $125 level. This means that the ETF will have to go up 3.6% before the investment begins to pay off. Some might consider this a hefty tax to pay for a broad-based ETF of 500 stocks. On a single stock, 3.6% is an acceptable amount of time value to offset, but probably not on this type of ETF.
- The 115 and the 120 both have reasonable BEPs and DPs that are within tolerance for SPY.
- The CaR is only $400 different between the 115 and 120 strike calls.

Based on just these factors, we choose the 115 strike as the better risk mitigation position. This is because the 100, 105, and 110 are too expensive, leaving too much loss potential. The 125 has too high of a BEP. And between the two finalists (the 115 and 120 strikes), for only a $400 difference out of pocket, only a 0.6% difference is needed to break even via appreciation.

As discussed in Chapter 20, "Married Puts," this is only one half of the equation. The reward portion is missing. You should include that when considering your upside potential calculations.

Figure 22.2 is the risk graph for the 115 strike call position.

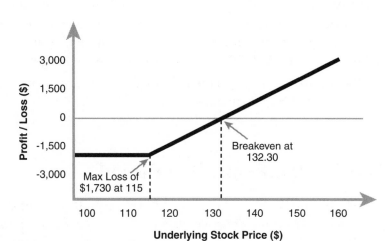

Figure 22.2 Deep ITM 115 SPY call

Does this chart look familiar? It should. It looks exactly like the married put risk graphs. This isn't a coincidence. Both define the downside risk below the current stock price and have unlimited upside potential. Sometimes choosing between these two tactics is a wash, and other times one tactic has an advantage over the other. Both define a hedge level that comes with a certain cost. Ultimately, the Options pricing and your investment bias on the underlying will drive you to select one tactic or the other.

The advantage that the deep ITM call has over the married put is that the deep ITM call requires significantly less money out of pocket to establish very similar upside exposure. Recall that the cost of the married put is the stock price plus the put premium. If you were to establish this married put at the 115 level, it would cost $130 for the stock and $2.40 for the put, totaling $132.40 per share, or $13,240 out of pocket. This compares to the $1,730 that the 115 ITM call costs in total for one contract.

However, sometimes you want to own the stock. Examples may include tax considerations (long-term capital gains rates versus short-term rates), or if you want to participate in dividends that come with SPY. You can't forget about the dividends.

Historically SPY has paid slightly over 2% annually in dividends to its shareholders. But this benefit goes only to shareholders, not call holders. Over the next six months this means that investors should expect 1% in dividends. This would help offset more than half the premium paid for the put. It's like a 50% off sale on the hedge!

These factors are left up to the individual investor's taste, but it's good to have options (pun intended).

Choosing the Expiration Period

The factors used to decide how far out to buy a protective put also apply to deep ITM calls. Time will decay just the same as the puts. And keeping with your long-term investment outlook, you'll want to go out six months again when establishing a new position. One thing to note is that as expiration approaches on the call—say, 30 to 60 calendar days—you may want to consider rolling forward to avoid the time decay.

Rolling forward is the act of closing the current call and buying another one for a future month. This is best to do when some time value is left in the current ITM call Option. Waiting until the Options are going through their rapid decay in time value makes it more expensive to roll forward the investment. Because you bought Options so deep in-the-money, this isn't a huge deal. But saving 1% on a roll can help over time.

In the case of the SPY 115 call Options, the current month has a cost of $15.78, and the next month has a value of $16.18. If the stock hasn't moved very much over this time period, and you want to continue to hold the investment, you should consider rolling to a month that is further out. Rolling before expiration in this case will let you keep an extra $0.40 toward your next call.

Of course, the decision to stay in the investment has to be based on the same analysis that got you into the investment in the first place. Be sure that your investment bias is still valid and that the investment is still desirable when rolling forward. This is clearly a decision to stay bullish despite being wrong so far. Sometimes it is just better to take what's left and come back to a different investment.

Many people ask us why they shouldn't just go with the ATM or OTM calls instead. There are even lower costs to doing this, and if you have a bullish bias, why not trust that analysis?

The minute you start going with OTM calls, you are speculating and no longer hedging. Emotions have probably got the better of you, and you will need a higher appreciation in the stock for it to pay off. From personal observation over the last 12 years, the authors think it is too hard to be a stock picker for that strategy. It's no exaggeration when we say we've seen hundreds of traders pick a stock, be correct with their bullish bias, and not make money from buying calls. When an OTM call is bought, it has no intrinsic value. None. Nada. Bupkis. This means that all of the value is extrinsic and is 100% speculative. As discussed in Chapters 15 through 18, the extrinsic value is influenced by many factors, including time until expiration, volatility, and interest rates. A lot can go wrong for an OTM call owner. These factors also exist for the ITM call owner, but real intrinsic value makes up most of the call's premium, so the price impact of these factors has a smaller effect.

A few strategies go hand-in-hand with the ITM call. One is to decide what to do once the call is profitable. As discussed in Chapter 14, "Harvest Your Gains and Losses," there are a few ways to do that. The call can be sold or rolled forward. Or you can even short the stock to lock in gains. These tactics are discussed in later chapters.

One advanced tactic this book covers later is using spreads. Recall that right after the married put, we introduced the collar tactic as a way to help pay for the hedge. A similar tactic can be applied to the ITM call. Writing another call against your long one creates something known as a spread. This will become one of the most effective hedging tools available to the individual investor interested in hedging.

Chapter Lessons

- Deep in-the-money calls are a means of controlling shares of stock for a discounted out-of-pocket cost and are considered a bullish investment.

- The cost of the deep in-the-money call defines the maximum loss possible and leaves unlimited upside potential.
- Use three calculations when deciding what strikes to use: capital at risk, break-even percentage, and downside percentage.
- Go at least six months when establishing a deep in-the-money call, and consider rolling 30 to 60 days if your analysis warrants staying bullish with your investment.
- The deep in-the-money call is similar in exposure to a married put. The two tactics should be compared on the underlying asset for dividend or tax advantages.
- Avoid at-the-money or out-of-the-money calls; these approaches are considered speculative and not hedges.

23

ETFs Will Look Great in Your Portfolio

"All right, Mr. DeMille. I'm ready for my close-up."

—Norma Desmond's (played by Gloria Swanson) famous
closing line in *Sunset Blvd* (1950)

ETFs have really had their moment in the spotlight in the last
several years. They have grown to become some of the most popular
investment tools for both small and large investors.

Ten years ago, managing a Buy and Hedge portfolio in a retail
brokerage account would have been very difficult. How have things
changed in the last ten years? Let me count the ways. Online tools have
evolved. Market data is more plentiful and easier to access. Options
volume has grown ten times. Bid/ask spreads have narrowed with dec-
imalization. New products such as ETFs have become mainstream
products for both hedging and portfolio asset allocation. Ultimately,
the evolution of the ETF marketplace deserves the most attention.

Ten years ago, how could you get good exposure to broad market indexes, sectors, and subsectors? More than likely you had to use
mutual funds. The ETF industry was in its early stages. Only a handful of ETFs existed—and they existed for only the very largest indexes
(S&P 500, NASDAQ, and so on). The Options volume on these ETFs
was somewhere between minimal and nonexistent. Although many
futures and index Options existed, they suffered from poor penetra-
tion, low volume, and little public awareness. Getting index exposure
meant buying a mutual fund, with its high management fees and end-
of-day pricing.

Today, all these hurdles have been overcome to varying degrees.
But the hurdle that has meant the most to the individual investor has

been the evolution of the ETF industry. ETF stands for exchange traded fund. For the first time ever, the total assets under management (AUM) for all ETFs surpassed $1 trillion in the first quarter of 2011. The ETF has been one of the fastest-growing products in the history of financial services.

But what exactly is an ETF? An ETF is a security that tracks an index, a commodity, or a basket of assets like an index mutual fund, but trades like a stock on an exchange. An ETF is legally organized just like an index mutual fund. But instead of getting priced only at market close like a mutual fund, the ETF trades with a changing bid/ask price throughout the day, when the markets are open.

The ability to purchase an ETF on an exchange like a stock is an obvious benefit. Being exchange-traded creates some nice additional benefits over mutual funds:

- Online brokers charge significantly less for commissions on ETFs than on mutual funds.
- Investors can short ETFs or purchase them on margin.
- ETFs have no minimum share requirements for purchase.

Here's the most important exchange-traded benefit:

- Many ETFs, being exchange-traded, have Options that the investor can buy and sell on the underlying ETF.

By now, you understand the importance of Options to the Buy and Hedge strategy. Options are the most effective way to manage and hedge the underlying securities you want to place in your portfolio. ETFs that have Options offer that flexibility. No mutual funds have Options that trade on the mutual fund.

Although Options on ETFs was a key breakthrough for the Buy and Hedge investor, the evolution of ETFs has helped define the strategy endorsed in this book. ETFs have several other important benefits for the Buy and Hedge investor:

- ETFs offer broad diversification, which helps the Buy and Hedge investor manage risk in his portfolio. The indexes available in ETFs range from the broadest indexes all the way down to the narrowest subsectors. However, even these subsector ETFs are still often diversified in a basket of many stocks and assets. These investments are excellent choices for filling out the asset allocation strategies outlined in Chapter 12, "Constructing a Long-Term, Diversified Portfolio."

• ETFs are low cost. Cost is always a factor in generating positive long-term returns. Since ETFs are based on indexes, they are considered "passive" investments. Passively managed funds such as ETFs are really managed mostly by a computer, not by a well-paid stock picker wearing a $3,000 custom-made suit and sitting in an office on Wall Street. As a result, the funds offer a lower cost structure that is passed on to the investor.

• ETFs, in general, tend to be more tax-efficient than mutual funds. Mutual funds, when they have significant redemptions, are sometimes forced to sell investments in the fund to meet redemption requests—and create a taxable event for all mutual fund holders. ETFs do not have that problem. Being exchange-traded, they always have a buyer and a seller.

• ETFs have expanded to cover so much of the investment universe that the Buy and Hedge investor can really create portfolios custom-built to manage risk. The ETF industry has expanded well beyond the large, well-known indexes such as the Russell, Dow Jones, S&P, and NASDAQ. ETFs now exist for every subsector of asset class. And many sub-subsectors exist as well. In addition, many alternative ETFs actually enhance or modify exposure to indexes and commodities, such as leveraged and inverse funds. New ETFs are being introduced every month, producing even more ways for the investor to create custom exposure to a specific investment hypothesis.

The alternatives now available to the retail investor in the ETF space are impressive. The space is growing very quickly. The Buy and Hedge strategy recommends that you use ETFs to fill out both the stock asset class and bond asset class in your asset allocation approach. We stepped you through this in Chapter 12.

ETFs can also be very effective for unleashing your inner guru (remember Chapter 13, "Unleash Your Inner Guru"?). To the extent that you choose to make individual and unique investment decisions in your portfolio, Buy and Hedge recommends considering sector and subsector ETFs for those decisions. If you feel strongly about a stock, ask yourself if you feel this way because the sector or subsector will increase. It is less risky to invest in a sector/subsector versus an individual stock. Individual stocks carry individual company risk that ETFs reduce by spreading the investments around many stocks.

Finding the Right ETFs for Your Portfolio

But how do you find these ETFs? It's easier than you think. The Internet has leveled the playing field for individual investors and offers an amazing amount of research and information about ETFs. First, sites such as Morningstar.com, SmartMoney, and CBS Market-Watch all offer free ETF screeners to help you find the ETFs that meet your investment criteria. The investor can even sign up for premium subscriptions to get more advanced screeners. The authors use the tools offered in these premium subscriptions (such as advanced ETF screeners).

Second, the online brokers have all launched free ETF information websites. Most will include a screener as well as offer investment profile information on ETFs. Not to mention, the sites are available to noncustomers. Why do online brokers offer these tools and content for free to noncustomers? At this point, ETFs represent between 10% and 20% of all trades at the online brokerage companies. This percentage was less than 5% just ten years ago. These brokers have an incentive to promote these products given the growth these investment products represent in their business.

Third, ETF issuers provide tools and information about their own family of funds on their sites. The tools and content usually are specific to their own family of funds, but many times the tools offer objective comparisons to other ETFs. The most tools can be found on the iShares and SPDR sites. Every ETF issuer also provides a prospectus about each fund it offers on its website. Sometimes, it really pays to research these funds on these sites. In fact, we recommend that you always read the prospectus for any ETF you purchase. However, we especially recommend that you read the prospectus for any ETF that is either a niche sector, subsector, or niche index or that has a total AUM of less than $100 million.

The Largest, Most Popular ETFs and ETF Issuers

The five largest ETF issuers in the world account for 91% of all the AUM in ETFs issued in the U.S. These issuers, from largest to smallest, are iShares, State Street Global Advisors (which issues SPDR funds), Vanguard, PowerShares, and ProShares. We have met someone in management from every one of these fund families. These are well-run companies, and they offer ETFs worthy of your consideration.

ProShares is the only provider on this list that offers leveraged and inverse ETFs. If you choose to use its leveraged funds, be sure to read the prospectus to understand the fund design. The leveraged funds are designed for short-term traders. Keep that in mind.

Figure 23.1 shows the 25 largest ETFs, along with their total AUM. These funds have significant liquidity, and many of them offer Options on the ETF.

ETF Symbol	ETF Name	Morningstar Category	$AUM (Millions)
SPY	SPDR S&P 500	Large Blend	93,574
GLD	SPDR Gold Shares	Commodities Precious Metals	58,876
VWO	Vanguard MSCI Emerging Markets ETF	Diversified Emerging Mkts	46,808
EFA	iShares MSCI EAFE Index	Foreign Large Blend	39,647
EEM	iShares MSCI Emerging Markets Index	Diversified Emerging Mkts	38,376
IVV	iShares S&P 500 Index	Large Blend	26,872
QQQ	PowerShares QQQ	Large Growth	22,569
TIP	iShares Barclays TIPS Bond	Inflation-Protected Bond	20,369
VTI	Vanguard Totlal Stock Market ETF	Large Blend	19,151
IWM	iShares Russell 2000 Index	Small Blend	15,834
LQD	iShares iBoxx $ Invest Grade Corp Bond	Long-Term Bond	13,634
IWF	iShares Russell 1000 Growth Index	Large Growth	13,274
EWZ	iShares MSCI Brazil Index	Latin America Stock	12,371
IWD	iShares Russell 1000 Growth Index	Large Value	11,591
AGG	iShares Barclays Aggregate Bond	Intermediate-Term Bond	11,524
IJH	iShares S&P MidCap 400 Index	Mid-Cap Blend	11,120
SLV	iShares Silver Trust	Commodities Precious Metals	11,081
MDY	SPDR S&P MidCap 400	Mid-Cap Blend	10,491
BND	Vanguard Total Bond Market ETF	Intermediate-Term Bond	10,079
DIA	SPDR Dow Jones Industrial Average	Large Value	9,449
VNQ	Vanguard REIT Index ETF	Real Estate	9,093
XLE	Energy Select Sector SPDR	Equity Energy	8,694
HYG	iShares iBoxx $ High Yield Corporate	High Yield Bond	8,686
CSJ	iShares Barclays 1-3 Year Credit Bond	Short-Term Bond	8,189
SHY	iShares Barclays 1-3 Year Treasury Bond	Short Government	8,035

Figure 23.1 The 25 largest ETFs by AUM as of june 2011

Using Sector ETFs in Your Hedging Tactics

You should notice in the list of the 25 largest ETFs that they are mostly very broad index ETFs. The broadest market ETFs house the most assets. Index strategies rely on these ETFs, just like the asset allocation strategies in this book rely on the largest index ETFs to provide your portfolio with diversification.

Notice that the list of the 25 largest ETFs has only a handful of sector ETFs and no subsector ETFs. (Although it contains a few commodity ETFs.) But sector and subsector ETFs are very common among the midsized ETFs offered by the top fund families. In particular, iShares and State Street SPDRs offer many sector ETFs that also offer Options that trade on the ETF.

Sector ETFs can be very effective tools for hedging—particularly when the ETF offers Options. You might find a stock that you like and want to add to your portfolio as one of your inner guru investments. But the stock might not offer any Options to help you create a protective position. Or the stock might offer Options positions, but the prices for the Options might be very high or have very wide bid/ask spreads. These Options on the stock might be priced very high because the stock has a very high implied volatility. Building a hedge for that stock could get very expensive. And you know the first Iron Rule of Buy and Hedge: hedge every investment. What are you to do? You have to hedge, but the hedge is expensive!

One alternative to building a more cost-effective hedge might be to use the Options on a sector ETF. Identify the sector that your stock is part of, and find the sector ETF that has Options that trade on it. You can purchase out-of-the-money put Options to create a "pseudo hedge" to your position. Essentially you are using the same technique as creating a married put, just with a put that is not perfectly correlated. The put Options on a sector ETF are very likely to be less expensive than the put Options on the individual stock in that sector. Remember that the ETF is diversified within that sector and therefore should be significantly less volatile than any stock in that sector. That reduced volatility should always drive a lower cost for the Option.

You learned in earlier chapters that the best hedges are the ones that offer direct Options on the investment that you want to hedge. That rule is still key to follow in the Buy and Hedge strategy. But sometimes you can consider changing the nature of your risk and hedge by using a sector ETF that has Options. Let's look at how the risk profile changes in one example when you hedge with a sector Option.

Let's say that you are interested in the company Apple (AAPL). This company is the darling of Wall Street, but historically it carries high volatility. You learned in earlier chapters that the cost of hedging is directly driven, in large part, by the volatility of the underlying stock/ETF. So, building a hedge for AAPL can be expensive.

The implied volatility for AAPL based on current Option pricing for October 2011 is 31%. The implied volatility of a technology sector ETF that has Options (symbol XLK) for September 2011 is 22% (XLK did not have an October Option available yet). This data implies that the same downside protection as a percentage will be cheaper for XLK than it will be for AAPL. Of course, with the diversification in that ETF, the risks are lower, so the volatility is lower also.

Let's say you want a hedge with downside protection of 10% in AAPL between now and the fall of 2011. Today, it is May 2011. Instead of buying the put for AAPL and a married put tactic, you can consider buying the OTM put for XLK (a technology sector ETF) at roughly 10% downside from the current XLK price. When you build this protection using XLK, it is important to remember to adjust the number of put Options you buy for XLK according to the relative price of AAPL. At the time this book was written, AAPL was trading at $340, and XLK was trading at roughly $26. Divide the AAPL price by the XLK price, and you get a ratio of 13:1. So, for every 100 AAPL shares you own, you need to buy 13 put contracts on XLK. (Remember that one Option contract covers 100 shares.)

Now that you have your put protection in XLK, the tech sector ETF, and you own AAPL stock outright, what can you expect from this investment and hedge? The risk profile has changed. Direct movements in AAPL stock will be felt in your portfolio dollar for dollar. There is no direct hedge on AAPL. However, AAPL is a tech stock, and it influences the broader tech community. So, any movement in AAPL is likely to be felt in XLK, but there are no guarantees. AAPL could outperform XLK, or it could underperform XLK. Or the stock and the ETF could perform similarly. Those are the three outcomes: AAPL outperforms XLK, AAPL underperforms XLK, or AAPL and XLK perform similarly.

Ultimately, you want AAPL to appreciate in price per share. If AAPL outperforms XLK, but both decline in price, you won't be happy. However, if the XLK put ends up in-the-money, you will be glad you used the sector ETF. Not only was it less expensive, but it would have produced more ITM value than the AAPL put. Of course, the inverse is true also. If both AAPL and XLK decline in value, but AAPL underperforms XLK, you won't be happy—twice over! Your put in XLK likely won't be worth as much as the AAPL put would have been worth—and the AAPL stock lost money. However, at least you still paid less for the put protection.

In the scenario where AAPL went up in value, you are somewhat indifferent to whether it outperformed or underperformed the tech sector. The put is worthless, and AAPL appreciated in value. Life is good—and luckily the put protection you bought cost you less. Ultimately, when using a sector ETF to build a hedge for an individual stock, the investor needs to remember that the hedge won't be perfect. The protection of the hedge (the put) is linked not to the stock but to a broad, diversified set of stocks in that sector (the ETF). As a result, the investor magnifies the impact of a problem to that specific company. In other words, the individual company risk is still present in your portfolio, and it is not hedged. You must be comfortable with that risk profile to use sector ETF Options instead of the direct Options on your underlying stock. Keep that in mind!

ETFs with Options

We don't want to beat a dead horse, but the growth of the ETF universe combined with the expansion of the Options market is really the reason that a retail investor can build an effective hedged portfolio today. Ten years ago, this would have been a very difficult or even impossible undertaking for the retail investor.

Table 23.1 shows the top 100 ETFs by AUM and indicates which have Options available on them. We looked at the Options market for each of these ETFs and examined whether the market had sufficient volume to warrant safe consideration. Remember that this is the list as of July 2011; it will have changed by the time you read this book. Be sure you look at the Options market for the Options on any ETFs you might be considering. It is important that the open interest be meaningful and identify bid/ask spreads that are not too wide.

Table 23.1 Top 100 ETFs by AUM Along with Classification of Options Availability

	Ticker	Fund Name	Category	Net Assets	Options Available?	Sustained Open Interest?
1	VTI	Vanguard Total Stock Market ETF	Large Blend	167.88B	Y	N
2	VOO	Vanguard S&P 500 ETF	Large Blend	108.03B	Y	N
3	SPY	SPDR S&P 500	Large Blend	92.09B	Y	Y
4	BND	Vanguard Total Bond Market ETF	Intermediate-Term Bond	90.55B	Y	N
5	VWO	Vanguard MSCI Emerging Markets ETF	Diversified Emerging Mkts	64.55B	Y	Y
6	VXUS	Vanguard Total Intl Stock Idx ETF	Foreign Large Blend	60.80B	N	N
7	GLD	SPDR Gold Shares	Commodities Precious Metals	58.46B	Y	Y
8	EFA	iShares MSCI EAFE Index	Foreign Large Blend	39.40B	Y	Y
9	EEM	iShares MSCI Emerging Markets Index	Diversified Emerging Mkts	38.41B	Y	Y
10	VO	Vanguard Mid-Cap ETF	Mid-Cap Blend	29.40B	N	N
11	IVV	iShares S&P 500 Index	Large Blend	27.61B	Y	Y
12	VB	Vanguard Small Cap ETF	Small Blend	26.12B	N	N
13	QQQ	PowerShares QQQ	Large Growth	22.84B	Y	Y
14	BSV	Vanguard Short-Term Bond ETF	Short-Term Bond	22.05B	N	N
15	VUG	Vanguard Growth ETF	Large Growth	21.03B	Y	N
16	TIP	iShares Barclays TIPS Bond	Inflation-Protected Bond	20.59B	Y	N
17	VNQ	Vanguard REIT Index ETF	Real Estate	20.27B	Y	N

	Ticker	Fund Name	Category	Net Assets	Options Available?	Sustained Open Interest?
18	VXF	Vanguard Extended Market Index ETF	Mid-Cap Blend	20.10B	N	N
19	IWM	iShares Russell 2000 Index	Small Blend	16.22B	Y	Y
20	VTV	Vanguard Value ETF	Large Value	15.62B	Y	N
21	VEU	Vanguard FTSE All-World ex-US ETF	Foreign Large Blend	14.04B	Y	N
22	LQD	iShares iBoxx $ Invest Grade Corp Bond	Long-Term Bond	13.70B	Y	Y
23	IWF	iShares Russell 1000 Growth Index	Large Growth	13.54B	Y	N
24	EWZ	iShares MSCI Brazil Index	Latin America Stock	12.69B	Y	Y
25	SLV	iShares Silver Trust	Commodities Precious Metals	12.35B	Y	Y
26	BIV	Vanguard Intermediate-Term Bond ETF	Intermediate-Term Bond	12.05B	Y	N
27	AGG	iShares Barclays Aggregate Bond	Intermediate-Term Bond	11.85B	Y	N
28	IWD	iShares Russell 1000 Value Index	Large Value	11.64B	Y	N
29	IJH	iShares S&P MidCap 400 Index	Mid-Cap Blend	11.48B	Y	Y
30	MDY	SPDR S&P MidCap 400	Mid-Cap Blend	11.09B	Y	Y
31	DIA	SPDR Dow Jones Industrial Average	Large Value	9.64B	Y	Y
32	VBK	Vanguard Small Cap Growth ETF	Small Growth	9.20B	Y	N
33	XLE	Energy Select Sector SPDR	Equity Energy	9.01B	Y	Y
34	VEA	Vanguard MSCI EAFE ETF	Foreign Large Blend	8.94B	Y	N
35	VGK	Vanguard MSCI European ETF	Europe Stock	8.61B	Y	N

	Ticker	Fund Name	Category	Net Assets	Options Available?	Sustained Open Interest?
36	SHY	iShares Barclays 1-3 Year Treasury Bond	Short Government	8.46B	Y	Y
37	HYG	iShares iBoxx $ High Yield Corporate Bd	High Yield Bond	8.33B	Y	Y
38	CSJ	iShares Barclays 1-3 Year Credit Bond	Short-Term Bond	8.29B	Y	N
39	VIG	Vanguard Dividend Appreciation ETF	Large Blend	8.28B	Y	N
40	PFF	iShares S&P U.S. Preferred Stock Index	Miscellaneous Sector	8.00B	Y	Y
41	XLK	Technology Select Sector SPDR	Technology	7.50B	Y	Y
42	XLF	Financial Select Sector SPDR	Financial	7.31B	Y	Y
43	VBR	Vanguard Small Cap Value ETF	Small Value	7.30B	Y	N
44	IJR	iShares S&P SmallCap 600 Index	Small Blend	7.28B	Y	Y
45	EWJ	iShares MSCI Japan Index	Japan Stock	7.18B	Y	Y
46	IWR	iShares Russell Midcap Index	Mid-Cap Blend	7.08B	Y	N
47	FXI	iShares FTSE China 25 Index Fund	China Region	7.03B	Y	Y
48	IAU	iShares Gold Trust	Commodities Precious Metals	6.98B	Y	Y
49	IWB	iShares Russell 1000 Index	Large Blend	6.92B	Y	N
50	JNK	SPDR Barclays Capital High Yield Bond	High Yield Bond	6.86B	Y	Y
51	GDX	Market Vectors Gold Miners ETF	Equity Precious Metals	6.84B	Y	Y
52	IVW	iShares S&P 500 Growth Index	Large Growth	6.51B	Y	N
53	DVY	iShares Dow Jones Select Dividend Index	Large Value	6.43B	Y	Y

	Ticker	Fund Name	Category	Net Assets	Options Available?	Sustained Open Interest?
54	TBT	ProShares UltraShort 20+ Year Treasury	Trading-Inverse Debt	6.25B	Y	Y
55	DBC	PowerShares DB Commodity Index Tracking	Commodities Broad Basket	6.03B	Y	Y
56	SDY	SPDR S&P Dividend	Large Value	5.98B	Y	N
57	EWC	iShares MSCI Canada Index	Foreign Large Value	5.71B	Y	Y
58	MOO	Market Vectors Agribusiness ETF	Natural Resources	5.54B	Y	Y
59	VV	Vanguard Large Cap ETF	Large Blend	5.25B	Y	N
60	EWY	iShares MSCI South Korea Index	Pacific/Asia ex-Japan Stk	4.92B	Y	Y
61	XLU	Utilities Select Sector SPDR	Utilities	4.70B	Y	Y
62	IWN	iShares Russell 2000 Value Index	Small Value	4.50B	Y	Y
63	IVE	iShares S&P 500 Value Index	Large Value	4.47B	Y	N
64	VPL	Vanguard MSCI Pacific ETF	Diversifed Pacific/Asia	4.34B	N	N
65	SHV	iShares Barclays Short Treasury Bond	Short Government	4.33B	N	N
66	XLV	Health Care Select Sector SPDR	Health	4.24B	Y	Y
67	IWO	iShares Russell 2000 Growth Index	Small Growth	4.17B	Y	Y
68	BLV	Vanguard Long-Term Bond Index ETF	Long-Term Bond	4.12B	N	N
69	XLP	Consumer Staples Select Sector SPDR	Consumer Staples	4.07B	Y	Y
70	XLI	Industrial Select Sector SPDR	Industrials	4.01B	Y	Y
71	EPP	iShares MSCI Pacific ex-Japan	Pacific/Asia ex-Japan Stk	3.97B	Y	N

	Ticker	Fund Name	Category	Net Assets	Options Available?	Sustained Open Interest?
72	EWG	iShares MSCI Germany Index	Europe Stock	3.80B	Y	Y
73	IYR	iShares Dow Jones US Real Estate	Real Estate	3.72B	Y	Y
74	EWT	iShares MSCI Taiwan Index	China Region	3.45B	Y	Y
75	CIU	iShares Barclays Intermediate Credit Bd	Intermediate-Term Bond	3.45B	N	N
76	IEF	iShares Barclays 7-10 Year Treasury	Long Government	3.43B	Y	Y
77	IWP	iShares Russell Midcap Growth Index	Mid-Cap Growth	3.42B	Y	N
78	IWV	iShares Russell 3000 Index	Large Blend	3.38B	Y	N
79	IJK	iShares S&P MidCap 400 Growth Index	Mid-Cap Growth	3.27B	Y	N
80	RSP	Rydex S&P Equal Weight	Large Blend	3.26B	Y	N
81	EWA	iShares MSCI Australia Index	Pacific/Asia ex-Japan Stk	3.24B	Y	Y
82	DJP	iPath DJ-UBS Commodity Index TR ETN	Commodities Broad Basket	3.21B	Y	N
83	IWS	iShares Russell Midcap Value Index	Mid-Cap Value	3.15B	Y	N
84	DBA	PowerShares DB Agriculture	Commodities Agriculture	3.10B	Y	Y
85	RSX	Market Vectors Russia ETF	Europe Stock	3.10B	Y	Y
86	OEF	iShares S&P 100 Index	Large Blend	2.94B	Y	N
87	EMB	iShares JPMorgan USD Emerg Markets Bond	Emerging Markets Bond	2.93B	N	N
88	OIH	Oil Services HOLDRs	Equity Energy	2.92B	Y	Y

	Ticker	Fund Name	Category	Net Assets	Options Available?	Sustained Open Interest?
89	TLT	iShares Barclays 20+ Year Treas Bond	Long Government	2.88B	Y	Y
90	MBB	iShares Barclays MBS Bond	Intermediate-Term Bond	2.83B	Y	Y
91	XLY	Consumer Discret Select Sector SPDR	Consumer Discretionary	2.75B	Y	Y
92	XLB	Materials Select Sector SPDR	Natural Resources	2.67B	Y	Y
93	AMJ	JPMorgan Alerian MLP Index ETN	Equity Energy	2.67B	Y	N
94	ICF	iShares Cohen & Steers Realty Majors	Real Estate	2.65B	Y	N
95	VOT	Vanguard Mid-Cap Growth ETF	Mid-Cap Growth	2.44B	N	N
96	ILF	iShares S&P Latin America 40 Index	Latin America Stock	2.31B	Y	N
97	IJJ	iShares S&P MidCap 400 Value Index	Mid-Cap Value	2.29B	Y	N
98	RWX	SPDR Dow Jones Intl Real Estate	Global Real Estate	2.28B	N	N
99	VDE	Vanguard Energy ETF	Equity Energy	2.21B	Y	N
100	IGE	iShares S&P North Amer Natural Resources	Natural Resources	2.19B	Y	N

Index Options as an Alternative

Index Options are interesting investments that have been around for quite some time. They have really surged in growth and use in the last ten years in parallel with Options growth. An index Option is just what it sounds like: an Option that you can buy and sell that is based on an underlying index. These products are just like Options for stocks/ETFs. They include calls and puts; they are ITM, OTM, and ATM; and they have time premiums as well as intrinsic value. The big difference is that they derive their value from an index, not an underlying security. As a result, the Options are traded as European-style Options. European-style Options can be exercised only on the date they expire. And European-style Options expire at the open on the Friday prior to the third Saturday of the month. This means that the European-style Option stops trading on the Thursday before that Friday. The index Option is settled based on the opening-day price the next day—the opening on the Friday morning.

Index Options, when they expire, basically settle for their value in cash. Remember that there is no underlying stock to be assigned. The Index Option derives its value from an Index only. If it is in-the-money at expiration, it has intrinsic value only, and it is settled for that amount. If you bought the Option, on expiration you effectively sell it back for whatever it is worth. If you are short the Option, on expiration you buy it back for whatever it is worth. In either case, your profit or loss is the difference between the price you paid to buy it and the price you paid to sell it.

Chapter 28 explains the tax advantages of index Options in detail. Index Options are treated as Section 1256 contracts, so all gains and losses are taxed pro rata: 60% of the gain is taxed at your long-term capital gain rate, and 40% is taxed at your short-term capital gain rate.

Figure 23.2 shows some of the most popular Index Options available. It is not a complete list, but it can give you a start. To verify the special tax treatment on any of the index options shown in the figure, consult your tax advisor or broker.

Index	Exchange Symbol	Exchange	Classification
CBOE Exchange Index	EXQ	CBOE	Narrow
Dow Jones Industrial Average (1/100th)	DJX	CBOE	Broad
Dow Jones Industrial Average Jumbo (1/10th)	DXL	CBOE	Broad
ISE 250 Index	IXZ	ISE	Broad
ISE Bio-Pharmaceuticals Index	RND	ISE	Broad
ISE Electronic Trading Index	DMA	ISE	Broad
ISE Green Energy Index	POW	ISE	Broad
ISE Homebuilders Index	RUF	ISE	Narrow
ISE Homeland Security Index	HSX	ISE	Narrow
ISE Integrated Oil and Gas Index	PMP	ISE	Narrow
ISE Long Gold Index	HVY	ISE	Broad
ISE Nanotechnology Index	TNY	ISE	Broad
ISE Oil and Gas Services Index	OOG	ISE	Broad
ISE-Revere Natural Gas Index	FUM	ISE	Broad
ISE-Revere Wal-Mart Supplier Index	WMX	ISE	Broad
ISE Semiconductors Index	BYT	ISE	Narrow
ISE SINdex Index	SIN	ISE	Broad
ISE U.S. Regional Banks Index	JLO	ISE	Narrow
ISE Water Index	HHO	ISE	Broad
KBW Bank Index	BKX	ISE	Broad
Morgan Stanley Cyclical Index	CYC	NYSE Amex	Broad
Morgan Stanley Retail Index	MVR	CBOE	Broad
Morgan Stanley Technology Index	MSH	NYSE Amex	Broad
Nasdaq-100 Index	NDX	CBOE	Broad
Nasdaq-100 Mini Index (1/10th)	MNX	CBOE	Broad
NYSE Arca Airline Index	XAL	NYSE Amex	Narrow
NYSE Arca Biotechnology	BTK	NYSE Amex	Broad
NYSE Arca Mini- Biotechnology Index (1/20th)	BJE	NYSE Amex	Broad
NYSE Arca Natural Gas Index	XNG	NYSE Amex	Broad
NYSE Arca Oil Index	XOI	NYSE Amex	Broad
NYSE Arca Mini-Oil Index (1/20th)	BZJ	NYSE Amex	Broad
PHLX Gold and Silver Sector	XAU	PHLX	Narrow
PHLX Housing Sector	HGX	PHLX	Broad
PHLX Oil Service Sector	OSX	PHLX	Broad
PHLX Semiconductor Sector	SOX	PHLX	Broad
PHLX Utility Sector	UTY	PHLX	Broad
Russell 1000 Index	RUI	CBOE	Broad
Russell 2000 Index	RUT	CBOE	Broad
S&P 100 Index	OEX	CBOE	Broad
S&P 500 Index	SPX	CBOE	Broad
S&P 500 Mini Index (1/10th)	XSP	CBOE	Broad
S&P MidCap 400 Index	MID	NYSE Amex	Broad
S&P SmallCap 600 Index	SML	CBOE	Broad

Figure 23.2 List of index options

Chapter Lessons

- ETFs are a key product for creating diversification and meeting your asset class allocation needs.
- Sometimes, ETFs should be considered for individual exposure to sectors that the investor wants to overweight in his portfolio (unleash his inner guru).
- ETFs with Options are the most effective tools because the Options provide natural hedging alternatives.
- Sometimes, the investor can use an Option on a sector ETF to create a "pseudo hedge" to offset the risk of a stock within that same sector. But this approach does not enjoy the perfect correlation of Options on the same stock.
- Index Options can be very effective tools for creating index exposure—especially given their special tax treatment.

24

Portfolio Puts

"I am not going to sit on my ass as the events that affect me unfold to determine the course of my life. I'm going to take a stand. I'm going to defend it. Right or wrong, I'm going to defend it."

—Cameron Frye (played by Alan Ruck) in *Ferris Bueller's Day Off* (1986)

Cameron Fyre would be a great investor. He certainly understood the risk / reward relationship being friends with Ferris Bueller. Defending against the events that can affect you is the whole reason behind hedging. As you'll read in this chapter, portfolio level puts provide a broad-based level of protection for a portfolio.

The hedging tactics discussed so far (married puts, collars, and deep ITM calls) are all great ways to define risk and limit volatility in a portfolio. Of course, all these approaches have some drawbacks. The first drawback is that multiple investments mean that multiple hedges need to be managed. Although that may not be a challenge for many, it can get tedious and time-consuming. And let's not forget all the commissions paid to the broker for executing all those trades.

The other drawback is that you may be restricted to investing only in stocks that have Options traded on them. Usually this isn't a problem because almost every large- or mid-cap stock with any kind of volume has Options on it. But assets such as mutual funds don't have direct Options available; as a result, you're left without a direct hedge. Not to worry; the solution isn't that complicated. You can create a hedge for your whole portfolio. We recommend that you use broad market ETFs or indexes to create the hedge for the entire basket of investments in your portfolio.

This ties directly to the corollary to Rule #1 in Chapter 10, "Hedge Every Investment," which states: An alternative to hedging every investment is building a portfolio hedge.

This is similar to the approach covered in the preceding chapter that recommended using sector ETFs to hedge a stock in the same sector. The difference in this case is that you need to find an ETF(s) or index(es) that correlates well with your overall stock portfolio.

This chapter outlines a simple way to reuse what you've already learned to create a portfolio-level hedge. It is meant to hedge the collective group of investments that are unhedged. We call it a portfolio put.

Portfolio Put Defined

The portfolio put is when an investor buys an index or sector ETF put to create downside protection in the event of a broad market correction. In other words, it appreciates in dollar value when the market declines—hopefully offsetting your portfolio loss dollar for dollar (or close to it). This kind of hedge can cover an entire portfolio value or just parts that aren't already hedged. The hedge is simply long puts on an index that aren't married to a specific position but that are designed to kick in and hedge as soon as the broader market has declined enough. Think of this tactic as an umbrella insurance policy.

For example, let's say you have an unhedged portfolio valued at $250,000 made up of large-cap stocks. If you don't want to lose more than 10% ($25,000) at any given time, you can buy puts on the S&P 500 Index Option (symbol: SPX) to provide that protection. Because you've determined that you don't want to lose more than 10%, you look at puts with a strike price roughly 10% lower than the current market price of the index. The authors always like to consider the SPX first because it has a diverse representation of the top 500 companies in the U.S. and includes exposure to many sectors such as financials, energy, industrials, technology, consumer staples, retail, and defense. This index will probably be less volatile than the mix of stocks you chose to buy, but it should still provide adequate downside protection for a falling market.

Two immediate questions come up: How many contracts do you need, and what strike do you choose to hedge this $250,000 portfolio? At the time this book was written, the SPX was priced at approximately $1,300. As with most Options, the SPX has a multiplier of 100, which means that one contract controls 100 times the strike price of market value. If you were to buy a $1,300 strike put, you would control $130,000 worth of market value. This is the same way Options are used for stocks, but the SPX is an index Option. Index Options are cash-settled vehicles, which means there isn't any stock to trade, just the mathematical value of the Options. In other words, it's impossible to take delivery of shares of SPX, but the Option is settled with cash based on its intrinsic value at expiration. This basically means that the step of owning stock is skipped, and the monetary value just changes hands when Options are in-the-money. This was described in the preceding chapter.

Just like the married put tactic, it is cost-prohibitive to buy ATM puts for this kind of protection. But how do you determine the strike price? You've already decided that you don't want to lose more than 10%, or $25,000, so moving down 10% from the current market price of the SPX means you should consider a $1,175 strike put. The $1,175 strike will provide coverage on $117,500 worth of market value (100 times the strike price). Considering that you need to cover $225,000 ($250,000 − $25,000), you should buy two puts to create adequate coverage of $235,000.

The lesson here is that instead of thinking in terms of shares, you need to think in terms of portfolio dollars. This is not a hard concept, but skipping it can make the calculations confusing.

As always, the put comes with a premium price tag. The $1,175 strike put with an expiration six months out costs $25. Apply the 100 multiplier on two contracts, and it will cost $5,000 (2 × 100 × 25).

It's important to note that the perfect portfolio hedge is elusive. You should be more than happy to settle for coverage that gets you 90% of the way there. It just never works out that the vehicle chosen to create the hedge correlates exactly to the portfolio. For example, one of your investments may take a beating after a bad earnings report while the rest of the market stays strong. In that case, the SPX put wouldn't provide much protection. You'll need to rely on your diversification to provide some risk protection in that circumstance. Alternatively, you can create specific hedges on an investment-by-investment basis, as this book recommends.

The risk that is not hedged away when you create a portfolio hedge is the single stock risk. Sometimes this is also called the single company risk. However, if you look at a time when all stocks were in decline, such as October through December 2008, the SPX would have been a good hedge.

A version of the cost percentage (CP) that was taught in earlier chapters can be instructive when used with this tactic. That's unsurprising because the methods are so similar. But because you already own the assets in the account, you are simply adding a put to create the hedge. The equations change only slightly. CP for the portfolio put is determined by the put cost divided by the sum of the put cost and the dollars you are hedging. For the example, the equation would be CP = $5,000 / ($5,000 + $225,000) = 2.2%.

This tactic can seem almost too simple. Can buying two puts cover a quarter-of-a-million-dollar portfolio? But it *is* that simple. At just over 2% every six months, you can build downside protection so that you don't lose more than 10% in your portfolio. This simple tactic alone could have prevented billions if not trillions of dollars in losses to individual portfolios during the most recent financial crisis.

As with all long Option strategies, going out six months is preferred to avoid the accelerated time decay in the near months. By now, you're a pro at this concept.

What if part of your portfolio is already hedged via a married put or collar, or you used a deep ITM call? You won't have to cover these hedged investments with the portfolio put. You actually want to avoid overhedging because it inadvertently turns a bullish set of investments into a bearish bias in a hurry. In this situation, you simply figure out what capital is at risk without a hedge to protect it.

Let's look back at the $250,000 example from earlier in this chapter. Say you have a position in our old favorite, BIDU, of 400 shares. With the current price around $145, this means that your investment is $58,000. This is a volatile tech stock that deserves its own hedge to avoid single stock risk. This leaves the portfolio with $192,500 in broad-based investments. You want to continue to protect against a 10% decline, which is $19,250, so you look at the $1,175 strike put again to cover market risk of $173,250 ($192,500 − $19,250). One $1,175 put covers you for $117,500 (not enough), and two puts cover you for $234,000 (too much). This seems a little like Goldilocks and her porridge dilemma. You can't chose 1.5 contracts. If you consider lowering the strike, you have too much downside exposure. What to do? Pick a different index or ETF with Options, of course. Yes, that was a trick question.

You can decide to use the S&P 500 ETF (SPY) or go with the OEX, which is the S&P 100 index. The SPY trades about one-tenth of the SPX index, and the OEX trades about one-half of the SPX at $590. Although it is a little less liquid than the SPY, at times you may prefer the OEX. You won't need as many contracts, and you can save on the commission costs, not to mention the favorable tax treatment. Watch your trade prices with the OEX because the bit / ask spread is wider than the SPY Option prices.

If you decide to go with the SPY as the hedging vehicle, the numbers look similar. You still need to hedge $173,250 of your portfolio. 10% below the $130 SPY price is the strike you want to choose, and that is $117. With the 100 multiplier, each $117 contract covers you for $11,700 worth of SPY decline. $173,250 / $11,700 = about 15 contracts. The price of each contract is $2.50, so the total out of pocket is $3,750 (15 × $2.50 × 100).

If you wanted to use the OEX, the same process applies. With the OEX at $590, a 10% decline brings the strike level to $530. Therefore, each contract covers $53,000 worth of market value. This brings the number of contracts to three ($173,250 / $53,000). Currently the $530 strikes six months out are going for $13 each, meaning your hedge will cost $3,900 (3 × $13 × 100).

Here are the steps of executing the portfolio put tactic:

1. Determine the dollar amount of the portfolio that is unhedged.
2. Determine the percentage you are willing to leave as capital at risk. The authors recommend a range between 8% and 10% for a diversified portfolio.

3. Determine the right hedging vehicle, whether an index or an ETF that accurately reflects the portfolio investments.

4. The CaR percentage determines the strike price of the protective puts. Each put covers a dollar value of the strike price times the multiplier.

5. Go at least six months out when choosing the expiration period.

6. The number of contracts is determined by dividing the amount to hedge by the coverage of each put.

7. Determine the cost of the hedge by dividing the dollar cost of the put by the sum of the put cost plus the amount you are hedging. If this percentage is too high, consider lowering the strike price of the put or choosing an index or ETF with a lower volatility. This cost should range from 5% to 8% annually.

As a closing note on this tactic, feel free to choose an index or ETF that more accurately reflects the diversification of your specific portfolio holdings. If tech is predominantly held in your portfolio, consider the NDX index (NASDAQ 100) or the QQQ's ETF (NASDAQ 100). Also consider the tax implications of the hedged index. Index Options receive advantageous tax treatment because they are considered Section 1256 contracts.

Chapter Lessons

- A portfolio hedge can be used to provide umbrella protection to an overall portfolio as a replacement for position-by-position individual hedges.
- A portfolio put is bought to cover a specific dollar amount by purchasing an index put that controls a market value equal to the amount to be protected.
- The portfolio put has seven steps to execute the tactic.

Part V
Advanced Tactics

Congratulations. You've made it through the basics of the Buy and Hedge methodology. You've learned about the Immutable Laws, the Iron Rules, the basics of Options, how to incorporate ETFs, and the basic hedge tactics that give you the tools to hedge effectively. We know this is a lot to digest. And Part V offers even more information for the advanced learner. So before going any further, be sure you understand the material in Parts I through IV. They are the foundation for the next set of advanced tactics.

In this part, you will learn about vertical spreads and diagonal spreads as two more tactics that take the concepts of single-legged options to the next level. You will also learn some valuable lessons about managing all that cash you have sitting around. The book finishes with a chapter on how to manage your tax liabilities while you hedge.

25

Vertical Spreads

Harry Burns: *"There are two kinds of women: high mainte-nance and low maintenance."*

Sally Albright: *"Which one am I?"*

Harry Burns: *"You're the worst kind. You're high mainte-nance, but you think you're low maintenance."*

—From *When Harry Met Sally* (1989)

There are many iterations for spreads, and investors need to be careful to ensure they are using the right combination of options to meet their risk parameters. As Harry (played by Billy Crystal) said to Sally (played by Meg Ryan) in the preceding quote, its easy to make the mistake that you're one thing when in fact you are something else. In spreads, you'll need to be sure of the bias you've established and exposure you've created but don't let the warnings scare you away. Spreads are by far our favorite means of hedging.

Now that you're familiar with some of the Option basics, it's time to discuss how combining multiple Options can create hedged invest-ment exposure. Spreads are the combination of multiple Options (always at least two legs, but sometimes more) to create specific bull-ish or bearish exposure to a stock, ETF, or index. As the name sug-gests, there is some sort of "distance" between the Options. This is known as the *spread*, and it can be on the strike prices, month of expiration, or both.

Spreads that have the same month but different strike prices are known as vertical spreads or verticals. Spreads that have the same strike price but different monthly expirations are known as calendar spreads or calendars. Spreads that have different strikes and different expirations are known as diagonal spreads or diagonals. Spreads with different numbers of contracts in each leg are known as ratio spreads.

Spreads, just like single-legged Options, create a net debit or credit. Also like single-legged Options, the exposure created can be bullish or bearish. A debit spread costs money, and a credit spread pays you money. Spreads can be done with puts or calls or, in some cases, both. They can be ITM or OTM or straddle the current market price. It quickly becomes clear that combining two Options that have multiple variables creates more combinations than we care to recommend. For our purposes, this book mainly discusses the different aspects of verticals, with some information on diagonals thrown in.

Vertical spreads are two-legged Option positions that have the same expiration month and number of contracts but different strike prices. One Option is sold, and the other is bought. Debit spreads result when the two trades create a net cost to the investor. This is similar to buying a single-legged Option: it creates a debit on the account to make the trade. The opposite is true for credit spreads: they create a net credit in the account, just like selling an Option, which adds cash to an account.

You can create any investment bias using spreads, just like you could with the other tactics taught earlier in this book. A debit spread has the same bias as being long that Option type. In other words, a debit call spread is like being long a call, so the investment is considered bullish. A debit put spread is like being long a put, so it is considered a bearish investment. This is the same for credit spreads. A credit call spread has a similar bias to a short call. Verticals are often referenced as either their cash impact or their bias, but these mean the same thing.

A bull call spread is the same as a debit call spread.

A bear call spread is the same as a credit call spread.

A bull put spread is the same as a credit put spread.

A bear put spread is the same as a debit put spread.

Traders may use these terms interchangeably, so it helps to learn the naming methodology and how each one is derived.

Although the strikes of the spread can vary, the relationship of the long and short will remain the same. The long or the short will always be at a higher price than the other to create the debit or credit. You can't have a credit spread that creates a debit, and vice versa.

A debit call spread always includes of a long call at a lower strike than the short call.

A credit call spread is created with a short call at a lower strike than the long call.

A debit put spread always consists of a long put at a higher strike than the short put.

A credit put spread is created with a short put at a higher strike than the long put.

If these dynamics ever seem out of alignment when you place a trade, check your math, your investment bias, and the strike prices you selected, because something weird is going on. If Option prices really do create the wrong kind of cash impact, stay away, because this should not be the case. Executing this trade can be perilous, and it's usually done by people who are much more sophisticated than you ever need to be.

Why would anyone go through all this effort to create multiple leg positions when the bias is the same as simply creating a single-legged position? The answer is that it either makes the trade more affordable or lowers the risk. In all four of the vertical examples, the spread creates a natural hedge and defines the investment's risk.

Debit spreads are often used to help pay or subsidize the cost of the original desired long Option exposure. Credit spreads are often used to limit the investment downside by creating a floor to the potential loss on the short side.

Let's look at a bull call spread example using Goldman Sachs Group (GS) as the underlying stock. When this book was written, GS was trading at $150 per share. As you learned in Chapter 22, "Stock Replacement Tactic That's Easy on Your Cash," you can gain the upside exposure on GS by owning a call that is in-the-money without putting up $150 per share. In addition, that same ITM call limits your downside and establishes a maximum loss for your investment equal to the purchase cost of the Options.

Following the rules for deep ITM calls, you establish a long position of 1 GS JAN12 135 call at $21. Here is how the percentages work out:

- Capital at risk (CaR) is $2,100.
- Break-even percentage (BEP) is 4.0%.
- Downside percentage (DP) is 10%.

This investment allows you to participate in all the upside potential as soon as GS has risen 4% to get past the break-even level of $156. As a review, the breakeven is calculated as the time value of the

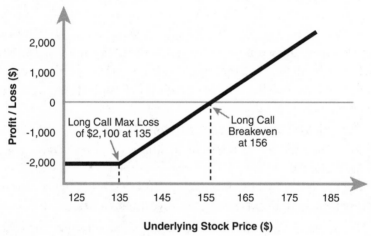

Figure 25.1 GS 135 long call

premium divided by the price of the stock. In this case the intrinsic value is $15 ($150 − $135), and the total value is $21. Therefore, you calculate the time value to be $6. $6 plus $150 = $156, the break-even price. Figure 25.1 is a risk graph of this GS 135 long call.

Let's say you now couple a short call Option with the long ITM Option. You sell 1 GS JAN12 160 call @ $7. You have now created a $25 spread. You are long the 135 call and short the 160 call. Here is what a risk graph looks like for this spread. By selling this call, you have sold your upside in GS above $160 per share. Figure 25.2 is the risk graph for this GS 135/160 bull call spread.

The first thing to note is that the downside loss has been lowered by $700 to $1,400 and remains capped at the $135 level. No additional risk has been taken by writing this additional call. Actually, you've lowered the risk. How is this possible, considering that a short call has unlimited loss potential? The answer is found in the second observation about the risk graph for spreads: the two call positions work in tandem to adjust the risk of the total investment. By forfeiting the

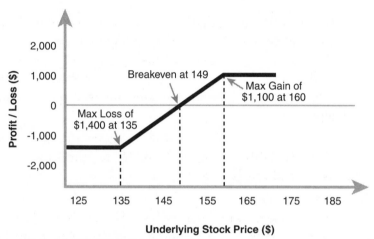

Figure 25.2 GS 135/160 bull call spread

unlimited gain potential of the long call, you have offset the unlimited loss of the short leg. They net out, and that is why there are no more gains after the $160 level is reached. If the stock runs to $300, the gains are the same as if it goes to only $160. The short call now offsets the long call.

Everything has a price in the market. In this case, lowering the maximum loss and out-of-pocket expense comes at the cost of giving up unlimited gains. You can usually live with that, because most investments won't experience unlimited gains. The maximum gain is $11 per share. Gains occur when GS trades between $149 and $160. Another way to look at this is that the maximum gain is the difference between the spread strikes and the out-of-pocket cost. In this case, it's $25 – $14. Either approach is a legitimate way to calculate the reward potential.

The third point that is key for spreads is that because you've lowered the maximum loss, you've also lowered the break-even point. The long call by itself had $6 in time value. When you sell the OTM 160 call, you've just offset that cost by selling $7 of time value. Your net is –$1, and your breakeven is now $1 below the current market price of $150. Said another way, if GS ends up right where it is now at $150, come expiration in JAN12, the investment will be profitable by $1.

Fourth, it is worth noting that you have not changed the number of shares you control: 100 shares corresponding to the one contract. The spread includes a right to buy from the long call and an obligation to sell from the short call. Of course, this all depends on where the stock is trading at the time before you know if any of these circumstances happen.

If GS is trading below the lower strike of $135, both Options are OTM, and the spread becomes worthless. No assignments or exercises take place, and you incur the maximum loss.

If GS is trading between the strikes of 135 and 160, the long call is ITM and has value, and the short call is OTM and is worthless. At expiration, both Options will be removed from the account, and 100 shares of GS at a cost of $135 a share will be added to your portfolio. The investor usually closes out the spread ahead of expiration to avoid the broker's autoexercise. Many investors/traders don't want to pony up the $13,500 needed to buy the shares. However, if you are auto-exercised, you'll have the ability to sell the shares in the open market the next trading day. The exception to this is indexes. With index Options, the exercise is a cash transaction, and upfront cash isn't necessary; just the net profit or loss is posted.

If GS is trading above $160, both Options are ITM and have value. The long call is profitable, and the short call has a loss. For every dollar above $160, each call appreciates dollar for dollar. But these two moving dynamics net each other out, because they are equally opposite dollar-for-dollar changes in value on an equal number of shares. At the time of expiration the Options are removed. One hundred shares are posted into the account at $135 per share from the long call and then are immediately delivered out of the account due to the short call at $160. A gain of $25 per share occurs that came at a cost of $14 when the spread was established. This is a net profit of $11.

Like all Options, vertical spreads provide the benefit of leverage. You may recall that when you buy a call, all the money necessary to establish the position is debited from the account's buying power. This is just like buying stock. The cash in your account is reduced, and the long Option value increases. With vertical spreads, the maximum potential loss is also withheld against the cash position. This means that buying power is reduced by the potential maximum loss of the spread trade. Every broker treats this slightly differently, but investors should expect the maintenance withholding of the trade to be reflected when the investment is established.

In the GS example, the maximum loss is $14 for the $25 spread. This means that $1,400 comes out of the account's Option buying power. If the maximum gain of the investment is $11, the maximum gain percentage is $11 / $14, or 78%. The maximum loss remains at $14, or 100%.

As previously stated, spreads are our personal favorite. As strange as it might sound, they are the most fun to create as an investment. So many dynamics are associated with a spread trade that it's difficult to outline a specific recipe that covers them all. The rest of the chapter details the rationale for using each Spread type and the details of trading them.

Bull Call Spreads

As you just learned, a bull call spread occurs when a long call is purchased and another call is sold at a higher strike price that has a net debit cost. The bull call spread, as the name suggests, is used for a bullish or bullish/neutral bias.

When both Options are ITM, the bull call spread has two Options that have strikes below the current market price. This strategy can be considered bullish/neutral. As with all bull call spreads, the maximum gain occurs when the underlying stock price is higher than the upper strike price of the short leg. In this case, that upper strike price is already below where the market is right now. So if the market stays where it is, goes up, or even declines slightly, the ITM bull call spread will be profitable. Losses occur when the market price of the underlying drops below the break-even point and the maximum loss is realized if declines continue below the lower strike price. Usually this kind of investment has a higher probability of success, but some upside potential is returned in exchange for that higher probability. As with all things on Wall Street, there are always trade-offs.

For example, if General Dynamics (GD) is trading at $75, a bull call spread example might look like this:

- One long GD JAN12 65 call @ $11.75
- One short GD JAN12 70 call @ $8.15
- Net debit/maximum loss of $3.60
- Maximum gain of $1.40

The risk graph shown in Figure 25.3 has the added notation for the current market price of GD to illustrate how both strikes are ITM. The breakeven for this 65/70 bull call spread is $68.60. This is calculated by adding the maximum loss to the lower strike price—$65 + $3.60. Anything above that level is profitable. You can also see that as long as GD stays above $70 a share, this trade will yield the maximum

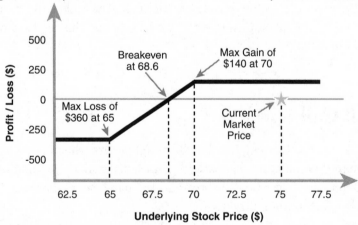

Figure 25.3 GD 65/70 bull call spread

gain of $1.40 or 39% ($1.40 / $3.60). This is worth repeating: if the stock goes up, stays flat, or even drops by $5 (~6.7%), the investment will realize its maximum gain of 39%. This is why this strategy is classified as bullish/neutral. The investment benefits when the underlying stock rises or doesn't change. Plus, there is a cushion even if the underlying drops a little.

A bullish bias can be applied with a bull call spread when the long Option is ITM and the short Option is OTM. Typically the breakeven on these kinds of strategies is right around the current market value. In this situation, the long spread investment doesn't reach its maximum potential until the upper strike is reached. This means that the holder of this spread wants the stock to go up—hence the bullish bias.

Here's an example using GD again, but with a ten-point spread, while it's trading at $75:

- One long GD JAN12 70 call @ $8.15
- One short GD JAN12 80 call @ $3.05
- Net debit/maximum loss of $5.10
- Maximum gain of $4.90

From the risk graph shown in Figure 25.4, you can see that the maximum loss of $5.10 per share happens if the stock drops below

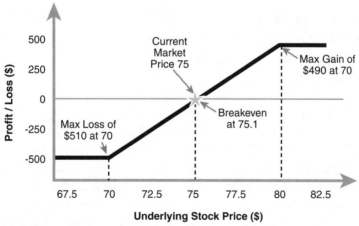

Figure 25.4 GD 70/80 bull call spread

$70. The good thing is this is a defined risk, so no matter how badly the stock drops, you're capped out at the original investment of $5.10. The breakeven is at $75.10. Again, that is calculated by adding the maximum loss to the price of the lower strike ($70 + $5.10). The maximum gain of $4.90 or 96% ($4.90 / $5.10) occurs if the stock goes up to $80 or higher.

This strategy is used to create a bullish exposure—similar to owning the stock. But with a spread, you reduce the investment volatility compared to owning the stock. In this case the gains and losses are both capped if the stock moves only $5 in either direction. The wider the strikes, the wider the range becomes.

Bull call spreads in which both Options are OTM are classified as a bullish strategy, but this is a speculative investment. Remember that bull call spreads have a maximum loss when the underlying trades below the strike price of the long leg. In the case of the OTM bull call spread, that is how the investment begins—totally OTM. However, that risk is offset slightly by a lower maximum loss and a higher gain percentage. Investments made with a speculative bias should have a higher reward due to the greater risk. The authors don't recognize this as a sound investment strategy because too often these investments end up being worthless, and the maximum loss is realized.

Let's look at one more example of an OTM bull call spread on GD still trading at $75:

- One long GD JAN12 80 call @ $3.05
- One short GD JAN12 85 call @ $1.80
- Net debit/maximum loss of $1.25
- Maximum gain of $3.75

The risk graph shown in Figure 25.5 shows that anything below the $80 level will result in the maximum loss of $1.25, and breakeven is at $81.25. The maximum gain of $3.75 occurs when the stock is over $85 a share with a percentage of 300% ($3.75 / $1.25). The high payoff would seem to be incentive enough for making the investment, but notice the $10 point move that the stock would have to make to realize it. This example shows just how speculative an OTM bull call spread can be.

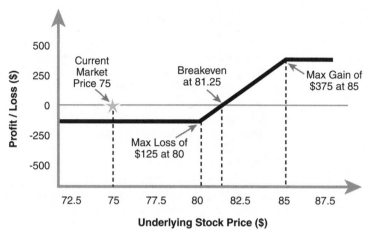

Figure 25.5 GD 80/85 bull call spread 1.25

Risk Metrics

This is a good time to review the risk metrics of spreads. Iron Rule #2 of Buy and Hedge is to know your risk metrics. These metrics should all be considered when using spreads, as shown in Table 25.1.

Table 25.1 Considerations for the Four Risk Metrics

Risk Metric	Considerations for This Tactic
Capital at risk	For a net debit spread, the CaR is the total net debit collected in dollars when the investment is initiated.
	For a net credit spread, the CaR is calculated as the difference between the strike prices of the two legs times the contract multiplier (100 times the number of contracts) minus the net credit collected in total dollars for initiating the position.
Volatility	Spreads are an effective tool for controlling the volatility of an investment.
	The volatility is similar to the volatility of a collar, because the potential gain/loss is range-bound.
	As long as the investment is range-bound, the investment volatility can be well controlled.
	If you use spreads to drive the leverage of your portfolio past 1.0x, spreads begin to lose their effectiveness for controlling volatility. This is especially true when the underlying asset trades in a range between the strikes.

Risk Metric	Considerations for This Tactic
Implied leverage	At a portfolio level, this is the most important risk metric to watch when using spreads. Spreads require less capital to create exposure to the underlying stock. As a result, spreads always have an implied leverage greater than 1.0x.
	Remember that the Buy and Hedge investor uses only spreads that are not speculative in nature. This means that for debit spreads, one leg will be ITM. When you have Options that are ITM, your implied leverage will always exceed 1.0x for that investment.
	ITM spreads are inherently leveraged. The implied leverage for a spread investment is calculated as the total market value of the implied equity controlled by the ITM leg divided by the CaR for that spread.
	It is important when using spreads to keep your overall portfolio's implied leverage below 1.0x. Be careful not to control so much "implied equity" that your overall portfolio controls more stock than you could purchase outright with your portfolio.
	Monitoring your overall portfolio's implied leverage is critical when using spreads. The incentive to leverage up your portfolio might exist when using spreads. Fight that urge, and keep your overall portfolio's implied leverage below 1.0x.
Correlation	Correlation is a calculation that is not impacted by the hedge tactic chosen.
	When you structure your portfolio, you consider the correlation statistics of the underlying stock. That correlation is not directly impacted by your use of an Option tactic such as spreads.

It is worth spending a little more time on the impact of spreads on your implied leverage. Implied leverage has a tendency to increase with spreads. This is because so many shares are controlled with the low capital requirements that spreads present. We said in Chapter 11, "Know Your Risk Metrics," that a handful of advanced tactics drive implied leverage well past 1.0x; spreads are one of them.

Let's return to the first bull call spread example with GD. Here's the data used in that example:

- GD is trading at $75.
- One long GD JAN12 65 call @ $11.75
- One short GD JAN12 70 call @ $8.15

- Net debit/maximum loss of $3.60
- Maximum gain of $1.40

Establishing this position will cost $360 per contract, allowing control of 100 shares of a $75 stock. You can execute this spread at $360 versus putting up $7,500 to buy the stock. When you buy stock, all the money used to buy the stock is considered capital at risk. If you wanted to put the same capital at risk ($7,500), you could buy 20 contracts of this spread instead. The $5 spread with the $360 per contract maintenance lets you control over 20 times the number of shares versus buying the stock.

Back up the truck and load up on this one, right? No way. That is not the Buy and Hedge approach. Although that is a potential use of your cash, it doesn't mean you're reducing your risk—specifically, the implied leverage. This position of 20 contracts on a $75 stock effectively controls $150,000 (20 × 100 × $75). When $7,500 can add the exposure of $150,000, expect the implied leverage of the entire portfolio to spike.

Using Probability to Compare Spread Trades

Spreads let you create cushion and build in some room for error. Because of the depreciating aspect of time value, spreads can allow the investor to make mistakes and still turn a profit. For example, ITM bull call spreads let the investor reach the maximum gain even if the stock doesn't go up. Remember, this is a bullish/neutral strategy that pays out the maximum even if the stock doesn't go up. The same can hold true for bearish outlooks. A bear put spread that is already ITM pays out the maximum even if the stock doesn't move from its market value when the trade is placed.

Here is where probabilities come into play and become an effective tool for comparing different spread trades. Most online brokers today provide probability data in their Option chain quotes. This data is derived from the current price of the Options and the implied volatility at each strike. We won't ask you to calculate this data yourself because your broker will provide it.

Table 25.2 compares three Amazon (AMZN) bull call spreads and the probability that they will hit the maximum loss and maximum gain. As a reminder, a bull call spread is when the investor is long the lower strike and short the higher strike. The net premium is a debit, and that debit is the maximum loss the investment can incur. The probabilities are derived from the percentage chance of expiring ITM in the Option chain. AMZN is trading at 200. Let's examine spreads about six months out.

Table 25.2 AMZN Bull Call Spreads

AMZN Bull Call Spread Strikes	Maximum Loss/ Premium	Maximum Gain (Percentage Gain)	Probability of Maximum Loss	Probability of Maximum Gain
175/185	$6.90	$3.10 (45%)	29%	61%
195/205	$5.35	$4.65 (87%)	52%	42%
225/235	$3.30	$6.70 (203%)	74%	19%

If the investor is confident in his research and believes that the stock will go up, the ITM/OTM spread of 195/205 may be best for him. There is a 52% chance that the maximum loss will occur, and the breakeven is only $0.35 away from where it is trading now. Essentially this strategy would give the holder a high correlation to the underlying stock. As AMZN moved between 195 and 205, the spread would feel like being long shares. If the stock goes up $5, the spread will gain nearly $5. If the stock goes down $5, the spread loses a little more than $5.

If the investor likes AMZN but has some reticence about the investment, he could consider the ITM/ITM spread of 175/185, where both legs are already ITM. Remember that calls with strikes below the market price are considered ITM. In this case, there is a 61% chance that the spread will yield the maximum gain, and only a 29% chance that the maximum loss will be incurred. The breakeven is $181.90 ($175 + $6.9). The built-in cushion of $18.10 ($200 − $181.9) means that the stock can drop nearly 9% before losses begin. This cushion comes at a cost. The maximum loss is higher at $6.90 versus $5.35, a 29% increase. The maximum profit of the investment is lower at \$3.10 versus \$4.65, a reduction of 33%. However, the probability of success jumps from 42% to 61%, which is nearly a 50% increase. This kind of strategy will initially lower the portfolio's volatility. As the stock moves, that may change, but out of the gate, it provides some safety.

The last strategy from Table 25.2 consists of two OTM spreads and is purely speculative. It is included here to show the probability associated with it. This spread has the lowest capital at risk and the highest percentage return if it hits the maximum gain. However, the probability of incurring the maximum loss is the highest at 74%, and the chance of hitting the maximum gain is only 19%. Said another way, three out of four times this trade is attempted, it is expected to hit the maximum loss, and it will hit the maximum gain only one out of five times. With a payout of only 200%, the probabilities do not work in its favor. If you decide to take a risk, the payoff needs to be worth it. In this case it clearly is not. Again, we urge investors to avoid using long OTM spreads.

Bear Call Spreads

Bear call spreads are the opposite of bull call spreads with regards to outlook, risk, and structure. As the name suggests, these spreads benefit from a downward movement in the underlying stock. A bear call spread is established with two Options in the same month with the same number of contracts where the short call strike is below the strike of the long call leg. In other words, you are short the call that is deeper in-the-money.

Let's return to the original GS example. The stock trades at \$150. Instead of a bullish outlook, adopt a bearish one. Instead of going long the 135 call, you short it for the \$21 in premium. You know that a short call (also known as a naked or uncovered call) has unlimited risk, so you hedge by buying the 160 call. The cost is \$7, but this protects you, because as soon as the stock goes over \$160 in value, the long call will appreciate as fast as the short call depreciates. The net credit is \$14 (\$21 – \$7). Figure 25.6 shows the risk graph for the GS 135/160 bear call spread.

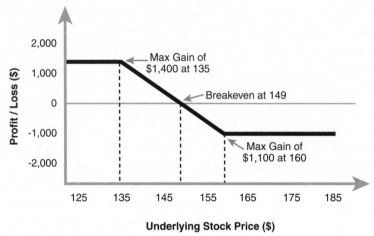

Figure 25.6 GS 135/160 bear call spread

The breakeven for this spread $149, just like the bull call spread, but you start to make money as the stock goes down. It's more accurate to say that you get to keep more of the premium received as the stock goes down. Remember that a bear call spread is also known as a credit call spread because it generates cash when the trade is placed. In this case you are given the $14 in cash. You can keep it all if the underlying drops below the lower strike price of $135 at expiration. The maximum loss occurs if the stock appreciates to above $160. In that case you would lose a net of $11. The spread itself would be worth –$25, the difference between the strikes. The $14 of premium you wrote for the spread would offset some of that to net out at $11.

You may notice that the bear call spread writer actually gets his maximum gain up front, so the net credit received is the maximum gain, and the difference left in the spread is the maximum loss (the CaR).

Just like bull call spreads, bear call spreads can contain Options that are ITM, OTM, or both. However, this time we recommend that you avoid bear call spreads where both Options are ITM. This is the exact opposite of what you learned with bull call spreads. It stands to reason that if ITM call spreads provide the best advantage for the bulls, they provide a less-desirable position for the bears. OTM bear call spreads offer the highest probability of success. Remember that the writer of a bear call spread wants the Options to expire worthless to keep the entire premium generated. So having the initial investment start where both Options are OTM offers the best chance for them to expire worthless. Worthless Options at the time of expiration are good for the writer/seller.

If a call spread writer wants to have the same exposure of being short stock, a spread with one Option ITM and one OTM is the best way to do so. There is a one-for-one move in spread value with the stock while it is between the strikes.

One advantage for the writer of spreads versus the long side is that time is on your side. At expiration, time is 0 for everyone, and only the mathematical calculation of intrinsic value gives Options any worth. But up until that point, time plays a part. As time ticks away every day, Options lose some value, and ultimately that time value goes to 0. So it stands to reason that time is an advantage to the seller of Options but works against the buyer of Options. This is true for single-legged or multilegged Option holders. Spread writers will always feel like there is an advantage, because time is on their side.

Vertical Put Spreads

Bull put spreads are a bullish investment created with two put Options with the long put leg at a strike price lower than the short put leg. The P/L graph for the bull put spread will almost always be virtually identical to the bull call spread. The difference is that the bull put spread generates income from a net credit, whereas the bull call spread is a net debit transaction. These two strategies are almost interchangeable. Their usage depends on which one gives the investor a slight pricing advantage based on Option premiums.

In a bull put spread, the Option writer wants the Options to expire worthless at the end of the Option cycle so that he or she can keep the premium generated from the transaction. Let's return to GD trading at $75 to run some scenarios.

Here is an OTM bull put spread:

- One long GD JAN12 65 put @ $3.05
- One short GD JAN12 70 put @ $4.50

- Net credit/maximum gain of $1.45
- Maximum loss of $3.55

I know you're getting pretty good at reading these by now, but let's review the important points of the risk graph shown in Figure 25.7. The maximum loss of this investment occurs below the $65 level, the trade is profitable above the break-even point of $68.55, and maximum gain occurs above the $70 mark.

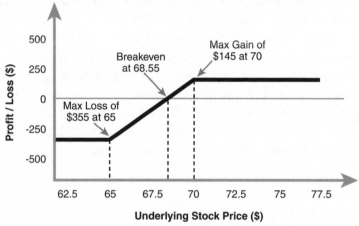

Figure 25.7 GD 65/70 bull put spread

Recall that although cash is generated from this transaction, the broker holds aside the maximum loss in what is called a maintenance requirement. In this case, that maintenance requirement is $3.55. Since that is the capital that is tied up in the trade, use it as the denominator to figure out the profitability. In this case it is 41% ($1.45 / $3.55). Notice that this is very close to the profile of the bull call spread from earlier in the chapter. The difference is most likely because of the dividend that GD pays. In other words, if all things stayed the same, the stock would tend to decline by the dividend amount. This in turn makes the puts slightly more valuable and able to hold a greater premium.

Just as the bull put spread mirrors the bull call spread, the bear put spread takes on the same aspects as the bear call spread. The bias is bearish, with upper and lower limits defined by the strike prices. Even the risk graphs look the same. The difference is that one generates a credit (bear call spread) and the other generates a debit (bear put spread).

Number of Contracts

The last piece of the spread puzzle relates to the size of the trade. As indicated in the risk metrics, spreads can result in the unintended overuse of leverage by creating too large of a position. Therefore, it is very important to accurately determine how many contracts you want to enter into when creating a spread.

As always, you begin with your portfolio allocation model and determine how much market value you want to control. That dollar amount is invested by owning shares outright or creating an equivalent control with the power of Options. Investing dollars divided by market price will give you the number of shares you intend to control. This is no change from what every investor does when entering any investment.

When you know the number of shares you want to control, divide by the option multiplier, and voilà—you have the number of contracts needed for the spread.

Here's an example. Suppose you have $15,000 to allocate to an investment in General Dynamics (GD) trading at $75. $15,000 of a $75 stock is 200 shares ($15,000 / $75). Divide the 200 shares by the 100 multiplier, and you come up with two contracts. From this point you determine that the following bull call spread is appropriate for your hypothesis:

- General Dynamics (GD) is trading at $75.
- Two long GD JAN12 70 call @ $8.15
- Two short GD JAN12 75 call @ $5.15
- Net debit/maximum loss of $3.00
- Maximum gain of $2.00

The requirement for two contracts of this spread would be $600. That is calculated by taking the number of contracts, two, times the multiplier, 100, times the net debit, $300. (2 × 100 × $300) = $600.

Again, the benefit of Options leverage allows the Buy and Hedge investor to create $15,000 worth of exposure by putting up only $600 out of pocket.

Here's how we want you to think about using spreads:

1. Start with the portfolio allocation model. This should define the amount allocated to any single investment and the underlying asset to be used.

2. Determine the projected performance of the underlying. The analysis should define the expectations and in turn define the upper- and lower-level expected price movements.

3. Use the performance projections to determine the tactic and relevant strike prices, and then choose the Options that meet the criteria.

4. Define the size of the trade by calculating the number of contracts you want to enter into.

5. Track your implied leverage at the portfolio level. Avoid situations that cause the overall implied leverage of your portfolio to exceed 1.0x.

Chapter Lessons

- Vertical spreads consist of two Options of the same type (calls/puts), with the same underlying asset, expiring in the same month, with the same number of contracts. The strikes will vary, and their difference creates the spread.

- Spreads will net a debit or credit and can use Options that are ITM, OTM, or a combination of the two.

- Spreads are inherently a hedged investment and can create any market bias you want as well as define your downside risk.

- Risk factors get slightly different treatment for spreads, but be sure to watch the implied leverage at portfolio level.

26 — Diagonal Spreads

Chung Mee: *"Speed is important in business. Time is money."*

Lawrence Bourne III: *"You said opium was money."*

Chung Mee: *"Money is Money."*

Lawrence Bourne III: *"Well then, what is time again?"*

—From *Volunteers* (1985)

Although *Volunteers* is one of Tom Hanks and John Candy's less popular movies, the quote is spot on because in options, time *is* money. The diagonal spread tactic is completely based off the concept that time depreciates at different rates along the expiration cycle.

Diagonal spreads are very similar to vertical spreads, except that the monthly expiration and strike prices are different. This extra dimension significantly increases the number of iterations we can add to the spread list. The good news is that we will focus on only a few for the purposes of this book. When talking about multiple months, we'll use the following as a point of reference: The month that is closest to expiration is called the near month, and the month that is further out is called the far month. That should be easy to remember.

We recommend that if you use diagonal spreads, you focus on spreads that are long the far month and short the near month. You do this to take advantage of time decay multiple times on the short leg and pay it only once on the long leg.

With a vertical spread, time decay happens simultaneously for both legs because they have the same expiration date. Of course, this is not a 100% equal rate of change, but at the end of the expiration month, they both have a time value worth 0. As discussed in

Chapters 15 through 18, time decays faster as expiration approaches. When long a spread (meaning a debit spread), the long side provides most of the value. This is the case regardless of whether calls or puts are used to create the spread. When in a debit spread, the holder wants it to appreciate in value before expiration. Essentially the debit spread has the same characteristics as being long. Appreciation of the long leg is driven by how ITM the long Option is.

Generally speaking, time depreciates most quickly during the last three to six weeks. Dramatic changes in volatility can play havoc with that statement, but generally this is the case.

Time decay is actually good for the short side of the spread. Essentially, selling an Option pays for part of the long side. As the adage says, sell high and buy low. In the case of short Options, buying low means expiring worthless.

Combining the two concepts, the desire for slow time decay on the long side and rapid decay on the short side leads the investor to use diagonals. Instead of choosing the same expiration month for both Options, go long an Option that has a further-out expiration month, and go short an Option that has a nearer expiration, with a plan to roll the near-term Option multiple times. Said another way, you should buy the long leg and pay for it by writing the short side multiple times. Here is an example of the legs for a long diagonal spread:

- One long GE JAN12 18 call
- One short GE OCT11 20 call

JAN12 will expire after OCT11, so there will be a chance to write calls in NOV11, DEC11, and JAN12 to generate multiple payments against the long JAN12 call.

Figure 26.1 shows how the short Option depreciates to 0 time value multiple times during the term of the long far-dated Option.

Because you want to go out six months when creating the Option position, you should be able to pay for the long side by writing six calls—one each month. Typically, you can expect to pay for the long side in the first four months, which leaves the final two months as upside income.

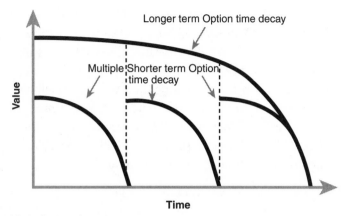

Figure 26.1 Option time decay

With diagonals, you should keep a few factors in mind. The first is that all the risk metrics discussed in the preceding chapter still apply, and capital at risk is still a key metric. Second, as the underlying moves over time, the distance between the strikes might have to be adjusted. Actually, count on that happening. You want to establish a wide enough spread to allow for adjustments in the upper strike price to generate enough premium. Worse yet, the stock can move so that even the long Option is OTM and the maximum loss is realized before having enough time to generate income to pay for it. Also, diagonal spread holders have to watch if the short call goes ITM. In this case, the investor needs to be prepared for an assignment. Although these risks exist with verticals, they are minimized, because at expiration, all the Options positions are netted out at the same time. With diagonals, the chance is higher, because you will be short the near-month expiration in many cases.

All these factors are why we like to call this an advanced tactic. But fear not. These are very manageable situations—but they probably will require more attention than other tactics.

Let's look at an example that will force us to make a few of these decisions along the way.

One way you should think about diagonals is to treat them like a deep ITM call with a monthly call written against it to help subsidize the cost. Let's look at Apple Inc. (AAPL) between the months of May 2010 and January 2011.

On May 24, 2011, you notice that AAPL seems to be trading in a range between $230 and $270 based on the previous few months. AAPL is trading at $247. You decide that due to AAPL's high share price, you will use an ITM call to gain exposure to the upside while limiting the capital at risk. You go long the JAN11 230 call that is trading for $44 that is eight months out. The plan is to write an Option every month that is OTM that is 20 to 30 points above the current market price. So you short the JUN10 270 call for $3.55 to help pay for the long position. Here are the investment details:

- One long AAPL JAN11 230 call @ $44
- One short AAPL JUN10 270 call @ $3.55
- Net debit/maximum loss of $40.45 per share

You continue to write Options each month against the long call position, keeping in mind that if the short side ends up in the money, you'll have some decisions to make. Remember, if the short call is ITM at the time of expiration, you'll get assigned and have to deliver 100 shares of AAPL at $270, putting you into a short position.

Fast-forward to the JUN10 expiration: AAPL is trading at 274 as it approaches the close on expiration Friday. The short position is now ITM and is worth $4. So the net on that short call is –$0.45 ($3.55 – $4.00). The long call position is now worth $58.75, a gain of $14.75 ($58.75 – $44). The value of both Option legs nets to a positive $14.30 per share. What do you do? Here are your choices:

- Trade out of the long and short positions entirely, and take the net $14.30 profit.
- Keep the long call, buy to close the short side, take the $0.45 loss, and write another call for the next month.
- Do nothing, and get assigned on the short call after expiration.

The first choice is a perfectly good selection. The stock reached the upper limit in one month. Although you always invest for the long haul, getting there early isn't a bad thing. Taking the gains and closing the investment is a viable decision, and you've eliminated emotion from the equation. The investment grew by $14.30 on a $40.45 requirement—a 35% gain. No one's ever gone broke making 35% a month.

The second choice should be the action if you feel there is more room for Apple's share price to grow. Maybe some news during the month makes you believe you should push up the upper limit. Regardless, you should be sure to reaffirm your investment bias on AAPL before taking this move. One way to do this is to buy-to-cover the short Option and immediately sell another Option for the next month. For example, the JUL10 290 call was trading at $4.25 at the time. This allows for another 16 points of AAPL appreciation and generates another $4.25 of income (time value you sold).

The third choice will result in a short position of 100 shares of AAPL. The total investment in AAPL would look like this:

- One long AAPL JAN11 230 call @58.75
- –100 shares AAPL (short position) @ 270

This might seem like a terrible situation, because right out of the gate, you have a neutral-to-bearish bias. You are neutral down to $230 price in AAPL and then bearish on your exposure below $230. This seems counterintuitive to your original bullish bias. And the biggest issue is that you're now short shares that have the potential to generate an unlimited loss. However, these factors do not actually create an adverse scenario. Believe it or not, this can actually be a good outcome for situations where stocks have risen too fast too quickly.

First, remember that you generated $3.55 originally from selling the call, so the net loss on the short stock is still only –$0.45. Second, this action allows you to harvest some gains. Every dollar that AAPL now declines (depreciating your long call position) is offset by an appreciation in the short shares. You've locked in the intrinsic gains. The time value of $14.75, however, remains unhedged, but this is now the maximum you can lose on the investment. The maximum loss on the long call was $40.45 before, and now it is $14.75, and you have dramatically reduced the capital at risk. Third, the short stock is covered by the long call. No matter how high the stock goes (that is where the risk is for the short stock holder), the long call will offset the loss by going up the same amount. But why do this? There is good money on the table with the profit of the investment. The reason to ultimately pursue this tactic is if you have changed your investment hypothesis on AAPL. If you are now neutral-to-bearish on the stock, you can leave the short AAPL stock rather than replace it with an OTM call in the next month.

Here's a case in point. It turns out that AAPL actually did pull back during the next expiration month and closed the JUL10 expiration period at $250. Here is how that would impact the positions on expiration Friday, July 16, 2010:

- One long AAPL JAN11 230 call @ 42 is a decrease of $16.75 ($58.75 to $42). Total net on the investment is –$2 from the original buy price of $44.
- –100 shares AAPL @ 250 is an increase of $20 ($270 to $250).
- Let's not forget the short call that was a –$0.45 net as well.
- Add all these up ($20 – $2 – $0.45), and the net investment has a $17.55 gain.

This is another $3.15 you've added to the previous months' gains, and you reduced the capital risk in the process.

These steps are illustrated in Figure 26.2

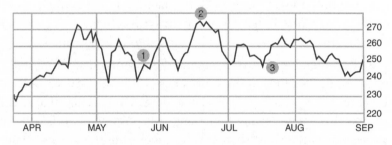

Figure 26.2 AAPL APR2010-SEP2010

The biggest issue with this approach is that it requires you to change your bias in a relatively short period of time. Granted, the stock hit your original sell point, but going from sell to being short is taking it one step further. You are hedged with the long call, and you locked in your profits, but new decisions about potential movements in the stock that are dictated by the market need to be carefully considered. We don't recommend timing stocks or markets. So, pursue this strategy only if your investment bias on AAPL changed at assignment.

Another issue with this approach is the cash requirement necessary to short 100 shares of AAPL. Shorting generates cash, but it's not cash available to invest. It is held as a maintenance requirement and reduces your portfolio's buying power. Technically speaking, shorting requires trading on margin, and even though you're not borrowing money to make the trade, it is considered a margined position. We mention this only because we realize in Chapter 11, "Know Your Risk Metrics," we never recommend borrowing money to invest. We still maintain that rule here, but we realize that brokers classify the trade itself as a margined position.

Diagonals Aren't Always the Best Solution

Not all diagonals end up delivering the best results. Sometimes, the vertical is a better solution. Let's return to our General Dynamics (GD) example and go back in time to June 2010. From this point in time we gathered real Option data to show how a diagonal would have worked compared to a vertical bull call spread.

Our example of the vertical ITM bull call spread from the preceding chapter consisted of a long call about eight months out and a short call with the same expiration. That vertical looked like this:

- One long GD JAN12 65 call @ $7.40
- One short GD JAN12 70 call @ $4.85

Let's turn this into a diagonal by replacing the short leg with a short-dated leg and create the following investment while GD is trading at $66:

- One long GD JAN11 65 call @ $7.40
- One short GD JUN10 70 call @ $0.85
- Net debit/maximum loss of $6.55

The net debit is $6.55 ($7.40 – $0.85), and yes, this is the maximum loss as well. If you could write an Option worth $0.80 every month from now until JAN11 when the long Option expires, you could potentially generate that 80 cents eight times. As cautioned earlier, the movement in the stock price will make that a challenge—not to mention potential assignments. Table 26.1 illustrates the actual data for the eight months and the cumulative impact of writing eight calls.

Table 26.1 The Cumulative Impact of Writing Eight Calls

Opening Date	GD Price	Option	Premium (Opening)	Closing Price	P/L	Cumulative
Short Call Positions						
5/24/10	$65.95	JUN10 70 call	$0.85	$0	$0.85	$0.85
6/21/10	$66.78	JUL10 70 call	$0.35	$0	$.35	$1.20
7/19/10	$58.60	AUG10 70 call	$0.05	$0	$0.05	$1.25
8/23/10	$59.33	SEP10 70 call	$0.05	$0	$0.05	$1.30
9/20/10	$63.63	OCT10 70 call	$0.05	$0	$0.05	$1.35
10/18/10	$64.37	NOV10 70 call	$0.20	$0	$0.20	$1.55
11/22/10	$66.26	DEC10 70 call	$0.25	$0.30	–$0.05	$1.50
12/20/10	$70.01	JAN11 70 call	$1.45	$2.97	–$1.52	–$0.02
Long Call Position						
5/24/10	$65.95	JAN11 65 call	$7.40	$7.97	$0.57	$0.55

In this example, the net gain after managing nine positions is a mere $0.55. GD during that time went from $65.95 on May 24, 2010 to $72.97 on January 21, 2011. The vertical you didn't choose would have hit its maximum gain of $2.45. The diagonal was unable to generate sufficient time premium from the OTM 70 strike calls each month.

This is a lesson to be sure when choosing diagonals. The time value written every month will vary based on the movements of the underlying stock. Sometimes, verticals are the better choice.

Chapter Lessons

- Diagonals are spreads with the same number of contracts and on the same Option type, but they have different strikes and different expiration months.
- Diagonals sell the near month Option multiple times to pay for a far month long position; this makes them a suitable replacement for verticals.
- Diagonals are at risk of changing the spread range due to movement in the underlying asset.
- Diagonals require more attention than other tactics because you almost always have an Option expiring in the near month.
- Diagonals aren't right for all vertical replacement scenarios.

27

Managing the Cash in Your Portfolio

(Eddie Felson, Vincent Lauria, and Carmen enter a pool hall.)

Eddie: *"Do you smell that?"*

Vincent: *"What? Smoke?"*

Carmen: *"No. Money."*

—From *The Color of Money* (1986)

Of course we cannot smell the money in our online brokerage accounts. But when your account has excess cash, you will tend to think about it a little more often—usually because you are trying to figure out something to do with it.

Many hedged portfolios maintain significant cash positions at all times. Chapter 11, "Know Your Risk Metrics," described leverage—specifically, how Options create natural leverage. Options, by their very mechanics, create leverage. The investor can control many more shares in a bullish or bearish direction using Options compared to just buying the shares. The result in the portfolio is significant excess cash.

Not every hedge tactic taught in this book creates excess cash in your portfolio. Collars, married options, and portfolio hedges do not use Options to leverage a portfolio. Instead, the Options in these tactics are used to create downside protection only. The tactics that result in significant excess cash are spreads and in-the-money calls and puts.

In many cases, the capital needed to create $100,000 worth of exposure to a stock or ETF using ITM Options or a spread is only about $20,000 (or even less sometimes). The Buy and Hedge approach does not recommend an implied leverage for your overall portfolio that exceeds 1.0x. So, to build a portfolio, for example, with $100,000 using these specific tactics, the result could be as much as $80,000 in excess cash in the portfolio.

The investor who uses tactics that create excess cash needs to decide how to manage the excess cash in his portfolio. The investor without excess cash still has cash as part of his allocation. Cash management should be important to this investor also. But this investor doesn't have to stare at large cash positions in his portfolio and wonder whether his return on that cash is sufficient.

Investing Your Normal Cash Allocation

Remember from Chapter 12, "Constructing a Long-Term, Diversified Portfolio," that your portfolio allocation includes cash as an asset class. In most cases, the allocation is only 10%—and it never increases until the portfolio is in its liquidation stage (such as retirement). For most portfolios, the cash can be left in the brokerage account, and nothing needs to be done with it. Your brokerage may sweep the money into an FDIC insured account, or you can direct your brokerage to just keep it in cash. You'll earn very little on the cash in your brokerage account either way. And if you keep the cash in your brokerage account, it is ready and available to use if you have a new investment idea.

However, if the cash portion of your asset allocation is large enough (say, greater than $100,000), you might want to consider seeing what other cash equivalent securities your broker offers. You could purchase a money market mutual fund, or the brokerage might offer a sweep program with a higher interest rate yield. If the cash in your portfolio is large enough, the increased yield might be worth the extra effort to manage the cash investments more closely.

Warning

Cash and cash equivalents are not always as safe as we once thought. You learned this lesson in 2008 with bank collapses and money market funds breaking the buck. When managing the cash in your account, you need to consider the investment quality of the brokerage. Every top online brokerage offers SIPC coverage, which insures your account up to $500,000 in the event that your brokerage fails and cannot return your assets. And most of the large brokerage houses also offer additional insurance they purchase on your behalf from third-party insurers. You need to talk to your broker and establish the extent of the coverage. Never have more cash in your account than your brokerage will insure in the event of the broker's failure.

In the case of cash equivalents, such as cash sweep programs and money market mutual funds, you need to investigate the specifics of each investment alternative for your cash. In many cash sweep programs, FDIC insurance is applied (but not in all of them, so ask your broker). Currently, FDIC insurance covers the first $250,000 of cash you have in that sweep program. Having more than $250,000 would be a risk. You might want to consider taking the cash in excess of $250,000 and finding a CD that is FDIC insured. Every different bank CD you invest in would come with the $250,000 guarantee.

For money market mutual funds, the quality of the fund matters. This is another lesson many people learned the hard way in 2008. For the first time, a money market mutual fund "broke the buck," meaning that it failed to return $1 to the investor for every $1 invested. The credit crisis turned some formerly AAA-rated bonds into worthless investments, which affected several of the money market mutual funds. The quality of the fund matters. Be sure to invest only with funds at a large bank or institution that stands behind the fund.

And if that doesn't satisfy you, stick to CDs—and put no more than the FDIC insured limit with any one bank. Remember that the FDIC guarantee is a guarantee for the *bank*, not the CD. So do not buy all your CDs from the same bank if the total exceeds the insured amount (currently $250,000).

Cash Management Tactics for the Advanced Hedging Client

The cash management tactics just described work great for the portfolio with modest cash amounts. Modest in this case means about

10% to 20% of the overall portfolio value. But the client who predominantly uses spread tactics and in-the-money Options tactics will need to spend more time managing the cash in his portfolio. We outlined the reason earlier in this chapter: significant excess cash is generated by these Options hedging tactics.

Let's look at an example. Assume that your portfolio is $275,000 in total value. Your underlying investments include a handful of ETFs and stocks, and you have used in-the-money call Options to create bullish exposure to each investment. Let's also assume that the calls were in-the-money by roughly 15% on average, meaning that on a $20 stock, the ITM call had a strike price of $17. Add a bit of time value—maybe 5%—and this portfolio can use ITM Options with a market value of roughly $45,000 to control $250,000 worth of stock and ETFs. Your cash allocation is recommended to be 10%, so about $27,500. However, the *real* cash total in your portfolio is about $230,000, or about 80% of the total portfolio. Why? Because the actual cash in your portfolio includes both the cash allocation *and* the cash freed up by using Options tactics that include leverage.

This is a lot of cash to manage. Any of the cash-management tactics described in the preceding section would be appropriate for managing this cash. The most important thing that the investor can do, however, is to pay attention to this large cash position. It would be a wasted opportunity for this cash to earn a yield lower than the market could bear. This is especially true if the investor plans to keep using ITM Options and spreads as a primary tactic, because this means the cash balance would always be large.

Warning

We have large cash balances when using these two tactics because we keep our implied leverage at or below 1.0x. As Buy and Hedge investors, we avoid leverage. That is what causes our portfolio to have this excess cash.

The following advanced cash management approach is the exception to that rule! It will cause your implied leverage for the overall portfolio to exceed 1.0x. But it only exceeds 1.0x because of the advanced cash management technique applied. Applied correctly and your risk will still be well controlled.

Now for the advanced cash management tactic. Over the years, Options and ETFs have grown in volume, makeup, and design to the point where an individual retail investor can create custom exposure to a specific sector, subsector, or class of investment. ETFs have even broadened to the fixed income asset class. The investor can now purchase a fixed income ETF that is full of bonds of a specific asset quality. And many but not all of these fixed income ETFs have Options that the investor can use to hedge the exposure to the ETF. The flexibility this can afford the creative investor is very helpful.

Earlier chapters covered using Options while investing in ETFs. With that knowledge base, the investor can design a solution for higher yield for the cash in his portfolio. Let's focus first on the ETF side of the equation.

Fixed income ETFs typically are organized to create exposure to a specific credit quality within the fixed income/bond universe. In addition, the fixed income ETF typically is built to mimic a certain duration—meaning the typical time until the fixed income is set to finish paying interest and return the capital. Remember that fixed income (or bonds) products are financial instruments issued by corporations and government entities to borrow money. The bond is a two-part obligation from the issuing party to pay interest on the borrowed money at some rate of return for the duration of the loan and to return the loan amount at the end of the loan duration.

A fixed income ETF usually focuses on one type of credit quality and a certain average duration for the ETF's overall portfolio. These two factors generally influence the total interest rate profile of the ETF. Most fixed income ETFs pay interest every month, although some pay interest quarterly. Be sure you know which schedule your ETF uses for paying interest. Take a look at the average dividends the ETF pays, and understand the commitment to pay dividends that the ETF makes. Typically, each ETF passes through all the interest payments to the ETF holders.

So, if you used all your excess cash to buy these ETFs, you would technically be violating two of the key rules of Buy and Hedge that we taught you in Chapters 11 and 12. First, your portfolio would be adding significant leverage—specifically, implied leverage. Remember that in this case, using the tactics with higher implied leverage can leave as much as 80% of your portfolio value in cash. But your overall portfolio can still have an implied leverage of about 1.0x, even with the significant cash position. If you take that 80% that is cash and invest it in a fixed income ETF, you would have an implied leverage that is now around 1.8x. This violates our rule about excess leverage.

Just as important, you would be violating the rule for your portfolio asset allocation. You would now have a very large bond allocation that could be as high as 30% to 40% of your total portfolio value. But your planned fixed income allocation might have been 0% to 10%. These two changes will modify your portfolio's performance and risk profile. So what is the advanced strategy for cash that uses fixed income ETFs?

Breaking the Rules for the Right Reason

If you decide that you want excess yield for your cash *and* you are willing to slightly increase the capital at risk in your portfolio, Buy and Hedge has an advanced cash strategy for you to consider. The strategy has you take that excess cash and invest it in a vehicle that can generate some excess yield (a higher interest rate than cash equivalents such as money market mutual funds or CDs). But the markets give no free lunches. Cash equivalent securities have a very low risk profile. If you want more yield, you have to take more risk. *There is no way around it!* Never forget that.

The authors endorse one tactic for increasing your yield while controlling your risk adequately: a married put on a fixed income ETF. You need to find a fixed income ETF that has Options *and* sufficient volume in out-of-the-money puts that can offer you protection. You should remember that in Chapter 23, "ETFS Will Look Great in Your Portfolio," we listed the top 100 ETFs by total assets under management. Seventeen of the top 100 ETFs are fixed income ETFs. And of those seventeen, seven of them offer options with sufficient open interest to find the right put protection level. The symbols for those seven ETFs are LQD, SHY, HYG, JNK, IEF, TLT, and MBB.

Remember from Chapter 20, "Married Puts," that a married put includes ownership of an underlying security and then a put that is out-of-the-money that provides some downside protection for the underlying security. In this case, you buy the fixed income ETF and then purchase a put that is out-of-the-money that creates downside protection for the ETF. You need to decide how much protection will make you comfortable. Typically, the authors look to purchase protection that is about 10% to the downside from the current ETF market price. We recommend building a ladder of protective puts that you regularly roll and that has protection for as many Option months as there are between now and six to nine months from now.

In this tactic, the fixed income ETF pays a dividend every month or quarter. In fact, the ex-dividend date for some ETFs with Options is the same as the Option expiration dates. For many others, it is the first day of the month. This is convenient. It means comparing the dividends collected with the cost of the protective put you purchase. You get a dividend every month, and that dividend helps pay for the protection (the cost of the put). The dividend must exceed the cost of the put; otherwise, you are paying money to own fixed income. In other words, you have a negative carrying cost for the fixed income ETF. When your goal is to increase your yield, you must find dividends that are more than the cost of the protection.

Luckily, you will rarely find a fixed income ETF with Options in which the put protection costs more than the dividends collected over the corresponding time period of the protection. This should make sense to you: Fixed income is a lower-volatility investment vehicle. It does not fluctuate as much as equities, and default among bonds typically is an uncommon occurrence. As a result, the put protection on such a vehicle is unlikely to be very high. In fact, often the at-the-money put protection for a given month in the future for a fixed income ETF is the *same as* or very close to the total dividends that are expected to be paid on that fixed income ETF over the same corresponding time period.

Let's look at an example. One of the fixed income ETFs with a lot of share volume and significant Option volume is JNK, a junk bond ETF. Junk bonds are the highest yielding corporate bonds in the U.S. They are labeled "junk" because the companies that issue the fixed income have the lowest credit quality. In other words, these companies are the most at risk of defaulting on their debt and causing that debt to become worthless. Normally, the authors would not recommend this type of security except in very specific circumstances. But in this case, you can buy put Options, which act as downside protection. This is similar to buying credit-default insurance for junk bonds. Let's examine the Options available for JNK as of March 31, 2011. This is the day before the ex-dividend date for the April dividend payment, because JNK is one of the fixed income ETFs that does not have its Options expiration date and ex-dividend dates aligned.

JNK traded between $40.56 and $40.47 that day and closed at $40.51. The September 11 put with a strike of $40 is trading at a bid/ask of $1.45/$1.70. In other words, it would cost the investor about $1.55 to $1.60 to buy that put. From March 31 to the Options expiration in September, six ex-dividend dates will qualify the ETF owner to collect the dividend: April 1, May 1, June 1, July 1, August 1, and September 1. The dividend every month for this ETF has been 26 cents. So, the investor will collect $1.56 over these six months. The $1.56 is about the same as the protective put cost. In other words, the market is telling you that if you want to own this ETF and have virtually no downside risk in owning it for the next six months, you need to give up all its dividends. That is effectively the cost of credit-default insurance for this investment.

But this tactic is focused on finding some extra yield, so you are ready to take some risk. What about the September '11 puts with a strike price of $38? This is roughly 5% to 6% of downside risk from the current price. The put cost for those is $0.65/$0.90, or roughly 80 cents. So, the investor could take in $1.56 in dividends and pay 80 cents in protective costs. The investor nets 76 cents—which, on a $40.51 ETF price, means an annual yield of 3.75%. So, if you are willing to take some risk to the tune of 4% to 5% of your capital for the next six months, you can generate some real yield that is materially better than cash equivalents are yielding. (Cash was yielding less than one-fourth of 1% in brokerage accounts at the time this book was written.)

Take it a step further. Look at the September '11 put with a $36 strike price. It is trading at $0.25/$0.45. So the investor could expect to pay about 35 cents. Again, the investor would collect $1.56 in dividends. So, the net would be $1.21 retained. This is an annualized yield of 7.7%, but the investor has taken materially more risk, which is why the yield is so materially higher. A $36 strike price means that the ETF could decline by almost 11% before the protection would kick in. This is more risk, and with more risk comes more return (7.7% net annual yield).

The main point to understand is that fixed income ETFs that have put Options allow the investor to customize the yield he wants to receive by customizing the downside risk he is willing to take. The put costs typically are some discount to the dividends that will be collected between now and expiration of that put Option. Determine the risk you are willing to take, and you can define exactly the yield you really net from that ETF.

Remember that this investment has risk. It is *not* the same as investing in cash equivalents. Cash equivalents offer materially less risk of losing your principal. You need to consider this tactic carefully. It is not for everyone. However, the rule of thumb to consider is based on the total capital at risk in your portfolio. After constructing your portfolio based on your asset allocation, you need to compute the capital at risk for your total portfolio. When you take the excess cash and invest it in a fixed income ETF and purchase a protective put, you have increased your total portfolio capital at risk. Make sure that your new total capital at risk is not so large that you cannot sleep comfortably at night. A good rule of thumb is that the total CaR for your portfolio should not exceed 20% to 30% after the cash investment tactic is deployed.

Chapter Lessons

- Hedging strategies tend to produce excess cash in your portfolio.
- If your excess cash is sufficiently large, consider finding higher-yielding alternatives that your broker offers for investing your cash, such as CDs and money market mutual funds.
- If you use ITM Options and/or spreads, your portfolio will have even more excess cash than usual. Look to maximize the return on this cash in your portfolio.
- Consider investing your excess cash in fixed income ETFs that offer put Options for hedging your downside risk.

28

Managing for Tax Efficiency

Carl Spackler: *"This place got a pool?"*

Ty Webb: *"Pool and a pond.... Pond would be good for you."*

—From *Caddyshack* (1980)

I know this quote has nothing to do with taxes. Do you know how difficult it is to find quotes from quality movies about taxes? It is difficult. But along with tax advice in this chapter we offer one other piece of advice. At some point in your life you will be at a party or a hotel or some gathering and one of your friends will ask, "Does it have a pool?" My advice: Don't miss a beat. Immediately say, "... a pool and a pond.... Pond would be good for you." It is not only a cheap laugh but you'll instantly know whether your friend is a *Caddyshack* fan.

In Chapter 9, The Taxman Cometh," you learned about the impact of taxes on your real returns. Paying taxes on your investment gains is your obligation as a citizen of this great country. Ultimately, and ironically, the investor *hopes* to create a tax obligation through investing, because this means that the investor is generating gains. Wouldn't it have been better to pay taxes in 2008 on a gain instead of suffering the large losses that most investors did?

Learning to be tax-efficient is key to creating real spending power from your investment success. The investor can spend only the gains that remain *after* taxes are paid. This chapter focuses on optimizing for tax efficiency. By optimizing for efficiency, we mean creating the lowest tax bill possible and delaying tax payments whenever possible.

Our tax lessons fall into three categories:

- Tactics for tax-advantaged accounts
- Tactics for taxable accounts
- Tax-advantaged investment vehicles

Tactics for Tax-Advantaged Accounts

Tax-advantaged accounts are individual retirement accounts (IRAs) and defined contribution accounts (such as 401(k)s). Investors can grow their investments in these types of accounts without paying taxes on the annual growth. Instead, the investor is taxed when the investments are withdrawn. At that time, the investor is taxed at his normal income tax rate. When this tax bill is delayed, the power of compounding is given a chance to work its magic to the investor's benefit.

Our advice is to maximize your contribution to these types of accounts if you qualify. The government provides incentives to contribute to these accounts. Currently, if your income is not too high, you (and your spouse separately) can contribute up to $5,000 to an IRA annually, and this contribution results in a tax deduction on your returns. In addition, if your employer offers a defined contribution account such as a 401(k), maximize your contribution to that account also. The first $13,000 of your 401(k) contribution reduces your taxable income by the same amount, effectively delivering a $13,000 income tax deduction. Instantly, you will have saved significantly and created a base of investments to grow and compound on a tax-free basis.

Chapter 10, "Hedge Every Investment," introduced the first Iron Rule: Hedge every investment. Later in the book, we introduced the primary tactics (basic and advanced) for building hedged investments. You learned in Chapter 14, "Harvest Your Gains and Losses," that hedging requires regular maintenance, resulting in an above-average number of portfolio transactions. Remember that closing positions is what generates taxable transactions. So, it makes sense to think about these tactics from a tax perspective. The result is that some tactics create more taxable events than others.

In a tax-advantaged account such as an IRA or 401(k) (assuming that you have a self-directed brokerage account attached to your 401k), the fact that certain tactics generate more taxable events is immaterial. The investor doesn't pay annual taxes on the gains in a tax-advantaged account. So, any of the tactics recommended in this book will work well in a tax-advantaged account. When deciding which tactic to use in a tax-advantaged account, the investor can really just focus on the best fit of each tactic for his investment hypothesis and the pricing of the Options available for that tactic.

Tactics for Taxable Accounts

The conversation about tax efficiency for taxable accounts picks up right where we left the conversation about tax-advantaged accounts. Remember that some tactics used to hedge create more frequent transactions. Therefore, these tactics create more taxable events. In a taxable account, these taxable events create tax obligations. Certain tactics are more efficient for tax reasons in a taxable account.

Being tax-efficient is a function of two factors: the tax rate you pay, and the timing of your tax payments. You need to optimize for both of these to call your portfolio tax-optimized. Techniques exist for influencing each of these factors.

The first factor is your tax rate. Under the current tax code, set to expire in 2013, short-term capital gains and long-term capital gains are taxed at different rates. Long-term capital gains enjoy a lower tax rate and have enjoyed that lower rate for some time. We believe politicians have strong reasons to keep incentivizing investors to invest for the long term. This means that the beneficial tax rate for long-term capital gains could continue past 2013.

For a gain or loss to achieve the long-term designation for tax purposes, the individual position with the gain or loss must be held for at least one year or more. *All other gains and losses* are considered short-term—held for less than one year.

Short-term capital gains are taxed at the same rate as your regular income. Long-term capital gains are taxed at 20% starting in 2011, except in the case where the investor is in the lowest tax bracket—the

15% bracket. Most investors will pay the 20% rate. Given that most investor tax rates on regular income are between 28% and 39.6%, the advantage here is material.

As Buy and Hedge investors, holding investments for the long term is our default approach. So, finding opportunities to achieve long-term gains should be a priority. Three of our hedging tactics create very good opportunities for one-year+ hold times for positions—married Options, collars, and portfolio hedging.

The first two tactics, married Options and collars, by definition include either long or short ownership of an underlying stock or ETF. The investor uses Options to create the protection necessary to make the investment hedged. The Options positions typically have hold times of six months or less—and almost always less than one year. And when the investor has the right investment hypothesis, the gains typically will be embedded in the underlying stock or ETF. Holding the stock or ETF position for the long term is what creates the desired exposure consistent with the investment hypothesis.

Meanwhile, if the investor hypothesis is accurate, the Options that created the hedge are expiring worthless or being closed with losses. These losses are short-term and can be used to offset gains somewhere else in the portfolio. But most importantly, when you are right with your investment hypothesis, the stock or ETF has unrealized gains. These are gains that you will likely want to keep holding well past one year—hence the advantageous tax treatment from the long-term capital gains.

Additionally, the portfolio hedge approach is more likely to provide opportunities for long-term capital gains instead of short-term capital gains. The portfolio hedge approach has the investor purchase a hedge for the overall portfolio using a broad market index. The portfolio is constructed of mostly unhedged stocks and ETFs—which should be held for the long term—generating long-term capital gains instead of short-term. This tactic, in other words, has the same advantage as the two tactics discussed before it: underlying ownership of stocks and ETFs for the long term.

All the other tactics we recommend in Parts IV and V of this book will almost never produce long-term capital gains. These tactics (in-the-money Options and spreads) are constructed completely using

Options, with no underlying ownership (or short position) in the stock or ETFs. And at Buy and Hedge, we never recommend using LEAPS (Options with expirations more than one year from today). As a result, using these two tactics will never produce a long-term capital gain. The investor will always be closing the position or rolling the position forward to a new expiration date in less than one-year windows. All gains and losses will be short-term by the tax definition.

Sometimes, the best tactic for your investment hypothesis is an ITM Option or a spread. When that is the case, you can still make that investment in a taxable account. Just be aware that you have guaranteed that you will pay taxes on these gains at your regular tax rate. No benefits from long-term capital gains rates will apply. However, we recommend that you use collars, married Options, and portfolio hedges in your taxable accounts, all things being equal. We are not saying that you can't use spreads and ITM Options in your taxable accounts. Just be sure you are predisposed to using the tactics that are most tax-efficient.

The second factor in tax efficiency is the timing of making tax payments. When an investor has a gain, putting off the tax obligation for that gain for an extra year gives the portfolio extra capital to put to work. That extra capital has a chance to compound its growth and give the client more portfolio power. You learned about the power of compounding in Part II, "The Immutable Laws of Investing."

We examined the techniques for delaying tax obligations or harvesting tax gains/losses in Chapter 14. We won't review them again, except to say that come October of any tax year, the investor needs to start examining his portfolio closely to look at opportunities to manage his tax obligation prior to the next April tax bill.

Tax-Advantaged Investment Vehicles

In our many years in the online brokerage business, several interesting investment vehicles have come along and changed the landscape for investors. We think the single most important product to be introduced is the ETF, covered in depth in Chapter 23, "ETFs Will Look Great in Your Porfolio." However, another interesting product gained real traction in the latter half of the preceding decade—and this product has special tax treatment.

The product is called an equity index Option. These indexes typically mimic exposure to a broad market. The most heavily traded equity index Option is the SPX, which provides ideal exposure to the S&P 500 index. These equity index Options are listed as Options only; there is no underlying security that you can buy. However, the underlying index has a price—from which all the Options derive their prices. You already know that Options are ideal for constructing hedges and for limiting the total risk of any particular investment you want to make.

So, equity index Options can be nice alternatives to ETFs for creating exposure to broad market indexes—while also building a hedge. But there must be a reason why we included this product in a discussion of taxes, right? The U.S. government treats equity index Options, for tax purposes, as Section 1256 contracts. And these types of investments get special tax treatment.

What kind of special tax treatment? All gains and losses from Section 1256 contracts are taxed 60% as long-term capital gains/losses, and the remaining 40% of the gain/loss is taxed as a short-term gain/loss. Long-term capital gains tax rates are materially lower than the short-term rates. This kind of tax treatment can be a real advantage to the taxable account holder who likes to use spreads or ITM Options to create hedged exposure.

Two mechanical observations about the tax treatment for Section 1256 contracts are important to point out. First, all gains/losses are taxed using the 60/40 split, regardless of hold time. Even if you hold the Section 1256 contract for more than one year (the standard point to achieve long-term gain status), the taxes are still treated 60/40. Second, the investor must "mark" all Section 1256 contracts still owned at year-end. "Marking" an investment means valuing it based on its last price on the last trading day of the tax year and then calculating the gain or loss based on the "marked" value compared to your investment basis. The gain or loss is treated as a taxable gain/loss. In the next tax year, if you sell the Section 1256 contract you marked at the end of the prior year, you would calculate the gain/loss based on the year-end "marked" value.

A current list of the equity index Options that are useful replacements for ETFs in your portfolio can be found on our website, http://www.BuyAndHedge.com. The equity index Options that qualify for Section 1256 contract treatment are highlighted. Figure 28.1 shows a current list of the Equity Index Options that you can invest in.

Index	Exchange Symbol	Exchange	Classification
CBOE Exchange Index	EXQ	CBOE	Narrow
Dow Jones Industrial Average (1/100th)	DJX	CBOE	Broad
Dow Jones Industrial Average Jumbo (1/10th)	DXL	CBOE	Broad
ISE 250 Index	IXZ	ISE	Broad
ISE Bio-Pharmaceuticals Index	RND	ISE	Broad
ISE Electronic Trading Index	DMA	ISE	Broad
ISE Green Energy Index	POW	ISE	Broad
ISE Homebuilders Index	RUF	ISE	Narrow
ISE Homeland Security Index	HSX	ISE	Narrow
ISE Integrated Oil and Gas Index	PMP	ISE	Narrow
ISE Long Gold Index	HVY	ISE	Broad
ISE Nanotechnology Index	TNY	ISE	Broad
ISE Oil and Gas Services Index	OOG	ISE	Broad
ISE-Revere Natural Gas Index	FUM	ISE	Broad
ISE-Revere Wal-Mart Supplier Index	WMX	ISE	Broad
ISE Semiconductors Index	BYT	ISE	Narrow
ISE SINdex Index	SIN	ISE	Broad
ISE U.S. Regional Banks Index	JLO	ISE	Narrow
ISE Water Index	HHO	ISE	Broad
KBW Bank Index	BKX	ISE	Broad
Morgan Stanley Cyclical Index	CYC	NYSE Amex	Broad
Morgan Stanley Retail Index	MVR	CBOE	Broad
Morgan Stanley Technology Index	MSH	NYSE Amex	Broad
Nasdaq-100 Index	NDX	CBOE	Broad
Nasdaq-100 Mini Index (1/10th)	MNX	CBOE	Broad
NYSE Arca Airline Index	XAL	NYSE Amex	Narrow
NYSE Arca Biotechnology	BTK	NYSE Amex	Broad
NYSE Arca Mini- Biotechnology Index (1/20th)	BJE	NYSE Amex	Broad
NYSE Arca Natural Gas Index	XNG	NYSE Amex	Broad
NYSE Arca Oil Index	XOI	NYSE Amex	Broad
NYSE Arca Mini-Oil Index (1/20th)	BZJ	NYSE Amex	Broad
PHLX Gold and Silver Sector	XAU	PHLX	Narrow
PHLX Housing Sector	HGX	PHLX	Broad
PHLX Oil Service Sector	OSX	PHLX	Broad
PHLX Semiconductor Sector	SOX	PHLX	Broad
PHLX Utility Sector	UTY	PHLX	Broad
Russell 1000 Index	RUI	CBOE	Broad
Russell 2000 Index	RUT	CBOE	Broad
S&P 100 Index	OEX	CBOE	Broad
S&P 500 Index	SPX	CBOE	Broad
S&P 500 Mini Index (1/10th)	XSP	CBOE	Broad
S&P MidCap 400 Index	MID	NYSE Amex	Broad
S&P SmallCap 600 Index	SML	CBOE	Broad

Figure 28.1 List of index options

Keep these tax tips in mind as you manage your portfolio. Your overall portfolio returns improve as you minimize your tax obligations. As always, be sure you consult a tax professional for your specific situation. The tax laws are always changing, and the tax situations described in this chapter could easily change!

Chapter Lessons

- Maximize your contributions to tax-advantaged accounts.
- In a taxable account, the tactics that include stock and ETF ownership provide the best opportunity to achieve long-term capital gains and lower your tax bill. These include married Options, collars, and portfolio hedges.
- Equity index Options offer advantageous tax treatment in many cases. If you prefer to use spread tactics or ITM Options and are investing in a taxable account, we recommend using equity index Options.

29

Conclusion: Putting It All Together

"Show me the money!"

—Jerry Maguire (played by Tom Cruise) in *Jerry Maguire* (1996)

Finding Your Investor Tempo

The Buy and Hedge investment approach is built for the long haul. When you execute on the Five Iron Rules, your investment portfolio can achieve the goals you have planned for it. But do you know what is at least as satisfying as seeing your investment portfolio grow? It is the feeling you get from knowing *you* were the person who made that growth happen. But it doesn't happen without some effort.

Being a do-it-yourself investor requires a real commitment. You need to build a real routine for regularly examining your portfolio's risk and return. The Buy and Hedge approach requires regular portfolio maintenance and a pledge to manage risk. This effort takes time—which is undeniably the most important commodity you can't afford to waste. So you need to be able to build a routine for your portfolio management using the Five Iron Rules. At Buy and Hedge, we call this your investor tempo.

You know what tempo is; it is the relative rate or rapidity of movement. It is synonymous with rhythm and cadence. Finding your tempo is often associated with dancing. It is the ability to make sure your body moves with the beat. If you are a golfer, you know what a good "swing tempo" is. When you are playing well and shooting low scores, your friends say your swing tempo looks great. And your swing feels like it all works well together. Typically, this means your swing speed looks coordinated from beginning to end—from backswing to downswing to impact to follow-through.

Play-by-play announcers at sports events often refer to an athlete's tempo—especially in sports that require regular repetitive effort. When a baseball pitcher is pitching well, he often takes the same amount of time between pitches and maintains the same speed in his windup and follow-through. Quarterbacks on the football field can achieve a good rhythm working on timing patterns with their wide receivers. These players are achieving coordinated tempo.

Tempo is important when you need to regularly repeat a pattern—especially when the pattern requires practice and discipline to repeat. This should sound familiar to you as a Buy and Hedge investor. The Buy and Hedge approach requires you to *repeat a pattern* (building and maintaining hedges) that *requires practice* (unleashing your inner guru) and *discipline* (eliminating emotion). Finding your investor tempo as a Buy and Hedge investor makes a lot of sense.

Finding your investor tempo as a Buy and Hedge investor means you spend just enough time managing your portfolio to make sure that you successfully execute on all five of the Iron Rules. Perfect tempo means that you spent just enough time complying with the rules—not a minute more or a minute less. If you realize that you have broken one of the Iron Rules, and your excuse is a lack of time spent on your investments, you have *not* achieved the proper investor tempo. If you spend too much time on your portfolio, and that causes you to break one of the Iron Rules, you *still* have not achieved the proper investor tempo.

The authors recommend that you create a regular routine for reviewing your portfolio and executing any necessary account maintenance. We recommend that you set aside time one or two days a week to execute the Five Iron Rules. You should be able to achieve very good investor tempo with that kind of time commitment. If you can find time only once a month, you might be able to be a successful Buy and Hedge investor, but you have handicapped your chances significantly. Conversely, if you like to log in every day and track your portfolio, you can be successful in this way also. But that kind of time commitment can lead to excessive, emotionally driven portfolio changes. So be careful!

Good investor tempo comes from having a regular routine and adjusting it only if you find yourself breaking the Iron Rules. Let your compliance with the Five Iron Rules act as your indicator of whether you have achieved good investor tempo. If you find yourself always in compliance, keep up the same routine you have today. If you are not, examine whether you are spending too much time on your portfolio— or, the more likely culprit, whether you are not spending enough time on your portfolio.

...While Executing the Five Iron Rules

Ultimately, the Five Iron Rules of Buy and Hedge are the most important lessons you need to take away from this book. Executing the Five Iron Rules will deliver success in your portfolio. You can learn to master the risk/return dynamic in your portfolio when you transform yourself into a Buy and Hedge investor.

The Five Iron Rules were selected because when they are combined, they transform your portfolio's potential. In other words, in this case, $1 + 1 + 1 + 1 + 1 =$ more than 5! The Five Iron Rules create a holistic approach to constructing and managing your investment portfolio. Your investment performance has the most potential when all five of the Iron Rules are executed together in one portfolio. But interestingly, if you implemented any one of the Iron Rules by itself in your existing portfolio, you would likely improve your portfolio's performance. In other words, each rule stands on its own and can improve your existing investment approach. But we still recommend that you apply all Five Iron Rules to your portfolio.

The Five Iron Rules were selected because they directly address the Immutable Laws of Investing. You cannot avoid the Immutable Laws as a do-it-yourself investor. In the markets, these Immutable Laws are like the laws of physics: *they affect everyone!* Think about one of the laws of physics: the law of gravity. If you jump off a diving board, you know what comes next: an exhilarating but short drop into refreshing water. If you jump off the Brooklyn Bridge, you also know what comes next: a not-so-short drop into cold, murky waters at a speed of impact that will injure or kill you. You understand the law of gravity, and as a result, you understand that its application can be both exhilarating and perilous. And because you understand it, you can adjust for it—and make good decisions.

The Immutable Laws of Investing work the same way. You should endeavor to remember the Immutable Laws and what they represent. The proper application of Buy and Hedge technique can give you an advantage over the Immutable Laws. In this case, the proper application of technique means executing on the Five Iron Rules.

Let's wrap up with one last recap of the Laws and Rules. Here are the Immutable Laws that affect all investors:

- Capital lost is capital that cannot grow.
- Risk is the input; return is the output.
- Emotion is the enemy.
- Volatility is kryptonite.
- The return that matters is after-tax return.

These Immutable Laws cannot be avoided. But when you apply the Five Iron Rules, you can overcome the negative impact of the laws:

- Rule #1: Hedge every investment.
- Rule #2: Know your risk metrics.
- Rule #3: Smart portfolio = long-term outlook + diversification.
- Rule #4: Unleash your inner guru.
- Rule #5: Harvest gains and losses.

Now it's time for you, as a Buy and Hedge investor, to implement what we have taught you in this book. You know the Five Iron Rules, and you understand the Immutable Laws. It is time to fly on your own and start beating the market. But you aren't really on your own. The authors maintain a blog at http://www.BuyAndHedge.com with regular articles on investment ideas and hedging tactics. You also can access other educational resources at our site.

But don't forget that this book is also a reference tool. It was written so that you can reference and reread any chapter on its own. Each chapter is a lesson in itself. Regularly return to the book and read any chapter when you need to refresh your memory on a certain Buy and Hedge technique. You will especially find Parts IV and V helpful reference tools when executing your first hedged transactions.

Good luck and happy hedging!

Index

U

V

W-Z

FINANCIAL TIMES

In an increasingly competitive world, it is quality
of thinking that gives an edge—an idea that opens new
doors, a technique that solves a problem, or an insight
that simply helps make sense of it all.

We work with leading authors in the various arenas
of business and finance to bring cutting-edge thinking
and best-learning practices to a global market.

It is our goal to create world-class print publications
and electronic products that give readers
knowledge and understanding that can then be
applied, whether studying or at work.

To find out more about our business
products, you can visit us at www.ftpress.com.